The Political Consequences of Anti-Americanism

Anti-Americanism as a concept is confused, often used in a contradictory fashion and invariably driven by emotion rather than intellect. Nevertheless, it casts a long policy shadow with adverse consequences (both real and potential) for actors including those who may not support the concept.

This book puts anti-Americanism into a contemporary context and analyses some of its political consequences. The argument of the book is that ideas matter: they shape actions and have policy consequences. With the case of anti-Americanism, even superficial ideas can reflect deep-seated emotions that might, at first sight, appear real. These can range from the rhetorical flourish and smart comment occasioned by a presidential gaucherie through to a deeply embedded, visceral hatred of all things American. The contributors to this volume discern the difference between these two ends of the anti-American spectrum and assess the varying degree of 'political consequence'. Divided into three parts, items addressed include:

- Networks, Culture and Foundations – consisting of the role of influential foundations and think tanks in combating anti-Americanism, and the link between the political establishment in Washington DC and the popular culture industry;
- Security and Anti-Americanism;
- Regional and Country Studies – including those of Canada, Australia, East Asia, Latin America, Greece and France.

The Political Consequences of Anti-Americanism will be of interest to students and scholars of politics, international relations, security studies, American politics and American foreign policy.

Richard Higgott is a Pro Vice-Chancellor and Professor of Politics and International Studies at the University of Warwick, United Kingdom.

Ivona Malbašić manages the Open Society Fellowship Program at the Central European University (CEU), Hungary.

Routledge/Warwick Studies in Globalisation

Edited by Richard Higgott and published in association with the Centre for the Study of Globalisation and Regionalisation, University of Warwick.

What is globalisation and does it matter? How can we measure it? What are its policy implications? The Centre for the Study of Globalisation and Regionalisation at the University of Warwick is an international site for the study of key questions such as these in the theory and practice of globalisation and regionalisation. Its agenda is avowedly interdisciplinary. The work of the Centre will be showcased in this series.

This series comprises two strands:

Warwick Studies in Globalisation addresses the needs of students and teachers, and the titles will be published in hardback and paperback. Titles include:

Globalisation and the Asia-Pacific
Contested Territories
Edited by Kris Olds, Peter Dicken, Philip F. Kelly, Lily Kong and Henry Wai-chung Yeung

Regulating the Global Information Society
Edited by Christopher Marsden

Banking on Knowledge
The Genesis of the Global Development Network
Edited by Diane Stone

Historical Materialism and Globalisation
Edited by Hazel Smith and Mark Rupert

Civil Society and Global Finance
Edited by Jan Aart Scholte with Albrecht Schnabel

Towards a Global Polity
Edited by Morten Ougaard and Richard Higgott

New Regionalisms in the Global Political Economy
Theories and Cases
Edited by Shaun Breslin, Christopher W. Hughes, Nicola Phillips and Ben Rosamond

Development Issues in Global Governance
Public-Private Partnerships and Market Multilateralism
Benedicte Bull and Desmond McNeill

Globalizing Democracy
Political parties in emerging democracies
Edited by Peter Burnell

The Globalization of Political Violence
Globalization's Shadow
Edited by Richard Devetak and Christopher W. Hughes

Regionalisation and Global Governance
The Taming of Globalisation?
Edited by Andrew F. Cooper, Christopher W. Hughes and Philippe De Lombaerde

Routledge/Warwick Studies in Globalisation is a forum for innovative new research intended for a high-level specialist readership, and the titles will be available in hardback only. Titles include:

The Political Consequences of Anti-Americanism

Edited by Richard Higgott and Ivona Malbašić

Routledge
Taylor & Francis Group

LONDON AND NEW YORK

E·S·R·C
ECONOMIC
& SOCIAL
RESEARCH
COUNCIL

Centre for the
Study of
Globalisation and
Regionalisation

First published 2008
by Routledge
2 Park Square, Milton Park, Abingdon, Oxon OX14 4RN

Simultaneously published in the USA and Canada
by Routledge
711 Third Avenue, New York, NY 10017

Routledge is an imprint of the Taylor & Francis Group, an informa business.

Typeset in Times New Roman by Pindar New Zealand (Egan Reid)

First issued in paperback in 2013

British Library Cataloguing in Publication Data
A catalogue record for this book is available from the British Library

Library of Congress Cataloging in Publication Data
  The political consequences of anti-americanism / edited by Richard
  Higgott and Ivona Malbašić.
  p. cm. – (Routledge/Warwick studies in globalisation ; 18)
  Includes bibliographical references and index.
  ISBN 978-0-415-46391-1 (hardback : alk. paper) – ISBN 978-0-203-
  92654-3 (e-book : alk. paper) 1. Anti-Americanism – History. 2. Anti-
  Americanism – Case studies. 3. United States – Foreign public opinion. 4.
  United States–Foreign relations – 1945–1989. 5. United States–Foreign
  relations – 1989– I. Higgott, Richard A. II. Malbašić, Ivona.
  E840.2.P65 2008
  327.73009'04–dc22
  2007048586

ISBN 13: 978-0-415-74670-0 (pbk)
ISBN 13: 978-0-415-46391-1 (hbk)
ISBN 13: 978-0-203-92654-3 (ebk)

Contents

Tables

Contributors

Donald E. Abelson is Professor and Chair, Department of Political Science and Director, Centre for American Studies, at The University of Western Ontario where he specializes in American Politics and United States Foreign Policy. He is the author of several books, including his most recent study, *A Capitol Idea: Think Tanks and US Foreign Policy* (McGill–Queen's University Press, 2006). His work has also been published in several edited collections and academic journals, including: *Global Society, Presidential Studies Quarterly, The Canadian Journal of Political Science* and *Canadian Public Administration.* In addition to his research and teaching interests, Donald Abelson has served as a consultant for several governmental and non-governmental organizations in North America and Europe.

Ariane Chebel d'Appollonia is Associate Researcher at the CEVIPOF/Center for Political Research (Sciences Po). She teaches at several universities in France (including Sciences Po and Paris III-Sorbonne) and in the United States (New York University, University of Pittsburgh, Northwestern University). She specializes in the politics of immigration in Europe and the United States, racism and xenophobia, extreme-right-wing movements, political theory and public policy. Among her numerous publications, she is the author of *Histoire politique des intellectuels en France* (Complexe, 1990), 'National and European Identities between Myths and Realities', in Ulf Hedetoft (dir.) *Political Symbols, Symbolic Politics: European Identities in Transformation* (Ashgate Publishing Company, 1998); and 'European Nationalism and European Union', in Anthony Pagden (ed.) *The Idea of Europe from Antiquity to the EU* (Woodrow Wilson Center, Cambridge University Press, 2002); and edited in collaboration with Simon Reich, *Immigration, Integration, and Security. America and Europe in Perspective* (University of Pittsburgh Press, 2008).

Davis B. Bobrow is Professor Emeritus of Public and International Affairs and Political Science at the University of Pittsburgh. His books include *Policy Analysis by Design* (1987, with John Dryzek) and *Defensive Internationalism* (2005, with Mark Boyer). He has held senior staff positions and consultancies with major US government agencies; visiting appointments in policy-related programs in East Asia, Europe and Israel; and the presidencies of the international

Studies Association, the National Association of Schools of Public Affairs and Administration, and the Association of Professional Schools of International Affairs.

Ann Capling is Professor of Political Science at the University of Melbourne. Her main areas of expertise are the politics and political economy of trade policy, the multilateral trade system, and global economic governance. In 2007 she was a member of the Warwick Commission on the future of the Multilateral Trade System. Her recent books include *All the Way with the USA: Australia, the US and Free Trade* (University of New South Wales Press, 2005) and *Australia and the Global Trade System: From Havana to Seattle* (Cambridge University Press, 2001). She has also written extensively on free trade agreements, 'democratic deficit' problems in global governance, and the political economy of Australian Rules football.

Michael Cox is Professor of International Relations at the London School of Economics and Political Science. He is also Chair of the United States Discussion Group at Chatham House, London, and Chair of the European Consortium for Political Research. Professor Cox's areas of expertise are in the foreign policy of the United States and American grand strategy. He is also concerned with Britain and the US, world politics after 11 September, the trans-Atlantic relationship in crisis, the history of the Cold War and post-Cold War international relations. Professor Cox was a Research Fellow at the Nobel Institute in Oslo in 2007. In 2008, he was made a Director of 'IDEAS' at the LSE, a new Centre for the Study of Diplomacy and Strategy. Professor Cox is the author of many books and articles, some of which include: 'A New American Empire', in D. Held and M. Koenig-Archibugi (eds) *American Power in the 21st Century* (Polity Press, 2004); 'Empire By Denial? Debating US Power', *Security Dialogue* 35, no. 2 (2004), pp. 228–36; 'American Power Before and After September 11', in R. Singh (ed.) *Governing America: The Politics of a Divided Democracy* (Oxford University Press, 2003, pp. 467–79); 'Dizzy with Success? American Power Before and After 11 September', *International Affairs* 78, no. 2 (2002).

Heribert Dieter is a Senior Fellow in the Research Unit – Global Issues at the German Institute for International and Security Affairs, Berlin. Since 2000 he has also been Associate Fellow, Centre for the Study of Globalisation and Regionalisation (CSGR), University of Warwick. Heribert Dieter is a member of the European Network of Excellence GARNET, where he co-chairs the research project on global governance and market regulation. He teaches at the Free University of Berlin and the University of Potsdam. He has worked on a broad range of issues related to the development of the world economy, such as regional integration in the Asia–Pacific region, Africa and Central Asia, monetary regionalism and the international financial system. Dieter's recent publications include *The Evolution of Regionalism in Asia: Economic and Security Issues* (Routledge, 2007), *The Future of Globalisation* (in German; Nomos, 2005) and 'The Limited Utility of Bilateral Free Trade Agreements', *Journal of Australian Political Economy*, no. 58 (December 2006), pp. 94–113.

Nicolas Guilhot is Research Fellow at the Social Science Research Council in New York. He has previously lectured at the London School of Economics and holds a Senior Researcher position at the CNRS (Centre National des Recherches Scientifiques) in Paris. His work focuses on the history of the social sciences and on international networks. He has recently published *The Democracy Makers: Human Rights and the Politics of Global Order* (Columbia University Press, 2005).

Richard Higgott is a Pro Vice Chancellor at the University of Warwick, where he has been a Professor of Politics and International Studies since 1996. He was Foundation Director of the Centre for the Study of Globalisation and Regionalisation and is a Senior Scientist and Director of the EU Framework 6 Network of Excellence on Global Governance, Regionalism and Regulation.

Ivona Malbašić manages the Open Society Fellowship program at the Central European University in Budapest. She has coordinated a three-year research project on political consequences of anti-Americanism at the Center for Policy Studies at the same University. Previously, she worked in international non-governmental organizations in Central and Eastern Europe, where she edited major publications, wrote policy letters and worked extensively on the post-war reconstruction in South-east Europe.

Helena Maragou is Professor of American Literature and Culture at the American College of Greece (Deree). In addition to literary subjects, such as the literature of US ethnic minorities, her recent research interests include the phenomenon of Greek and European anti-Americanism and the ways in which it impacts on the practice of American studies in social/cultural contexts inimical to US foreign policy.

Toby Miller is Chair of the Department of Media and Cultural Studies at the University of California, Riverside. His teaching and research cover the media, sport, labour, gender, race, citizenship, politics, and cultural policy. Professor Miller is the author and editor of over 20 books, and has published essays in more than 30 journals and 50 volumes. His most recent publications include *Política Cultural* (Editorial Gedisa, 2004, with George Yúdice); *International Cultural Studies: An Anthology* (Blackwell, 2005, associate editor, editors Ackbar Abbas and John Nguyet Erni); *Global Hollywood 2* (British Film Institute/University of California Press, 2005, with Nitin Govil, John McMurria, Richard Maxwell and Ting Wang); and *Cultural Citizenship* (Temple University Press, 2007). His current research covers the success of Hollywood overseas, the links between culture and citizenship, and anti-Americanism. He is the editor of *Television & New Media*, co-editor of *Social Identities*, and editor of the Popular Culture and Everyday Life series for Peter Lang. He has made many appearances in the print and electronic media and previously worked in broadcasting, banking and politics.

Kim Richard Nossal is Professor and Head of the Department of Political Studies at Queen's University, Kingston, Canada. His research interests include Canadian foreign and defence policy, Australian foreign policy, and the international relations of non-central governments. Professor Nossal is the author of numerous book chapters, articles, books and conference papers. Selected publications include: *The Politics of Canadian Foreign Policy*, 3rd edn (Prentice Hall Canada, 1997), *Diplomatic Departures: The Conservative Era in Canadian Foreign Policy 1984–93* (UBC Press, 2001, co-edited with Nelson Michaud), and *Politique internationale et défense au Canada et au Québec* (Les Presses de l'Université de Montréal, 2007, co-authored with Stéphane Roussel and Stéphane Paquin).

Inderjeet Parmar is Professor of Government and Head of Politics at the University of Manchester. His most recent book is *Think Tanks and Power in Foreign Policy: A Comparative Study of the Role and Influence of the CFR and RIIA, 1939–1945* (Palgrave, 2004). He has published several articles on the foreign policy roles of the Ford, Carnegie and Rockefeller Foundations in journals such as *Review of International Studies*, *Minerva* and *Global Networks*. He is currently writing a research monograph entitled *Foundations of the American Century: Ford, Carnegie and Rockefeller Foundations and America's Rise to Globalism, 1920–2005*.

Cintia Quiliconi is a PhD candidate in Political Science and International Relations at the University of Southern California. She holds a Master's degree in politics from the New York University and a Master's degree in international relations from the Latin American School of Social Sciences (FLACSO), Argentina. She has been a researcher in the Program on International Economic Institutions at FLACSO, Argentina (1998–2005) and is a member of the Latin American Trade Network (LATN). She has been Lecturer at the University of Buenos Aires and at the University of Quilmes in Argentina. Cintia Quiliconi has been a consultant for UNDP, IADB, World Bank, World Health Organization and the Argentine Ministry of Economy on topics related to international trade negotiations. Her main interests are focused on political economy of development and international and regional trade negotiations in developing countries and particularly Latin America.

Adam Quinn is Lecturer in International Relations at the Department of Politics and International Relations, University of Leicester, and will shortly be examined for his PhD at the Department of International Relations at the London School of Economics and Political Science. He previously worked as a teaching Fellow at the Department of Political Science and International Studies (POLSIS), University of Birmingham, and as a Visiting Lecturer at the Centre for the Study of Democracy (CSD), University of Westminster. Other recent publications include 'The Great Illusion: Chimeras of Isolationism and Realism in Post-Iraq US Foreign Policy', *Politics and Policy*, 35:3, September 2007, and '"The Deal": The Balance of Power, Military Strength and Liberal Internationalism in the Bush National Security Strategy', *International Studies Perspectives*, February 2008.

Skaidra Trilupaityte is a Fellow at the Culture, Philosophy and Art Research Institute in Vilnius; member of AICA (International Art Critics Association, Lithuanian section) and ISA (International Sociological Association); Lecturer at the Vilnius Academy of Arts. Skaidra Trilupaityte publishes on variety of subjects relating to post-Soviet cultural policies. Her academic interests include: artistic and institutional changes during post-Soviet transition, relations between post-Soviet and expatriate cultures, intellectual exchanges after the Cold War, and new artistic identities. During 2004 spring term she conducted research on cultural policies in post-Soviet Russia and Lithuania at the New School University (New York) as a Fulbright scholar.

List of Abbreviations

ABC	American Broadcasting Company
AEI	American Enterprise Institute
AFTA	ASEAN Free Trade Area
ALP	Australian Labor Party
ANZUS	Australia, New Zealand, United States Security Treaty
APEC	Asia–Pacific Economic Co-operation
ASEAN	Association of Southeast Asian Nations
ASEM	Asia Europe Meeting
APT	ASEAN + Three (Southeast Asian Nations + Japan, China and South Korea)
ATTAC	Association for the Taxation of Financial Transactions in Aid of Citizens
AUSFTA	Australia–United States Free Trade Agreement
BBC	British Broadcasting Corporation
BMD	Ballistic Missile Defense
CAFTA	US–Central American Free Trade Agreement
CBC	Canadian Broadcasting Corporation
CBS	Columbia Broadcasting System
CCF	Congress for Cultural Freedom
CFR	Council on Foreign Relations
CIA	Central Intelligence Agency
CNN	Cable News Network
CSIS	Centre for Strategic and International Studies
CSP	Centre for Security Policy
CTV	Canadian Television
DDB	Doyle Dane Bernbach
EAM	Communist National Liberation Front
ECLAC	Economic Commission for Latin America and the Caribbean
EDC	European Defence Community
EEP	Export Enhancement Program
EFIC	European Foundation for Intellectual Cooperation
EU	European Union
EU-15	Western European members of the EU

FDI	Foreign Direct Investment
FLASCO	Latin American School of Social Sciences
FTA	Free Trade Agreement
FTAA	Free Trade Area of the Americas
GATT	General Agreement on Tariffs and Trade
GDP	Gross Domestic Product
GMF	German Marshall Fund of the United States
IACF	International Association for Cultural Freedom
IADB	Inter-American Development Bank
IFIs	International Financial Institutions
IMF	International Monetary Fund
ISI	Import Substitution Industrialization
KGB	Committee for State Security (translated from Russian)
LATN	Latin American Trade Network
LSE	London School of Economics and Political Science
MIT	Massachusetts Institute of Technology
NAFTA	North American Free Trade Agreement
NASA	National Aeronautics and Space Administration
NATO	North Atlantic Treaty Organization
NGOs	Non-Governmental Organisations
NWICO	New World Information and Communication Order
OECD	Organisation for Economic Co-operation and Development
OSI	Open Society Institute
PIPA	Program on International Policy Attitudes
PNAC	Project for the New American Century
PTA	Preferential Trade Agreement
SARS	Severe Acute Respiratory Syndrome
UK	United Kingdom
UN	United Nations
UNCTAD	United Nations Conference on Trade and Development
UNDP	United Nations Development Program
UNESCO	United Nations Educational, Scientific and Cultural Organization
UNSC	United Nations Security Council
US	United States
USAID	US Agency for International Development
USSR	Union of Soviet Socialist Republics
USTR	United States Trade Representative
WMD	Weapons of Mass Destruction
WTO	World Trade Organization

Acknowledgements

This volume is the result of a lively debate organized by the Centre for Policy Studies at Central European University in Budapest, Hungary. The primary aims of the workshop were to discuss contemporary anti-Americanism and to shed light on both its potential and real political consequences. We are grateful to the Centre for Policy Studies for their continuous support in a three-year research project on the political consequences of anti-Americanism. Special thanks to Zsuzsa Gábor, Viola Zentai, Andrew Cartwright, Borbála Varga and Tamás Dombos.

This volume would not have been possible without advice and guidance from the project's Steering Committee, especially Diane Stone whose insights, suggestions and support throughout the project have been invaluable. We also wish to thank Thomas Carothers, Ian Buruma and Tony Judt for their insights and for help during the three years of project activities. Finally, the editors wish to thank the Tipping Point Foundation of Sofia for making this publication possible.

1 Introduction

The Theory and Practice of Anti-Americanism – a Brief Introduction

Richard Higgott and Ivona Malbašić

Aims of the book

Anti-Americanism as a concept is confused, often used in contradictory fashion and invariably driven by emotion rather than intellect. Nevertheless, it casts a long policy shadow with adverse (both real and potential) consequences for actors, including those who may not espouse the concept. It is the overall aim of this book to put anti-Americanism into a contemporary (twenty-first century) context and to analyse some of its political consequences. The argument of the book is that ideas matter. Ideas shape actions and have policy consequences. Ideas, even superficial ones, can also reflect often deeper-seated emotions than might at first sight appear to be the case. This is certainly so with anti-Americanism. It can range from the rhetorical flourish and smart comment occasioned by a presidential gaucherie through to a deeply embedded, visceral hatred of all things American. This book will examine the difference between these two ends of the anti-American spectrum (see Quinn and Cox chapter) and assess the varying degrees of 'political consequence' attendant on the depth of feeling that has clearly grown in the early years of the twenty-first century.

It is a further aim of the book to discern the difference between correlation and causation. For example, it is not unreasonable to discern the weakening of what we might call the North Atlantic political community. The last few years have seen those political and military institutions at the core of the community become increasingly contested as their ideational and social bases have become increasingly fragile. To what extent, we should ask, is this simply a correlation with the growth of anti-American rhetoric in Europe, and to what extant is the relationship causal? After all, in October 2003, 53 per cent of Europeans thought that the United States played a negative role regarding peace in the world. While this clearly has much to do with the US-led invasion of Iraq, Iraq is not the only reason.[1] The Pew's 2006 Report shows that the image of the US and support for the 'war on terrorism' has slipped even further since 2003.[2] The last few years, and especially since the Asian financial crises of the late twentieth century, have seen a distance emerge on a range of issues in the relationship between the US and its regional Cold War partners. Again, to what extent is this a correlation with the rise of anti-American rhetoric in the region and to what extent is it causally dependent on growing unpopularity of the US? The answer to this question is not easily discerned. In both cases, the changing nature of the relationship cannot simply be traced to the adverse effects of the behaviour of one contemporarily unpopular administration. Clearly, the George W. Bush administration has been, in part at least (how little or great is not clear), responsible for the deteriorating standing of the US in world affairs in the twenty-first century. Yet, as many of the chapters in this volume demonstrate, antipathy towards the US and its policies, even in the homelands of traditional allies, existed in the years prior to the advent of the second Bush administration and indeed has deep historical roots in some instances.

The degree to which anti-Americanism has political consequences – whether it is merely correlated with the said consequences or is in fact causal of them – is beside the point; anti-Americanism is a fact of everyday political life. It does matter, however, to those (both within the US and beyond its shores) who would wish to mitigate this process; especially since we have moved beyond rhetoric in a twenty-first century which has seen anti-Americanism 'go operational' in a range of policy domains. Unfortunately, there currently exists a dialogue of the deaf between, on the one hand, senior figures in the United States who seem to care little about attitudes of non-Americans towards them and their policies (*pace* Vice-President Cheney, former Defense Secretary Rumsfeld and their coterie of supporters in the early years of the twenty-first century) and, on the other hand, those for whom America's standing and moral authority abroad is a major element of US foreign policy capability (see Nye 2002).

The current era represents a dramatic change for the US from those heady days after the collapse of communism and the end of the Cold War. The world is no longer willing to accept order underwritten by a more or less benign US hegemony. Not to put too fine a point on it, 17 years after the end of the Cold War, disorder rules. The Atlantic community is at its loosest since the formation of the North Atlantic Treaty Organization (NATO), the US is in a seemingly unwinnable conflict in Iraq, and wider Middle East issues (especially the Israeli–Palestinian issue) seem increasingly intractable. China and India are emerging as truly global powers in both an economic and a political sense as new regional orders emerge. When accompanied by the tide of anti-Americanism that has arisen since the turn of the century, the US has serious global problems and dilemmas.

As Zbigniew Brzezinski, the former National Security Advisor to Jimmy Carter and leading opponent of the 2003 invasion of Iraq, would have it in a swingeing critique of contemporary American foreign policy: 'American leadership has lost much of its legitimacy, the worldwide credibility of the American presidency has been undermined. The moral standing of America has been tarnished.' Brzezinski's thesis in his new book is that anti-Americanism is in many ways the outcome of US's inability to turn victory in the Cold War into a post-Cold War consolidation of its material and ideational hegemony of the early 1990s when the US was clearly seen as the most readily acceptable steward of international security. Since that time (not simply since the arrival of George W. Bush), the US has dissipated all or at least much of the global standing that it had accrued by failing to understand the difference between what Brzezinski calls the 'power to destroy' and the 'power to control'. The issue for Brzezinski (2007) is this: what can the US do to row back from the current parlous position? Not a lot, is his answer since anti-Americanism has become an '… integral part of the shifting global demographic, economic and political balance'.

The problem outlined by Brzezinski is not simply one for the US, of course. Amongst intellectual and political actors in other parts of the world there is also a distinction to be found between those who see little or no good coming from US global interventions and the need to resist its hegemony (see the tradition from Servan-Schreiber 1968 through to Bello 2005) and those who, like Brzezinski, bemoan the immature use and abuse of American hegemony since the end of the Cold War and wish it to behave in a manner befitting both its historical intellectual agenda and its contemporary material power (see the tradition from Strange 1987 through to Mahbubani 2005). It is in this context that the essays in this volume come to focus on some key elements of contemporary anti-Americanism.[3]

Defining anti-Americanism

Anti-Americanism is to be found in a wide range of literatures, not all of which focus directly on anti-Americanism *per se*. Within the US there is a strong domestic tradition of work that is self-critical or even self-loathing of the US historical experience. This is not the focus of this volume and need not detain us here. In Europe there is a strong tradition that we can basically describe as being critical of the US global project on world order. Clearly the French tradition, epitomized in Jean-Jacques Servan-Schreiber's *Le Défi Américain* from the 1960s, is illustrative of this kind of literature. Accompanying this European literature is an increasing body of work emanating from the developing world which tends to conflate the negative impacts of globalization with the effects of US policy and indeed the US way of life. Hence anti-globalization is inseparable from anti-Americanism. This particular take on the role of the US as the principal agent of the negative aspects of globalization can be found in the work of key actors from the anti- or alter-globalization movement such as non-government organizations (NGOs) like the Third World Network (http://www.twnside.org.sg) and Focus on the Global South (http://www.focusweb.org).

Anti-Americanism is a complex phenomenon with many different forms, causes and consequences in different regions and countries. There have been many attempts to define the phenomenon, but there is no agreement on what anti-Americanism is or how to distinguish legitimate criticism of US foreign policies from anti-Americanism. This debate is very often emotional – especially in the US, where the political right tends to see every criticism of the US as anti-Americanism while the left argues that what is contested is not the US but its policies. Exogenous to the US there is, in many parts of the world certainly, an element of 'scapegoating' in the use of anti-Americanism for domestic political purposes (see Trilupaityte chapter on Russia and Nossal chapter on Canada). At the same time, specific policies of the current administration in Washington have contributed to the upsurge in negative attitudes towards the US (see Capling chapter on Australia).

Because of its complexity, 'it is more useful to think of [anti-Americanism] as a family of related attitudes rather than as a single entity' (Crockatt 2003). The upsurge of anti-Americanism might be a direct reaction to specific US policies, but at the same time it might be directed to the 'American system as such, its global power, its model of democracy' (Fabbrini 2004).

Markovits (2003) sees anti-Americanism as 'a particularly murky concept because it invariably merges antipathy towards what America does with what America is – or rather is projected to be in the eyes of its beholders'. He finds support for this notion in the fact that in Europe, 'particularly among the Western European elites, anti-Americanism has been about the essence of the United States, while in other regions the negative attitudes have been caused by US actions'. In the context of what America is, Markovits defines anti-Americanism as a prejudice, similar to other hostile predispositions such as racism or anti-Semitism. Hollander (1995) also defines anti-Americanism as some form of prejudice, as 'a particular mind-set, an attitude of distaste, aversion or intense hostility, the roots of which may be found in matters unrelated to the actual qualities of attributes of American society or the foreign policies of the United States'. It should be said, that these positions, while not uncommon, are not essentially testable so remain simply as asserted points of view.

Some analysts (Revel 2003a; Hollander 2002), like some senior American political figures (*pace* George W. Bush), argue that America, as the world's only superpower, is widely envied for its economic, political and cultural success. As Revel notes: 'ideological reasons for blaming America first are multiplied by simple jealousy of American power' (Revel 2003a). While envy, and prejudice, might be ingredients in some manifestations of anti-American sentiment, such definitions 'risk blurring the already problematic distinction between anti-Americanism and a critical stance toward particular aspects of American policy or culture' (Crockatt 2003).

On the other hand, it is very often possible that criticism of US policies can coexist with wider positive attitudes towards Americans as a people or the US as a country. In France, for example, 'attitudes towards the American administration are consistently more negative than attitudes towards American society and people' (Meunier 2005).

Crockatt (2003) argues that anti-Americanism cannot be fully understood without explaining a process of Americanization that first started in the US as a tool to 'turn immigrants into Americans', and later turned into a global phenomenon of promoting American economic, cultural and political ideas supported by American governments. Cultural diplomacy, academic scholarships and big US foundations (see Parmar's chapter) have regularly been employed to create positive images of the US. Yet as much as America provided a role model for some, it became a subject of strong resentment for others.

Another aspect that adds to the complexity of the phenomenon is the link between anti-Americanism, modernity and globalization. America is in some instances as much a concept or an idea that has very often come to symbolize the idea of modernity (Ceaser 2003). In some cases, 'anti-Americanism … is a reaction to modernity rather than to America itself; indeed, it could be said to be a reaction to globalisation, since the growth of American power and the spread of its influence coincided with the expansion of capitalism on a global scale' (Crockatt 2003). In Europe, argues Fabbrini, fear of Americanization has been intertwined with a fear of globalization and its negative consequences (Fabbrini 2004). This is especially the case for some sections of the French political class. Although the European economy shares, to a greater or lesser extent, the same values of free market enterprise, the negative consequences of globalization are largely attributed to the US.[4] Anti-Americanism as anti-modernism is also clearly a powerful force for resistance in certain, although not all, quarters of the Islamic world.

Thus our general starting point for the chapters in this volume is that anti-Americanism cannot be defined using simple, overarching explanations, which would indeed fail utterly to grasp the complexity of the phenomenon. As Meunier (2005) suggests, attitudes towards the US 'need to be desegrated according the issue-area – whether we are talking about foreign policy, entertainment, or food'. Anti-Americanism has an assortment of meanings that depend on historical, political and social contexts. It is our aim to shed light on some of its meanings by bringing the analysis from a wide range of studies such as political economy, international relations, security studies and cultural studies.

Structure of the book

This book is by no means a comprehensive overview of anti-Americanism; it rather focuses on issues and countries less studied in recent literature. Cultural and trade-related insights on the subject offer an important counterweight to more traditional, security studies-driven analysis of anti-Americanism. Contributors analyse in detail countries and regions that have been neglected in most of the recent literature on the phenomenon – such as Canada, Australia and, to some degree, East Asia.

The book has three main parts. The first part analyses the role of influential foundations and think tanks in combating anti-Americanism and the implications of democracy-promotion through the Open Society Network (OSI) on the phenomenon. It also studies in detail a link between the political establishment in Washington, DC, and the popular culture industry – mainly the Hollywood film industry.

Nicolas Guilhot analyses the emergence of cultural diplomacy as a non-state strategy promoted by private actors (intellectuals, philanthropic foundations, etc.) to combat anti-Americanism in Europe during the Cold War. He argues that the problem of anti-Americanism evolved over time, as the shape and main intellectual threads of the Cold War were changing. The chapter focuses on the way in which intellectuals have been involved in the ideological fight against anti-Americanism, through three interrelated organizations that, taken together, cover the whole span of the Cold War: the Congress for Cultural Freedom, the *Fondation pour une Entraide Intellectuelle Européenne*, and the Open Society Network created by George Soros.

The role of the US East Coast elite circles in combating European anti-Americanism is analysed in Inderjeet Parmar's chapter. He focuses on the roles of the Ford Foundation and the German Marshall Fund of the United States (GMFUS) in promoting Americanism and combating anti-Americanism through three historical and contemporary case studies: Henry Kissinger's Harvard International Seminar, the Salzburg Seminar in American Studies (both during the Cold War), and philanthropic trans-Atlantic unity-building initiatives since 11 September 2001. Parmar uses archival and other foundation records to examine American philanthropy's role and influence in constructing pro-American elite networks in Europe (and, to a degree, in Asia) as part of the East Coast American foreign policy establishment's post-World War II imperial drive to replace Europe as manager of the global system but within a context of US–European 'co-operation'. Highlighting some of the principal features of the cited seminars and more recent public diplomacy, this chapter shows that their effectiveness lay – and may still lie – in their attempts to engage authentically with their target audiences and in their careful selection of overseas participants. Parmar concludes that the Ford Foundation and GMFUS pursue(d) such initiatives because of their own social origins, cultural immersion and personal inter-connections with the American power elite.

Donald Abelson's chapter examines the extent to which a select group of US think tanks have, since the tragic events of 11 September 2001, both contributed to and become the target of anti-Americanism. At the beginning of the twentieth century, think tanks in the United States such as the Brookings Institution and the Carnegie Endowment for International Peace were regarded as neutral and scientific organizations engaged in policy analysis. However, by the early 1970s, a new generation of think tanks known for their efforts to combine policy research with political advocacy began to populate the American political landscape. Over the past three decades, many of these so-called 'advocacy' think tanks have embraced a host of domestic and foreign policy issues and, in the process, have attracted widespread criticism. This chapter explores how and to what extent a small band of conservative and neo-conservative think tanks have not only reinforced but sparked anti-American sentiment during President George W. Bush's war on terror. By looking closely at the efforts of think tanks to influence debates over such controversial issues as National Missile Defense and the ongoing war in Iraq, scholars can better understand the root causes and political consequences of anti-Americanism. Such an analysis will also shed light on the politicization of policy expertise and why scholars need to pay more attention to the individuals and organizations that seek to shape US foreign and security policy.

The place of popular culture in anti-Americanism has been widely debated recently. Analysing public opinion data and the views of opinion leaders and elites, Toby Miller argues that popular culture's contents are not clearly and demonstrably key contributors to anti-Americanism. Instead it is the corporate power and foreign and commercial policies of the US, notably its militarism, which are key sources of anti-Americanism today. However, the role of the US State in the success of popular culture is vastly greater than is normally recognized. The efforts of public diplomacy to eschew popular culture, to counterbalance it, lean towards a high-culture bias that will not address ordinary people's needs.

By comparing different political strategies of representation, Skaidra Triplupaityte analyses the relations between cultural anti-Americanism and identity politics in post-Soviet Russia. The question is raised of how Russian pro-Americanism of the early 1990s evolved into a previously unimaginable level of resentment towards the US, which in most cases reflected a common perception of 'unfair' US treatment of Russia. A comparison between formal governmental as well as informal non-governmental relations between the former leading Cold War powers provides an extremely rich background for analysing anti-Americanism in Russia within continuing Cold War rhetoric, since non-corresponding politics often revealed tacit cultural predispositions. The chapter shows how the US's intentions towards Russia could be interpreted in different, even opposing ways, although many explanations do not dwell on historical or empirical reasoning. Yet, in some discourses of new Russian nationalism, cultural anti-Americanism was employed as a useful instrument for representing subversive anti-Russian powers.

The second part of the book addresses two complex issues: trans-Atlantic relationships and security and anti-Americanism. Adam Quinn and Michael Cox analyse the relationship between the US and Europe that has become more strained in the twenty-first century, although one should not romanticize the period before President George W. Bush's inauguration as a golden age of trans-Atlantic harmony. The authors argue that anti-Americanism has already brought serious consequences for world politics, and could bring more in the coming years. One political consequence of rising public anti-Americanism will be the increased difficulty for European leaders in sustaining a pro-American stance or in supporting policies identified in the public mind with the United States, even when the leaders themselves might by their own instincts be disposed to favour such policies. In the world of growing threats to liberal democratic nations, advanced technologies and shifting power balances, Europe and the US have more interest in securing their partnership rather than in allowing a further drifting apart of their respective needs and interests.

The extent and nature of anti-Americanism in international public opinion provide one set of clues to likely international security stances of governments and movements. When faced with choices about how to respond to US government policy preferences, domestic public opinion provides political elites with incentives and disincentives to co-operate, stand aside from or even resist what Washington seems to want. The opinions of domestic publics also can be used to bargain with Washington for side-payments and compliance wavers. A lack of appreciation by US officials of negative or sceptical foreign public opinion can lead to mistaken judgements about likely foreign reactions to US security initiatives, argues Davis B. Bobrow in his chapter. An examination of numerous polls in the first years of the twenty-first century surely shows substantial increases in negativism about US policies, particularly in Western Europe. Yet it also shows that, with certain exceptions – the largest of which encompasses a number of Islamic populations – there seems to be no generalized anti-Americanism. Disagreements, for the most part, are with the policies associated with the second Bush administration. In many parts of the world, there remains a predominant conviction that the US should be an international leader and the superpower – a superpower with whom good relations are essential. That hardly suggests that most governments are under severe pressure to create an alternative international security order, or to reflexively resist Washington. It does suggest that American requests for security co-operation, or even toleration, will have to be persuasive on a case-by-case basis – and often they can be. Scepticism about America and its policies does not equate to anti-Americanism, nor does it have the same implications for international security.

The last part of the book offers regional and case studies and includes countries such as Canada that are very often neglected in the study of anti-Americanism. Furthermore, this part of the book tackles one policy aspect that has caused grave resentment in many parts of the world: the US foreign trade policy.

Kim Richard Nossal analyses the nature of anti-Americanism in Canada. Canadian anti-Americanism is unique not only because it is so old and enduring, but also because it is so weak and bland when compared with that of other regions and countries. While the economic anti-Americanism that had been a part of Canadian political culture for more than two centuries largely faded away after the signing of free trade agreement between the US and Canada in 1989, anti-Americanism has frequently been used to galvanize political support among the electorate. In the late 1990s in particular, the Liberal government of Jean Chrétien oxygenated anti-Americanism in Canada, legitimizing and sometimes actively encouraging anti-American sentiments. His Liberal successor, Paul Martin, did the same, seeking to use anti-American sentiment to shore up support in the 2004 and 2006 general elections. However, the type of anti-Americanism that characterizes contemporary Canada remains a low-grade and ultra-lite contingent anti-Americanism, where antipathy towards George W. Bush co-exists with an overall feeling of friendship towards Americans and the US.

Australian anti-Americanism, argues Ann Capling, has many distinctive elements that stem primarily from Australia's location and its role and position in the international economy. While geography has predisposed Australia to look to the United States as a protector and an ally, economics has often caused rancour in the relationship. This is especially true of the Australia–US trade relationship, where Australian and US economic interests have been in deep conflict over a long period. This chapter explains how US trade policies have generated resentment and anger amongst Australians, and how this particular form of anti-Americanism is manifested in Australian politics and political culture. While the Australian and US governments have managed to 'contain' trade-related anti-Americanism, Capling argues that the recent linking of trade and security concerns in the context of the Australia–US Free Trade Agreement has created a situation in which the anti-American sentiment that is generated by trade conflicts could spill over into the security alliance itself. The final section of the chapter explores the political consequences of anti-Americanism for both Australia and the US.

Asian countries offer another interesting case in trade relations with the US. Since the Asian crisis in 1997, countries in the region are intensifying their efforts for regional co-operation. In some cases, argues Heribert Dieter, these attempts have been accompanied by strong criticism of American economic and foreign policies. However, this does not equate with anti-Americanism. Rather, we are confronted with a puzzle: on the one hand, East Asian societies continue to follow American culture as well as maintain strong security ties with Washington. On the other, East Asian countries are very eagerly trying to reduce their dependence on institutions that are heavily influenced by the US, especially the International Monetary Fund (IMF). Dieter argues that the declining influence of the US in East Asia is the combined effect of a number of factors: the decreasing attractiveness of the US as an economic power, the increasing importance of China as well as its clever diplomacy, the disastrous policies of the American-led IMF in the Asian crisis, and the unfortunate foreign policy of George W. Bush.

Anti-Americanism in Latin America has a long history. Although the phenomenon has previously been related to security issues, it has more recently been the failure of Washington's consensus policies that has caused tensions in US–Latin America economic relations, argues Cintia Quiliconi. In some Latin American countries, mainly in the Southern Cone, this sentiment has been accompanied by a shift to left-wing governments that strongly and openly oppose American economic and foreign policies. Security issues have become intertwined with economic issues and the US is trying to exert soft power through economic relations with security aims. In this sense, the proliferation of bilateral trade agreements between the US and various Latin American countries shows a trend in which the expansion of international trade with the region is vital to US interests in Latin America.

Anti-Americanism has indeed been a complex phenomenon in Greek political history since World War II. Helena Maragou focuses on historical events that generated anti-American sentiments in Greece from 1946 until the late 1990s. One of these controversial events was the North Atlantic Treaty Organization (NATO) bombing of Serbia in 1999, which marked a turning point in Greek society's response to US foreign policy. Maragou traces the current political implications of anti-Americanism with an emphasis on the deep distrust held by Greeks towards the US's role in international affairs. Greek anti-Americanism is on the one hand a local manifestation of European anti-Americanism; however, it also exhibits distinctive characteristics which reflect the unique historical conditions that caused it. In short, Greek anti-Americanism is not, as many think, the result of collective paranoia or envy, or even an excuse for not facing up to domestic problems – irrespective of inherent contradictions and exaggerations based on sometimes gross stereotyping of America. Greek anti-Americanism is historically rooted, a tangible response to concrete historical conditions.

Ariane Chebel d'Appollonia analyses the origins and diversity of anti-Americanism in France, with an emphasis on political dimensions. She outlines the historical roots of the phenomenon, its sources in the French left and right, and common patterns of US criticism that are very often linked with anti-globalization movements and resistance to the 'Americanization' of French culture and France's welfare state. This contributor also deals with the impact of anti-Americanism in French–US relations, and the influence of the phenomenon on French foreign policy. Since the end of the Cold War, the French political elite has been uncomfortable with US 'unilateralism' and similarly with the policies of George

W. Bush's administration in the Middle East. Finally, the chapter offers analysis of contemporary anti-Americanism in France, especially after 11 September 2001.

Conclusion

Taken together, the chapters in this volume advance our understanding of anti-Americanism in several ways. First, they make it abundantly clear that the phenomenon exerts no homogenous force. Far from it, differences are to be found across the policy spectrum and across regions of the globe. A second insight that emerges from the chapters in this volume is the degree to which anti-Americanism emerges from what America does, rather than from what it is. This is not to say that there exist no strands of anti-Americanism that reflect what some would see as prejudice against and moreover jealousy of the world's most materially advanced and prosperous country – simply, this is clearly the minority reading of anti-Americanism. When accompanied by a belief that the US practices material and environmental profligacy, there is no doubt that the US is a source of considerable resentment amongst a growing range of actors and communities across the globe. It can be difficult to know, however, where this ingrained resentment/prejudice ends and where a genuine concern about the adverse impacts of the American policy process begins.

It becomes clear from the chapters in this volume that the principal source of anti-Americanism – although not the only one – is policy driven. To this extent, the principal source of anti-Americanism is US policy and behaviour itself. This is perhaps best illustrated in cases of the US's relationships with traditionally close security allies (such as Australia and Canada), among whom one would expect little anti-Americanism; yet the sentiment can indeed be found there, when other aspects of the relationship have at times been neglected or when the US treats the partner as 'an ally but not a friend', as former Australian Foreign Minister Bill Hayden once observed. In this regard, US trade policy, for example, can often be a source of anti-Americanism in what are otherwise strong and warm relationships. In most instances, the antagonisms stay at the level of policy. There is no doubt, however, that the 'securitization' of US foreign economic policy since 11 September 2001 has had the effect of enhancing anti-Americanism within the body-politic of some key American partners – this is especially the case in its policy towards bilateral trade agreements, where the US ostentatiously rewards those who support its security policy with agreements (for example, Australia, South Korea, Singapore) while at the same time declining negotiations with those who do not support its global military interventions (for example, New Zealand) (see Higgott 2004a). As Ann Caplinng notes in her chapter, the securing of a Free Trade Agreement with the US increased rather than diminished anti-Americanism in Australia.

Anti-Americanism as a deeper-seated hostility than is found in just the policy context is seemingly more evident in states that have traditionally held great power status at a prior historical stage and where there is a tendency to see US policy in a wider ideological context. As Ariane Chebel d'Appollonia demonstrates, for example, negative French attitudes towards US unilateralism in its foreign policy-making are actually located in wider, more deep-seated antagonisms to what we might call globalization as a world view as well as a reflection of policy. While French responses may have been ahead of global opinion, with a pedigree dating back at least to the early post-World War II era, the events of the last few years might suggest that it is appropriate to finish with a question rather than a series of definitive conclusions.

Is it possible to see anti-Americanism transforming from what we might call an essentially policy-driven phenomenon towards a more deep-seated set of entrenched hostile attitudes towards the United States? To seek an answer to this question, it is perhaps worth returning to the judgements expressed by Zbigniew Brzezinski at the beginning of this chapter. The title of Brzezinski's book is *Second Chance*. Explicit for Brzezinski is the issue of whether the US can recover from the gradual but, since the turn of the century, rapidly accelerating anti-Americanism that has been a characteristic of the last three presidencies.

Anti-Americanism as prejudice and resentment has clearly grown, but it is not globally embedded. For the tide to turn, however, policy must also turn. What is required, for Brzezinski, is not only a change of rhetoric on the part of US govern-ments but also a substantive change in the style of US foreign policy engagement with the rest of the world. To imagine that all that is needed is a reversion from unilateralism to multilateralism is far too simple, and misunderstands the complex nature of the post-World War II historical bargain. The difference has never been one of unilateralism versus multilateralism; the issue was one of institutionalism. The US used its post-war hegemony to underwrite a series of institutions of both an economic and political nature that created a global (essentially liberal) order. A principal characteristic of its behaviour was restraint and a willingness to engage in the act of hegemonic self-binding (see Ikenberry 2001).

Over the last decade, US policy has turned its back on the institutions it helped to create and underwrite. For sure, many of these institutions are in need of reform – perhaps even, in the cases of the UN and the IMF, for example, quite drastic reform. But there is a growing understanding that these institutions will not work properly without the application of 'responsible hegemony' by the US. They certainly will not function in the absence of the US's positive participation. Similarly, there is a growing recognition that the US cannot go it alone, in an institutional vacuum rather than through the pursuit of policies unilaterally. The option of unilateralism must always remain in the tool-box of a great state, but it cannot and must not be the normal *modus operandi* of that great state if it hopes to carry world opinion with it in and secure a functioning, albeit imperfect, system of world order. Brzezinski's 'second chance' for the US, and the prospects for stemming the growing tide of anti-Americanism in global affairs, will probably be determined by the ability of the next (and subsequent) US administrations to restore balance to the use of the whole range of foreign policy instruments and, especially, by the degree to which the US can lend support to the restoration of functioning global institutions in the early decades of the twenty-first century.

Notes

1 Eurobarometer, http://ec.europa.eu/public_opinion/archives/eb/eb60/eb60_rapport_ standard_en.pdf
2 The Pew Global Attitudes Project, http://pewglobal.org/reports/pdf/252.pdf
3 We are, of course, not alone in this regard. There has been considerable interest in and numerous publications on anti-Americanism in recent years. Of the recent literature, see, for example: B. O'Connor (ed.) (2007); R. Crockatt (2003); J.-F. Revel (2003a); P. Hollander (2005); P. J. Katzenstein and R. O. Keohane (eds) (2006); D. Lacorne and T. Judt (2005); R. A. Berman (2004); J. E. Sweig (2006); A. McPherson (2006); S. Faath (2006); E. Shiraev and V. Zubok (2000); S. Armus (2007); A. Stephen (ed.) (2006).
4 According to Eurobarometer *Report on Globalization* in 2003, 75 per cent of Europeans said that the US had too much influence on globalization. Available from http://ec.europa. eu/public_opinion/flash/FL151bGlobalisationREPORT.pdf

Part I
Networks, Culture and Foundations

2 Americanism and its Critics: From the Congress for Cultural Freedom to the Open Society Institute

Nicolas Guilhot

In *The Sociological Imagination*, Wright Mills observes that 'we cannot very well state any problem until we know whose problem it is' (Wright Mills 1959: 76). This is certainly the most reliable guideline one can follow when dealing with the twin notions of 'Americanism' and 'anti-Americanism', that too often seem to be atemporal concepts detached from any particular configuration of social forces and contexts. If there can be no *ex ante* definition of their meaning, it is because what they actually designate depends on the concrete situations in which they are used to trace distinctions and oppositions that evolve over time. Indeed, as categories indicating both identity and enmity, they are fundamentally weapons used in ideological struggles. Taking Wright Mills' advice and asking who regarded as an important political task the promotion of 'Americanism' and the defeat of its critique ('anti-Americanism') makes it possible to give a specific historical content to notions that are too quickly turned into intemporal, universally valid concepts.

This chapter argues that the defence of Americanism was essentially the problem of a specific group of intellectuals who, in the aftermath of World War II, operated the 'cultural' side of the US diplomatic offensive in Europe. They represented a very tight intellectual niche – socialists, Trotskyites, disillusioned communists united by their anti-communism – but enjoyed a high degree of international exposure and influence as they were propelled to the ideological frontlines of the Cold War by state agencies and philanthropic foundations. Through the constellation of organizations, journals and cultural initiatives coordinated by the Congress for Cultural Freedom (CCF), they developed a coherent picture of Americanism as a progressive ideology or social model. The way they defined it was influenced by their own intellectual trajectories, of course, but also by the nature of the resistances that the American proposition encountered.

The different strands of anti-Americanism, whether they stemmed from the conservative and elitist rejection of mass culture or from the Marxist persuasion in its various guises, defined the parameters of this exercise in cultural diplomacy. Cultural criticism and sociology appear as the two main fields where the opposition between Americanism and anti-Americanism was staged. In this context, Americanism combined both a principled defence of the 'free world' and a strong emphasis on its socially progressive virtues. It was construed, in other words, as an inclusive and consensual ideology, which sought to appear as a higher form of rationality than the old nineteenth-century ideologies. Yet, this particular construct was made possible by the fact that it reflected a broad intellectual consensus between individuals who otherwise represented different political and cultural traditions, but were united by anti-communism and adherence, albeit sometimes qualified, to the 'American proposition'. I argue that, as this 'anti-totalitarian consensus' began unravelling in the 1960s, the notions of Americanism and anti-Americanism that it had produced became no longer operative. Instead, a good deal of criticism of the American model was now internal to the liberal 'vital centre' of American politics, and to the very trans-Atlantic networks earlier involved in its defence: the ideals of productivism, technocracy and apolitical social reform were increasingly questioned, while some New Left ideas were echoed, albeit critically, by some intellectuals close to the CCF.

While the hard-core anti-communists and more adamant defenders of Americanism in the CCF evolved toward neo-conservatism and, ultimately, the democracy-promotion initiatives of the Reagan administration, others embraced some form of post-liberalism, even though they remained critical of what they perceived as the anti-Americanism of the New Left. I focus more specifically on this second, lesser-known intellectual legacy of the CCF, which informed in particular the evolution of one of its spawns, the *Fondation pour une Entraide Intellectuelle Européenne* (European Foundation for Intellectual Cooperation, EFIC). I argue that the EFIC outlined a particular path out of the cultural cold wars of the 1950s and abandoned the ideological framework defined by the opposition of Americanism and anti-Americanism, and the struggle against communism. Instead, it moved increasingly toward a post-national and liberal concern with 'human rights' and 'civil society' that eased its merger into the Open Society Foundation created by George Soros.

The rise of Americanism

When Gramsci provided one of the first analyses of 'Americanism' in the 1930s, he was not yet sure whether it represented a coherent model or simply a transient aggregate of largely autonomous developments. What was clear to him, though, was that the notion of 'Americanism' was chiefly a repulsive model put together by a variety of social groups fearing the disruptive effects of American modernity on their traditional status (Gramsci 1971). Taking stock from this observation, it may therefore be suggested that, in contrast to what linguistic structures indicate, anti-Americanism precedes and produces Americanism. With the onset of the Cold War, the variety of intellectual resistances to the new international role of the United States – whether they took the traditional form of a reactionary and aristocratic cultural pessimism rejecting American mass society, or of a diffuse Marxism denouncing cultural and economic imperialism – provided a very propitious context for a self-conscious effort at formulating an ideology of 'Americanism' meant to overcome these resistances.

With the launching of the Marshall Plan in 1947, 'Americanism' became a model properly speaking – it offered a template as an example to be replicated.

The Plan was no mere functional response to the economic crisis in Europe, nor solely a system of anti-communist aid, but it entailed a whole political economy cantered on the organization and the management of industrial societies (Milward 1984; van der Pijl 1984). In fact, the strategic rationale for the Plan was less the external threat represented by Soviet expansionism than the internal frailty of European societies, social discontent, and the disruptive effect of war and poverty on their very fabric.

The Marshall Plan thus internationalized a particular form of modernity that emerged in the 1920s–1930s around the problem of the governance of industrial society and that has given Americanism its core features (Vickers 2000). This model rested on the assumption that class conflict over the appropriation of surplus value could be overcome not by revising the social distribution of wealth but by raising productivity. Waste and scarcity, not social inequalities, were identified as the real causes of social unrest, and they could be eliminated by the rationalization of production, scientific management and the search for efficiency in all compartments of social life. These developments were promoted by a new caste of techno-political elites – engineers, social scientists, administrators, industrialists, philanthropic managers – who sought to develop responses to the crisis of traditional, *laissez-faire* liberalism, without calling into question the capitalistic nature of the economy. The 'techno-corporatism' that they promoted during the interwar period, which would later contribute to the formulation of New Deal policies, placed much control over public policy formulation into private hands, as the collaboration between business elites, social scientists and public administrators was encouraged by private intermediate organizations. It was, in many respects, an attempt at planning the economy without handing over control to the state – but rather, locating it into fluid private–public collaborative networks (Alchon 1985; Jordan 1994).

Science, rather than politics, would ensure that industrial society functioned harmoniously. This technocratic mindset certainly subtracted policy-making from public scrutiny and democratic deliberation: 'public administration' embodied this belief in rational and scientific management as opposed to the chaotic clash of individual opinions in the political sphere. Yet, the elites of the Progressive era did not abandon the principle of democracy as much as they reframed it. In their search to conciliate this technocratic faith in rationality and efficiency with the democratic ideals of the nation, they displaced the locus of popular participation from the political arena to the mass market. Taylorism, Fordism and, more generally, the frantic search for efficiency would raise the living conditions of the working classes. The material capacity to consume translated in the industrial era the classical political freedoms of the Constitution, and the Republican ideal of participation as participation of the workforce in the benefits of continuous economic progress. Access to mass culture was first and foremost a fundamental political principle of the new era, a form of economic citizenship (Paggi 1989). Efficiency, stability, democracy, the overcoming of class conflict through modernization and economic progress, mass culture as a democratic principle, and also a new role for generic intellectuals in the power structure, defined the core attributes of Americanism.

Yet, in a post-war Europe where Soviet prestige was high and communist parties strong, this export could be successful only to the extent that it was matched by a cultural or ideological offensive establishing its legitimacy (Scott-Smith 2002). The articulation of what Frances Stonor Sanders has called the 'American proposition' was chiefly the work of a trans-Atlantic network of intellectuals who sought to create cultural conditions supportive of American hegemony in Europe.

Cold War intellectual networks and the perceptions of anti-Americanism

Created in 1950, the Congress for Cultural Freedom primarily provided an institutional platform allowing the so-called 'non-communist left' to organize and internationalize itself. It gathered liberal and left-wing anti-communists (and a few conservatives) around an anti-totalitarian ideological platform that represented a self-styled 'vital center' of Western politics. Seminars, conferences, exhibitions, concerts and a vast network of cultural journals were used to disseminate and defend liberal ideas and to systematically oppose Marxist or communist influences.[1] Most of the CCF affiliates came indeed from the old left of the 1930s: Sidney Hook, Melvin Lasky, or Daniel Bell, for instance, belonged to the nebulous constellation of Trotskyite and social-democratic groups schooled in the political atmosphere of City College in New York. Some early participants, however, had more conservative positions – like Edward Shils – or moved earlier toward the right – like James Burnham. Among the Europeans, the CCF comprised members of the non-communist resistance, like Raymond Aron or Pierre Emmanuel, former communists like Arthur Koestler or Ignazio Silone, East European émigrés like Jerzy Giedroyc or Constantin Jelenski.

This broad alliance of intellectuals and cultural producers was formed around the opposition to 'totalitarianism', a concept that was instrumental in channelling the pre-1945 opposition to fascism toward anti-communism (Gleason 1995). Initially a staunchly anti-communist organization created spontaneously in opposition to Soviet sponsorship of the peace movement and of internationalist cultural events, the early CCF sought to strike a delicate ideological balance by reclaiming many progressive credentials of the left. As Leopold Labedz, a long-time adviser and collaborator of the CCF, wrote in retrospect:

> the Congress of the early 1950s used what may be called a 'popular front' technique, turning it against Communists. It provided a common platform against totalitarianism of Right and Left and it tried to pull out the left-wing intelligentsia from the orbit of the communist ideological influence [...] The original idea [was] uniting the widest possible range of intellectuals on a common platform of opposition to illiberal thought ...[2]

Constantin Jelenski, a Polish intellectual émigré who joined the Congress in the early 1950s, also considered that the task of the early CCF was to oppose Stalinism without accepting as allies all reactionary anticommunists. It was meant to show that one could be anti-Stalinian while going on fighting against every form of right-wing totalitarianism, every chauvinism, every 'neo-fascist' threat, every encroachment on freedom of expression within our very societies. The urgency of the struggle against the Stalinist threat, waged from 'liberal' positions [...] allowed the Congress to unite individuals coming from very different cultural and political traditions ...[3]

Its view of anti-Americanism also reflected the nature of this anti-totalitarian consensus and the attempt at striking a strategic balance between anti-communism and progressivism. As the Congress intellectuals saw it, European anti-Americanism chiefly expressed itself as the critique of 'mass culture'. This topic provided the focus of important debates in the 1950s and early 1960s that were central to the US effort at 'cultural diplomacy' (Berghahn 2001). At a conference on 'The Future of Freedom' organized by the CCF in 1955, Daniel Bell gave a paper on 'America as Mass Society' which captured most of the issues at stake. The rejection of American 'mass culture', he contended – denounced as being commercialized, vulgar, devoid of substantial content and real cultural traditions – could best be traced to 'a defence of an aristocratic cultural tradition' that was fundamentally undemocratic and feared the loss of control of the elites in shaping the cultural preferences of the masses (Bell 2000). His argument aimed at the 'cultural pessimism' of a conservative European intelligentsia who perceived American culture as the triumph of the market over the works of the spirit, but also at the 'theories of mass society' developed by German émigrés such as Hannah Arendt, Emil Lederer, Karl Mannheim and, later, prominent members of the Frankfurt School.

In this latter view, the rationalization of social life under conditions of pervasive use of technology and intensified capitalism severed traditional ties and dissolved social identities, giving rise to phenomena of social atomization that found in fascism their privileged political expression. In some of its formulations, this analysis overlapped with a wider diagnosis of the crisis of capitalism and dovetailed with the communist-inspired critique of Americanism in the wake of the Marshall Plan. The debate about mass culture thus made it possible to confront at once, and under the same label, two distinct forms of opposition to the American model, but also to combine anti-communism with an egalitarian democratic ideal. Against these critiques, indeed, Bell defended the positive value of mass society: modernization, secularization, the pluralization of values and the undoing of traditional community ties, he argued, contributed to emancipating individuals, allowing them to fulfil their aspirations independently from positions assigned by class or tradition. Mass society, in his view, was a positive development because it was fundamentally inclusive, as it brought into the polity and the economy groups that had been excluded, allowing for their participation and self-realization.

The intellectual struggle against anti-Americanism thus took the form of a sociological defence of 'industrial society', of which the United States was thought to offer the most accomplished example. By the mid-1950s, the mobilized intelligentsia of the CCF – and in particular its sociologists: Daniel Bell, Seymour

Martin Lipset, Edward Shils, and Raymond Aron in France – produced a particular redescription of the American model discussed above under the guise of 'industrial society'. Spread through various publications and conferences, this sociological discourse turned Americanism as the very ideal-type of industrial modernity and reflected many of its features: the faith in pragmatic and technocratic management; the belief that engineering, rather than politics, could solve social conflicts, and in particular the conflict between capital and labour; the idea that increased productivity would ensure the smooth inclusion of the lower classes into the polity, and so on. In particular, it posited that the complexity of modern, industrialized societies made political ideologies obsolete, since they were ill-adapted for the management of complex systems, and had to give way to more pragmatic and rational forms of governance. These discussions were encapsulated in the notion of the 'end of ideology' that provided for a while the rallying cry for most Cold War social scientists.[4] Coined during the 1955 conference organized by the Congress, this intellectual shorthand implied, as Lipset subsequently wrote (Lipset 1960), that

> the fundamental political problems of the industrial revolution have been solved: the workers have achieved industrial and political citizenship; the conservatives have accepted the welfare state; and the democratic left has recognized that an increase in over-all state power carries with it more dangers to freedom than solutions to economic power.

The end of ideology was thus related to an attempt at occupying a wide-ranging ideological middle-ground, a liberal centre attractive to both socialist intellectuals and moderates. Yet, it also sought to discredit any form of class-based politics. In the West, as Daniel Bell argued, class-based ideologies subsided because 'in a politico-technological world, property has increasingly lost its force as a determinant of power, and sometimes, even, of wealth. In almost all modern societies, technical skill becomes more important than inheritance as a determinant of occupation [...] What then is the meaning of class?' (Bell 2000). The point was also, obviously, to discredit the scientific pretences of Marxism as a sociological theory. For indeed, according to Bell, once the working class was considered to have economic citizenship and to enjoy social mobility, the only social group still attached to some utopian ideals of socialism were the intellectuals – precisely because mass culture and the market threatened their privileged status. The rise of revolutionary ideologies was thus explained away as a politics of resentment, led by intellectuals who refused that their cultural productions, which buttressed their social status, be democratically judged by the market.[5] The opposition of Marxist intellectuals to mass culture and their anti-Americanism could therefore be understood, in Bell's view, as the continuation, in the twentieth century, of this self-catering attitude.

The marketing of 'mass culture', 'industrial society' and the 'end of ideology' by the intellectuals associated with the Congress was as much an analysis of current societal trends as an attempt by former radicals to come to terms with their own ideological evolution and their endorsement of Americanism. It construed an image of American society conceived from a very specific perspective – that of an Old Left politicized in the polarized atmosphere of the 1930s before joining the liberal anti-communist fold after 1945 – and reading into America if not the ideal of a classless society, at least an open social system where mobility and strong redistributive tendencies ensured a high degree of egalitarianism. In a preface to a second edition of his *Political Man*, the book where he had developed various ideas closely related to the CCF, Lipset gave a rather candid explanation for his own endorsement of Americanism, where the reinvestment of a leftist past into the defence of Americanism comes to the fore: answering to some critics, he wrote that he still 'considered [himself] a man on the left', but added that the thought of the United States 'as a nation in which leftist values predominate' (Lipset 1963).

The 1960s, the end of the anti-totalitarian consensus and its ideological legacies

While the early Cold War was characterized by clear-cut ideological frontlines, and offered the possibility to stage a progressive fight against anti-Americanism, extolling the virtues of a democratic, egalitarian and inclusive industrial society, the social and political configuration of the late 1960s made this increasingly difficult. The revelation, in 1966–67, that the Congress for Cultural Freedom had been financed by the Central Intelligence Agency (CIA) since the beginning was certainly a major blow to the organization. For intellectuals who had claimed to defend intellectual freedom and independence, many of whom were unaware of the CIA backing, this came as a shock. Some of them, such as Raymond Aron, left the organization and no longer associated themselves with the CCF journals. As Constantin Jelenski put it shortly after, in a letter that reviewed the situation of the Congress in 1967, 'a considerable number of illustrious individuals from all countries, who represented a constructive, non-communist left that, if not pro-American, did not accept a systematically anti-American ideology, were first lured by the Americans, and then compromised by the Americans'.[6] In fact, the Congress entered a protracted crisis that its reorganization as the International Association for Cultural Freedom (IACF), under the auspices of the Ford Foundation, would never really solve. Yet, the CIA scandal was probably the symptom, rather than the cause, of a deeper, underlying crisis. The liberal centre of the 1950s and the anti-totalitarian consensus were unravelling, as the escalation in Vietnam made a number of liberals uneasy about the course of US foreign policy.

In the same letter to Emmanuel, Jelenski saw clearly that

> the very conditions for the cohesion between individuals representing such diverse political views, a cohesion motivated by a common struggle against an immediate totalitarian danger, are no longer present ... Our friends in Asia are in favour of the Vietnam war – the vast majority of our other friends are against it ...[7]

As the relevant ideological divides were increasingly cutting through the old liberal centre itself, anti-Americanism no longer provided a compass for understanding and articulating the cultural cold wars of the past.

The emergence of a New Left that contested the very foundations of the 'industrial society' that Congress intellectuals had so eagerly promoted in their writings was another major element accounting for the disorientation of this intellectual milieu. Not only did the social movements of the late 1960s seem to make irrelevant the notion of the 'end of ideology', but the 'industrial city' was contested both for its failure to deliver the goods it promised and for the forms of social control and domination embedded in it (Boltanski and Chiapello 1999). In this latter perspective, it was the conflation of social progress with productivism and the commodification of citizenship that were denounced from a perspective no longer emphasizing social benefits, but rather individual freedom and self-realization in a post-material perspective. Industrial modernity was attacked not for its failure to deliver, but for the very nature of its project. The whole intellectual paradigm on which the Congress sociologists and cultural critics had thrived for almost two decades was thus called into question by the generation that enjoyed the benefits of industrial society.

This new situation also contributed to the widening of internal rifts that came to the fore once the previous consensus was shattered. In particular, the 'social science' approach defended by the Congress sociologists (and especially the paradoxical form of intellectual anti-intellectualism implied in the 'end of ideology') was always at odds with the views of the European members of the CCF. If Raymond Aron was indeed a theorist of industrial society, who would be instrumental in diffusing the work of Bell in France, for instance, he still maintained an interest in philosophical theorizing and speculation. Pierre Emmanuel, a poet who was attached to a traditional conception of culture and the intellectual, was always critical of the pragmatic social scientific perspective peddled under the label of 'industrial society'. A Gaullist, he also resented what he considered an overwhelming American influence within the Congress and, later, the IACF. And though he was certainly very much involved in the sociological discussions about the end of ideology and mass culture, Jelensky had a much wider spectrum of cultural interests. More importantly, the different perspectives on the New Left adopted by the old liberal anti-communists in the US and the variegated network located in Paris account for much of the subsequent divisions.

For sure, all the different components of the Congress milieu reacted very strongly and critically *vis-à-vis* the New Left. On both sides of the Atlantic, the attack against industrial society was immediately perceived as a sign of 'irrationalism' – for such was the extent to which the traits of industrial modernity had come to represent the very embodiment of rationality. A generational gap also prevented most members of the CCF from really feeling the pulse of the new social movements. As a result, they tended to analyse the situation as a return to the 1930s. The denouncement of irrationalism and of a new form of fascism was therefore the common thread running through the statements and documents produced by the Congress intellectuals. And yet, this common language concealed diverging tendencies that, over the years, would become ever more pronounced.

The ideological realignments taking place within the old liberal centre no longer held together by a common anti-totalitarian, pro-American platform essentially took two forms.

On the one hand, the old guard of the Congress, and in particular the intellectuals who had crafted the 'end of ideology' and marketed 'industrial society', adopted an intransigent position and rejected *en bloc* the ideas of the New Left, which they saw as nihilistic. Paradoxically, those who had chanted the virtues of mass culture and its emancipatory functions were appalled by the forms it was taking, and moved towards a defence of traditional forms of authority and culture. This reaction was clearly identified – and felt to be somewhat unwelcome – by several European CCF members. Jelenski, in particular, observed that 'during the big debate about mass culture that took place between 1945 and 1955 [...] left wing intellectuals (Dwight McDonald, Marcuse, etc.) were against' while Shils and Bell were in favour. But he also noticed that the roles were inverted: 'today we see Edward Shils becoming a fanatical enemy of this youth which gives its real meaning to mass culture'; to refer to Shils and Bell, he used the word 'neoconservatives'.[8]

François Bondy, another influential member of the Congress, referring to the Committee for the Free World in which Labedz, Lasky, Shils and Lipset, among others, took part, refused to subscribe to their initiative, which he considered 'very much right-wing'.[9] In fact, this tendency within the Congress would contribute to the neo-conservative reaction and retreat toward other seats of cultural power, whether think tanks, political organizations or state agencies. Lipset and Bell, for instance, became both affiliated with the Coalition for a Democratic Majority and, later, the Committee on the Present Danger – two organizations which contributed to assembling the core of the neo-conservative movement. Pretty much on the defensive during the 1970s, this current would finally find political outlets under the Reagan administration, where it became chiefly responsible for the creation of 'democracy promotion' programmes through such institutions as the National Endowment for Democracy (Guilhot 2005).

But it is possible to delineate another, lesser-known legacy of the Congress for Cultural Freedom. Reactions within the Paris secretariat of the IACF and, even more so, within the Fondation pour une Entraide Intellectuelle Européenne (European Foundation for Intellectual Cooperation, EFIC), opened a different path out of the cultural cold war of the 1950s. The EFIC was a creation of the Congress that ran programmes in Eastern Europe and, to a lesser extent, in the Iberic peninsula. Its activities consisted mostly of sending social science and literature to a vast network of contacts across the Iron Curtain, and offering travel grants for scholars and artists when they were authorized to travel to Western Europe. When it was created in 1957, as an informal Committee of Writers and Publishers (it would be turned into a formal organization in 1967), the EFIC was closely following and promoting the 'revisionist' critique of communist regimes articulated in Eastern Europe by disillusioned young Marxists.[10] It provided, too, a bridge between non-conformist intellectuals in Eastern Europe and the critique of ideologies that the Congress stood for, and subscribed to the idea that industrial societies, whether capitalist or communist, were facing similar problems of governance that made ideologies obsolete. Although the EFIC was almost indistinguishable from the CCF, its intellectual leadership, as far as the analysis of East European trends was concerned, resided primarily with Constantin Jelenski (the other important figure was Pierre Emmanuel, who oversaw the programmes in Spain and Portugal). Yet, by the mid-1970s, the ideological framework under which the EFIC was operating had considerably changed.

There is no doubt that Jelenski subscribed to the criticism of the New Left which depicted it as a reaction against 'rationality'. However, his judgement was much more qualified for several reasons. While the neo-conservatives represented a domestic reaction against the New Left in the US, Jelenski had a more global view of the new social movements, and did not dissociate completely May 1968 in Paris from the Prague Spring the same year. He foresaw in the critique of productivism and the post-materialistic values of the New Left anti-authoritarian potentialities that represented a threat for communist regimes as well: 'One of the features common to the Western "New Left" is its challenge to a set of presuppositions which are common to all developed societies ("capitalist" and "communist" alike) and which one could call "productivist".'[11] Moreover, the EFIC was closely associated with the new Polish opposition, and especially with one of its main thinkers, Adam Michnik. It was thus exposed to the new language of dissent that was developing in Eastern Europe and had little to do with the revisionism of the 1950s. This language was now based on the defence of individual rights and a form of non-engagement with the state that focused instead on the expansion of an autonomous public sphere. It would soon define the two core notions of the democratization processes of the late 1980s: human rights and civil society.

This take on the Helsinki process is certainly important in explaining the delinking between the two main sensitivities present in the old CCF. For the neo-conservatives, indeed, the third basket of the Helsinki agreements was merely a blank cheque given to the USSR. In subsequent years, they would develop a very strong critique of international human rights law, considered to be a weapon playing in the hand of their liberal opponents and, ultimately, fuelling anti-Americanism. Liberals considered human rights to be a set of international norms ('international human rights') and institutions, and their human rights policy was intended to strengthen international organizations and their legal frameworks. The neo-conservatives, instead, shifted the emphasis away from law toward regime change: they defined human rights policy as the building of regimes based on human rights, that is, as 'democracy promotion'. Their understanding of American exceptionalism led them to insist on the benevolent nature of American power, and to conflate the pursuit of the national interest with the extension of human rights and democracy.

From the cultural cold wars to the promoting of 'open societies'

The position of the EFIC in the late 1970s set it on a different course. Following fund-raising difficulties in Europe, it gradually turned its attention to the United States.[12] The networks of intellectuals, dissidents and reformists that it maintained in Eastern Europe were also looking increasingly to the US for political and material support.[13] Generational change in the secretariat, as well as the deaths of Pierre Emmanuel (1984) and Constantin Jelenski (1987), deprived the EFIC of much of its programming and strategic capacity. While personal contacts with old members of the Congress (such as Daniel Bell) were still important, the EFIC also developed new contacts through the networks of the Ford Foundation, especially among the liberal circles of the emerging human rights movement.

It is in this context that it developed lasting ties with Aryeh Neier, the founder of Human Rights Watch, and George Soros, as it took part in an academic exchange at New York University by suggesting possible grantees. Soros, who was financing the scheme, became interested in the work of the EFIC, and offered to contribute financially to its efforts. Over the years, his participation would match, and then surpass, that of the Ford Foundation, turning the EFIC into an element of the emerging philanthropic network of Open Society Institutes (OSIs). When the democratization of Eastern Europe took place in 1989–91, the European Foundation for Intellectual Cooperation found itself largely unprepared to face the tasks ahead. Its know-how, which had been unique during the Cold War, became largely useless, as other organizations could now operate more or less freely in Eastern Europe, and its small budget made it ill-equipped to engage in the vast reform programmes being launched.

Yet, the network of intellectuals, scholars, reformers and dissidents that it had built in 25 years constituted a precious social capital, as many of these former protégés were already moving to new seats of cultural or political power. The winding down of the EFIC in 1991 should not obscure what is arguably its most important legacy: its incorporation within the expanding network of Soros philanthropies. During the spring of 1990, when it was already decided that the EFIC should be terminated, its director Adam Watson delineated an entire exit strategy, which consisted into 'handing over' the networks of EFIC contacts to existing organizations, the most important of which were 'the various bodies which George Soros is setting up in Eastern Europe'.[14] Highly symbolical of this continuity, the old EFIC secretariat in Paris, which generations of East European intellectuals had visited, was soon turned into the 'Open Society Institute – Paris'.

Retrospectively, it is not surprising that the post-liberal tendency within the Congress for Cultural Freedom, as it developed around the team of the European Foundation for Intellectual Cooperation, merged smoothly into one of the most globalized and powerful foundations of the late twentieth century. To a large extent, the initial mission of the OSI network in Eastern Europe – illustrated by the creation of the Central European University in 1991 – was perfectly aligned with the work accomplished by the EFIC: providing scholars of the region with cultural and scientific resources and travel grants. But more importantly, this continuity has deeper sociological and ideological roots.

The European Foundation for Intellectual Cooperation was not only an organization but, as Jelenski once put it, 'a network of influential friendships'. It gave a form to a cosmopolitan community of individuals, a liberal international counter-public sphere whose existence was dependent upon its ties to such organizations as the CCF or the EFIC, able to stir international public opinion and exert political influence. The European Foundation was itself a cosmopolitan milieu: Jelenski came from an aristocratic and intellectual Polish family, had studied in England, worked in Italy for the United Nations, and settled in Paris; Pierre Emmanuel was well acquainted with the United States, where he had lived as a child, and had very strong cultural ties with both Eastern Europe and, even more so, Spain; Annette Laborey, the secretary of the EFIC, was German but had studied in the United States for a while. This internationalized milieu was certainly congenial to Soros, who was himself a Hungarian émigré who had studied in London before moving to New York in 1956. He indeed shared several biographical traits with the constituency of the EFIC – among them an Eastern European background, the experience of exile and study opportunities in the West. This social proximity appears clearly in the fact that Annette Laborey was introduced to George Soros through a former Hungarian grantee of the EFIC, in 1981.

But the affinity of individual dispositions was also matched by the compatibility of the respective world views. The ideological core of Soros' philanthropic initiatives, articulated around the concept of 'open society', can be traced back to the liberal and anti-totalitarian influences of Karl Popper. During his formative years at the London School of Economics and Political Science (LSE), Soros was indeed exposed to the teaching of Popper, as well as to Lionel Robbins, who, along with Friedrich Hayek, were the main exponents of the Austrian School of Economics at the LSE in the late 1940s.[15] This intellectual milieu would play a leading role in the international revival of liberalism (or, rather, in the emergence of neo-liberalism) in the subsequent decades. More importantly, the liberalism defended by these Central European thinkers was shaped by their reaction to the traumatic collapse of early twentieth-century liberalism and the advance of corporatism, nationalism and totalitarianism. It saw in the free market and the rule of law the only possible form of democracy. It was also fundamentally internationalist and deeply suspicious of the national state.[16] This brand of liberalism resurfaces in several of Soros' writings on international markets and the need for liberal political institutions to ensure their smooth functioning (Soros 1997; Soros 2002). It also informed to a large extent his philanthropic efforts in Eastern Europe, and especially the founding of the Central European University, the main purpose of which was to train a liberal and anti-nationalist elite capable of carrying out the political transition to capitalism (Guilhot 2007).

The merging of the EFIC within the OSI network therefore appears as a natural outcome. One can indeed trace the intellectual antecedents of these organizations to two distinct expressions of the anti-totalitarian mood of the late 1940s. Moreover, by the late 1970s, the EFIC had carried out the transformation of the Cold War anti-communism of the Congress into a liberal anti-totalitarianism articulated around new actors (such as the journal *Contrepoint* in France) and the international human rights movement (Grémion 1995). It was therefore logical for the organization, when its operations became increasingly dependent upon the US context during the 1980s, to turn toward the liberal internationalist circles around the nascent OSI rather than to the neo-conservative tendency that had evolved out of the old CCF.

In fact, its internationalist strategy was very much at odds with the peculiar form of nationalism embodied by the neo-conservative movement, which was largely home-grown.

The notions of democracy and human rights which the neo-conservatives heralded were actually conflated with the American national interest which they universalized. They remained steeped in a national vision, which recast the opposition between Americanism and anti-Americanism in moral and universalistic terms. By contrast, the vision represented by the OSI reflects the decentralized nature of an organization spanning vast transnational networks. It addresses issues no longer from the perspective of a national viewpoint, but through the prism of a complex web of local and global agendas. And yet, this particular position does not prevent the OSI from being locally perceived as an agent of 'Americanism' – which to a certain extent it is, since it is also a channel for the exportation of models of governance, recipes for economic reform and an NGO culture largely 'made in the US', and its founder has become part of the foreign policy establishment. In fact, the OSI has recently deplored the upsurge of anti-Americanism, which impairs its activities in several countries.

Even though – or rather because – they occasionally clash (as occurred over the war in Iraq), these two different legacies of the Cold War illustrate the fact that Americanization is indeed a 'contested project', in the sense that it implies the exportation not only of specific models, but also of the conflicts around these models and the strategies used to fight these conflicts (Dezalay and Garth 2002). In that sense, the very opposition between neo-conservative thinking and the transnational, NGO-based deployment of American 'soft power' through such initiatives as the OSI is today one of the main ways of ensuring the international diffusion of the Washington-based debates around political and economic globalization.

Notes

1 On the Congress for Cultural Freedom, see P. Coleman (1989); P. Grémion (1995); F. S. Saunders (1999); G. Scott-Smith (2002).

2 Leopold Labedz, letter to Shepard Stone, June 1970, Constantin Jelenski Papers, Yale University, Beinecke Rare Book and Manuscript Library, Uncat. MSS, Vault 579, Box 6 (hereafter CJP), Folder 166, pp. 2–3.

3 Constantin Jelenski, letter to Pierre Emmanuel, 23 May 1967, CJP, Box 6, Folder 134.

4 On this whole debate, see the documents collected in C. I. Waxman (ed.) (1968).

5 This analysis, which takes shape in the conservative sociology of the 1950s, subsequently informs the analysis of communist regimes as establishing the rule of intellectuals as a class. This is, for instance, the line followed by G. Konrad and I. Szelenyi (1979).

6 CJP, Box 6, Folder 134, Letter to Pierre Emmanuel, manuscript draft (1967).

7 *Ibid.*

8 FEIEA, Box 16/2, C. Jelenski, Letter to R. Chenu, 5 July 1971.

9 FEIEA, Box 22/3, F. Bondy, Letter to A. Laborey, 3 November 1981. Born in Germany, François Bondy was an ex-communist who left the Party in 1939, at the time of the

Soviet–German pact. He joined the Congress for Cultural Freedom in 1950, as Director of Publications, before becoming the editor of *Preuves*, the French magazine sponsored by the Congress.

10 On the EFIC, see N. Guilhot (2006: 379–409).

11 CJP, Box 6, Folder 169, 'International Association for Cultural Freedom (Suggestions for a program)', p. 3.

12 After its separation from the IALC, the EFIC was financed directly by the Ford Foundation, which put it under pressure to match its funds by raising money autonomously.

13 Note Grémion (conclusion).

14 FEIEA, Box 26/5, Letter to Daniel Bell, 23 June 1990. Another of these organizations was the Institut für die Wissenschaften vom Menschen, in Vienna, that Soros had also sponsored initially.

15 On Soros, see N. Guilhot (2007: 447–77).

16 In fact, in the last chapter of *The Road to Serfdom*, Hayek calls for the constitution of an 'international authority' powerful enough to secure markets and to avoid the encroachment of national states while remaining limited in its operations by the Rule of Law (F. A. Hayek (1994)).

3 Combating Anti-Americanism: American Foundations and Public Diplomacy

Inderjeet Parmar

This chapter considers the political–intellectual responses of East Coast US elites to the rise of anti-Americanism, specifically the historical and contemporary public diplomacy initiatives of major philanthropic foundations. Periods of anti-Americanism – such as during the Cold War and after 11 September 2001 and the Iraq War – led the major American philanthropies (in this case, the Ford Foundation and the German Marshall Fund of the United States) to launch significant private initiatives that dovetailed in a semi-official division of labour with official state agencies' efforts to combat 'anti-Americanism' and to promote 'Americanism'. Some privately organized and funded public diplomacy initiatives were considered so successful by foundation and state officials that they were continued over several decades.

Three specific cases – two from the Cold War and one from the post-11 September and Iraq War years – are considered below: Henry Kissinger's Harvard International Seminar, the Salzburg Seminar in American Studies, and the trans-Atlantic unity-building activities of the German Marshall Fund of the United States (GMF). The historical evidence presented suggests that really effective public diplomacy requires critical engagement and exchange on a personal or small group basis rather than mere mass-oriented propaganda. It is also clear that there are limits to public diplomacy's effectiveness and influence due to differing national interests and world views. The chapter concludes that the foundations are strategically vital institutions which mediate corporate, state and elite intellectual interests in order for the US to pursue more effectively global hegemony or leadership through the construction of elite knowledge networks. The foundations are a deeply entrenched component of the American East Coast establishment and power elite; they therefore view America's position and role in the world in a manner very similar, if not identical, to that of the official makers of US foreign policy.

Given the identity of foundation trustees' and state officials' social origins, political affiliations, overlapping corporate directorships, club memberships, racial/ethnic composition, and the progressive era provenance of East Coast philanthropy (Arnove 1980; Berman 1983; Parmar 2000), it is unsurprising that there should be little general disagreement over their definitions of US national interests or anti-American threats to those interests. In addition, by World War II and the Cold War, those commonalities had coalesced institutionally through close relations with the US Department of State, in particular. The State Department's Division of Cultural Relations, formed in 1938 (Bu 2003), increasingly coordinated official and unofficial agencies' efforts, while the Department's research and analysis capacities were enhanced by foundation-funded operations involving think tanks like the Council on Foreign Relations (Shoup and Minter 1977; Parmar 2004a). Relations between private and state agencies – such as the Central Intelligence Agency and the Ford Foundation – were further cemented during the Cold War (Berghahn 2001; Scott-Smith 2002). During the latter period, a shared 'discourse of danger' (Campbell 1992) about a 'communist threat' united the American foreign policy establishment even more tightly in opposing all anti-Americans abroad (and, indeed, 'un-Americans' at home – Parmar 2005a), who were seen as fellow-travellers of communism.

Foundation officials viewed anti-Americanism as being variously sourced in foreign envy of American wealth, resentment of US power, failure to understand America's true intentions and values, or failure to master modernity (Friedman 2003a; Cunliffe 1986). 'They resent our success and hate our values', as President George W. Bush (Parmar 2005c) noted: this is a less sophisticated formulation than foundation representatives would publicly support, yet it sums up, in part at least, their effective position on the causes of anti-Americanism. They have taken 'America' or rather American foreign policy behaviour out of the causes of 'anti-Americanism', largely dismissing out of hand the idea that there could be a rational and reasoned basis for opposition to US foreign and military policies. The 'solution', in large measure, to the problem of such uninformed or unreasoned anti-Americanism, was and is better, more effective cultural or public diplomacy.

Viewed critically, however, it may be argued that fighting communism and anti-Americanism provided the United States with the 'defensive' cover through which to establish its own global hegemony. Identification of enemies and threats, and the construction of a series of 'defensive' military and other alliances, was the means by which America could mobilize its people and resources behind a globally hegemonic strategy. The major American foundations played key roles historically, and continue to do so, though latterly under the banner of a 'war on terror', as this chapter shows, beginning with two examples from the Cold War.

Foundations and post-war American hegemony

After 1945, foundation leaders developed a crisis mentality mirroring that within the American state. With the developing perception of a 'communist threat', foundation leaders increasingly saw the world in stark terms: America's friends and foes, the forces of freedom versus the 'evil empire' or the 'slave state', as the infamous NSC-68 (National Security Council paper 68) put it in April 1950 (Leffler 1992; McCarthy 1987). They saw 'anti-Americanism' as a part of the communist threat or, at the very least, its fellow-traveller. Within the mindset of the national security state, criticism of American society or government was seen as anti-American. The Carnegie, Rockefeller and Ford foundations lined up behind a programme of hegemonic expansion: promoting Americanism and combating anti-Americanism through public diplomacy were key dimensions of that project.

This is an under-researched but fundamental aspect of the foundations' activities during this period, rich in lessons about the nature of the foundations themselves in a time of global transitions – the rise of US power, the relative decline of Europe, and the formation of post-colonial states. As well, it offers valuable insights into how American 'soft power' – trying to persuade other powers to back US foreign policies, as opposed to using coercion – operated in a world of rising anti-Americanism (Nye 2003). The programmes contrast well with what some critics, as is shown later in this chapter, argue is inadequate in public diplomacy today: the focus on 'selling' or 're-branding' America, as indicated by the appointment of Madison Avenue advertising executive (and former CEO of the multi-billion dollar firm, Ogilvy and Mather) Charlotte Beers in 2001, rather than by engaging and debating with America's European allies (Gedmin and Kennedy 2003; Arndt 2005; Melissen 2005).

Henry Kissinger's Harvard University International Summer Seminar

As Scott Lucas argues, Kissinger's Harvard Seminar illustrates the degree to which the United States' hegemonic project integrated culture, the academy and American foreign policy, tightening the integration of a state–private network to wage a war 'defending' the American way of life (Lucas 2003: 258). The advantage of such state–private networks was that official policy objectives – promoting American interests and pro-American ideas and elites – could be met, or at least advanced, especially in 'sensitive' areas or issues, by purportedly unofficial, non-governmental means (Parmar 2006b). American foundations – who claimed to be independent of the state, non-political and non-ideological – were ideal institutional mechanisms for promoting Americanism and combating anti-Americanism.

The Seminar was originally formed by Harvard's William Y. Elliott, Central Intelligence Agency (CIA) consultant and Kissinger's doctoral supervisor, with initial funding (US$15,000) from the CIA in 1951. From 1950 (until 1971), Kissinger became the linchpin of the Seminar, developing its ideological rationale and recruiting the participants. By 1953, Kissinger had obtained financial support from the Farfield Foundation, a conduit for CIA finances. In 1954, the Ford Foundation began its sponsorship of Kissinger's Seminar, the beginning of a long relationship (Lucas 2003: 259). Public and private finances, therefore, were inextricably bound up in the origins of Kissinger's Seminar, fully exemplifying the state–private network concept.

The aim of the Seminar, Kissinger argued, was 'to create a spiritual link between the younger generation of Europe and American values', as Europeans were frustrated with the collapse of 'traditional values' and the rise of a seemingly unsympathetic United States, 'a bewildering spectacle of economic prosperity and seeming misunderstanding of European problems'. This attitude opened the way for 'neutralism' and communism to win European support. The Seminar would 'assist in counteracting these tendencies, by giving inwardly alive, intelligent young

Europeans an opportunity to study the deeper meaning of US democracy'. The programme, however, would fail if it were merely one of 'dogmatic indoctrination'; therefore, it had to be focused around *persuading* Europeans that Americans were genuinely concerned with 'abstract problems' and not just 'material prosperity'. The programme was to be a forum for '*disagreement and criticism*', with a view to *demonstrating* that 'self-reliance is a *possibility* despite the complexity of the present age and that the assumption of *personal responsibility* is more meaningful than unquestioning submission to an apparatus'. Just like communists, democrats needed to display 'the strength of their convictions' (Lucas 2003: 261–2; emphasis added).

Hence, this Seminar was no blunt-edged attempt at indoctrination: the deeper abstract and philosophical meaning of life in American democracy animated the programme by examining the concept of freedom, 'the striving for self-realization in art against the felt pressure of convention, the quest for a reconciliation of rationalism, personal responsibility and dogmatism in religion'. The Seminar aimed to produce no 'absolute solutions' to policy and social problems but rather to generate an '*elucidation of fundamental issues*', making 'social problems … *challenges for normative concepts* …' (Lucas 2003: 263; emphasis added).

The role of the Ford Foundation

Given the leadership of Ford in the early 1950s – men such as Paul Hoffman, John J. McCloy and Shepard Stone (all connected with the State Department or CIA) – the Foundation provided a perfect source for privately financing the Harvard Seminar (Berghahn 2001).[1] Between 1954 and 1959, Ford awarded US$170,000 to the Harvard Seminar, bringing together leaders and potential leaders from across Europe and Asia, networking them with Americans and familiarizing them with American values and institutions. In all, Ford contributed millions of dollars to the efforts of Kissinger and others to improve trans-Atlantic relations between 1954 and 1971.[2] For instance, the 1954 group of 40 participants – aged 35–40 years (a group that often sought refuge in 'a narrow nationalism', according to Kissinger)[3] – included a German diplomat, a British Member of Parliament, a French journalist, a Korean lecturer, and a Filipino lawyer, among others. Numbers were kept low to enable Seminar leaders 'to pay personal attention to each participant', with the selection policy being based 'as much as possible on the personal recommendations of reliable individuals'. It was clear to Kissinger that the success of the programme depended 'to a large extent on its selection process'. The Seminar received around 700 European applications annually; final selection was based on recommendations by American and European elites – the contributors to Kissinger's journal, *Confluence*, Seminar alumni, 'Harvard faculty with European connections' and the recommendations of international societies such as the English-Speaking Union and various Institutes of World Affairs. All recommendations were assessed for short-listing by Kissinger, his assistant, and by a national of the applicant's country of origin, then interviewed in Europe by a trusted representative. The final decision was made at Harvard, minimizing the chances of any 'dangerous' elements.

The Seminar was skilfully devised to provide a range of contacts with American life over a period of two months: seminars on politics, economics, philosophy, art, American democracy, and discussions on 'America's role in relation to other countries of the world'; evening lectures by outsiders and Harvard and other faculty, including a robust defence of the McCarthyite investigating committees by James Burnham; foreigners' presentations on their own nations' problems; visits to American business organisations, labour unions, newspapers, local families, and baseball games. Weaved into a complex programme aimed at appreciating America's role in the world were numerous meetings devoted to such seemingly irrelevant topics as 'the nature of the poetic', French theatre, the German novel after World War II, and the revival of religious art in France.[4] Yet, herein lay part of the strength of the Seminar, designed to illustrate the fabric and depth of American life, helping to achieve the Seminar's objective of overcoming 'national prejudices'.

It was argued that the Seminar members were 'prolific' writers and speakers upon return to their homes, spreading the Seminar's message far and wide. State Department and Institute of International Education representatives, who had observed the Seminar at close quarters, also endorsed its importance.[5] In 1956, Ford reported that the Seminar was yielding a number of positive effects on participants and for the United States in general. For example, the Seminar seemed to be an excellent forum in which to 'correct false impressions of the United States, notably among Asian visitors'; it attracted 'influential or potentially influential people' from strategic areas; its effects were felt beyond Harvard, as 'responsible' press comments suggested that other US universities were influenced by the Seminar through the participation of faculty and dissemination of Seminar publications; and it 'helps to develop understanding and a sense of common purpose between Americans and influential foreigners and among the foreigners themselves ...', some of whom had set up Seminar alumni clubs and even a regional seminar in India. Ford funded many of the alumni meetings and circulated Seminar literature to all alumni, helping to sustain the network.[6]

Social occasions were explicitly arranged in order to 'encourage the establishment of personal friendships with Americans', thereby creating emotional bonds between elites.[7] The genuine *engagement* between the participants and Seminar leaders provided a sense of *ownership* among the visitors.[8] Kissinger outlined the detailed programme to the Ford Foundation, showing the way in which political scientist Earl Latham had led discussion of the pluralistic character of the American political system and Massachusetts Institute of Technology (MIT) economist Charles P. Kindleberger had examined economic conditions in the world system. In detailed discussions, issues such as communist China, neutrality, and world communism, had been thoroughly aired and discussed. The social programme, Kissinger claimed, led to greater appreciation of American society than any formal lecture or reading courses. For Kissinger, the programme's most 'decisive' impact was the 'attitudes engendered in the minds' of participants in '*the crucible of informal conversations*' (emphasis added).

It was noted, for example, that 'Seminar members found that an evening's conversation with an American couple and their friends resulted in a more profound appreciation of the American society than months of reading prior to coming here'.[9] Through the intensity and close contact over eight weeks, Seminar members discovered 'a wealth of channels toward general international understanding ...' In these ways, the Harvard Seminar, Kissinger concluded, 'provided them with a unique opportunity to assess the qualities of the nation which bears the heaviest burden of responsibility in the Western World ... Each of them has carried away a deeper insight into what they had previously distrusted in America – an insight often resulting in elimination of their initial disturbance'. Working in the Widener Library at Harvard, participating in challenging discussions, and enjoying the performances of the Boston Symphony Orchestra, 'dispelled participants' initial ideas about the shallowness of American culture'.[10] In short, Kissinger declared the Seminar an unqualified success because it appeared to engender among elite Europeans and Asians empathy, understanding and appreciation of American society, its elite and its 'burden of responsibility' to the West.

According to the archival record, participants' evaluations of the Seminar were overwhelmingly positive. Kissinger passed on to the Ford Foundation excerpts from hundreds of letters of appreciation from participants as evidence of the Seminar's effectiveness. Participants reported that the Seminar was 'exciting, informative, and remarkable for *candour*'; that it was 'forming an [international] elite which is so badly needed' in building world unity; that the knowledge and understanding gained would help to *challenge* any 'false accusation thrown against the American people'; that the Seminar exhibited little of the stereotypical American 'conformism'; that 'your method of recruiting [American] speakers who are *critical and who tell us the worst as well as the best is far more disarming and successful than any sort of traditional propaganda ...*'. Alain Clement, a journalist with *Le Monde* – a leading neutralist newspaper (i.e. one supportive of the concept of an independent Europe wedded to neither superpower) – returned a convert to American culture, Harvard and Henry Kissinger.[11]

Kissinger thought that the Seminar, despite his own growing responsibilities (with the US State Department, National Security Council, US Arms Control and Disarmament Agency, and the RAND Corporation), was so effective and important that he would continue to organize it.[12] Notable alumni of the Seminar include such leaders as Japan's Yasuhiro Nakasone (1953), France's Giscard d'Estaing (1954), and Malaysia's Mahathir Mohammed (1968) (Isaacson 1992: 71). In form and content, the Harvard Seminar differed radically from the public diplomacy of the post-1989 and post-11 September 2001 periods. It provided to Seminar members 'a sense of actively participating rather than ... merely being recipients'.[13] The Seminar, however, was just one part of an impressive array of public diplomacy operations at the time.

Salzburg Seminar in American Studies: 'the faint odour of cultural imperialism'[14]

The Salzburg Seminar in American Studies was, in effect, the overseas counterpart of the Harvard Seminar:[15] it targeted European men and women at the cusp of leadership positions in their own society – in law, politics, business, academia – and was run on the basis of candid exchange, criticism, and intellectual engagement. It represented a kind of public diplomacy – as opposed to propagandistic advertising – that some today hope to restore, as the tide of anti-Americanism rises around the world (Gedmin and Kennedy 2003). It began in 1947 as a co-operative venture between the Geneva International Student Service and the Harvard Student Council to improve Europeans' understanding of American society. By the late 1960s, 6500 Fellows had attended courses at the Seminar's castle, Schloss Leopoldskron.[16]

The aim of the Seminar was simple: to improve trans-Atlantic understanding (because even highly educated Europeans regarded the US in 'a distorted and negative light')[17] through '*dialogue* between people who count and who are going to count'. According to the president of Columbia University, the Seminar was designed to have its 'greatest effect upon men ... who must be counted upon by the public opinion-forming groups in their respective countries'.[18] It was further noted for its attempt to put forward the '*unvarnished facts* about the United States', and to explore trans-Atlantic issues 'with *candour and in depth*'. If a 'true' picture were to be painted, 'it is not always flattering'. (emphasis added)

Great emphasis was placed on critical engagement among participants and American Seminar faculty, the flavour of which is captured by key terms recurring through every report on the Seminar: problems to 'hammer out' between faculty and participants, 'candour tempered by tolerance', 'seeking together', 'finding together', avoiding propaganda.[19] For Grayson Kirk, a keen Seminar supporter, the value of American resources expended on 'propaganda' was questionable.[20] It was the concept of a 'two-way avenue of learning' that motivated Seminar organizers, which was to bear fruit.[21] This was evidenced by a Czech Fellow's comment in 1967: 'Your propaganda is the best propaganda, because it is not propaganda at all.'[22] On the basis of that 'non-propagandistic' propaganda, European elites were to spread their understanding far and wide through their organizations, newspapers, books and lectures.[23] As Salzburg officers argued in 1960, 'in Europe, more than in America, public opinion is moulded by a relatively small number of people. They disseminate their re-orientated [in light of their education at Salzburg] ideas on American life through their newspapers and periodicals, schools and universities, trade unions ...'[24]

An analysis of Seminar Fellows by occupation (1951–59) reveals its success in recruiting emerging elites in its aim to 'educate' Europe's opinion leaders: of the 2,878 participants, there were 718 graduate students, 564 teachers/academics, 376 journalists, editors and writers, 343 government officials and civil servants, 260 lawyers and 60 union leaders. Fellows were drawn from a range of countries: the best represented were Germany (585), Italy (478) and France (411) – all pivotal Continental states.[25]

In their grant applications, Salzburg officers consistently differentiated their (American) ideas, methods and outlook from those of their European Fellows. Europeans were elitist in attitude, while the Americans were more egalitarian. Europeans were constantly impressed by American openness in contrast to their own reticence. For example, even the open-access character of the library facilities and resources at Salzburg (10,000 books, 100 periodicals, a wide range of newspapers, etc.) was reportedly 'a source of amazement to Europeans unused to such "open" procedures and is, again, an experience for them with a basic American characteristic'.[26]

The Ford Foundation began financial support for the Seminar in 1955, and covered 20 per cent of its financial costs for the next 20 years – total funding of almost US$1 million. The State Department and the Fulbright programme furnished much of the rest. The Fulbright programme was inaugurated in 1946 to increase mutual international understanding through exchange of scholars across the world. Ford believed that the Seminar was 'one of the most effective of all American Studies programmes', offering opportunities to further connect East and West European leaders, as attested by State Department officials.[27] The Seminar's board of directors included Harvard's Dean (and later National Security adviser to the Kennedy and Johnson administrations, and Ford Foundation president) McGeorge Bundy, Emilio G. Collado of Standard Oil, and Massachusetts Institute of Technology's Walt Rostow.[28]

In operation, the Seminar's schedule was intense. Run over four weeks (three times a year), the Seminar featured morning lectures, afternoon small group work, and evening discussions and private reading in its well-stocked library. The 'seemingly informal' aspects of the programme, as organizers put it, were fundamental: 'The continual extra-curricular discussion among Fellows, faculty, and staff, all of whom live under the same roof throughout the session; the recreational activities in which everyone participates; in fact, the actual teaching method itself – the constant opportunity for questions during lectures and the close association with faculty which differs so radically from the European method, all give impressions in the understanding of America as a working democracy and, as such, are as important as the actual subject matters taught.'[29]

The specific effects are difficult to gauge. An internal Ford report surprised its own author as to the Salzburg Seminar's effectiveness over a period of two decades. Sociologist Daniel Bell lauded the Seminar as educating and bonding together European intellectuals, and launching the careers of several young scholars such as Ralf Dahrendorf (author, most famously, of *Class and Class Conflict in Industrial Society* in 1959, and director of the London School of Economics, 1974–84) and Michel Crozier (author of *The Bureaucratic Phenomenon* in 1964). He also indicated that Seminar alumni were now teaching at Columbia and Stanford universities.

For Bell, Salzburg alumni were immediately distinguishable at the Congress for Cultural Freedom seminars he had directed during 1956–57.[30] Seminar president, Dexter Perkins, noted the formation of alumni clubs – 'Salzburg Circles' – that held reunions to 'discuss American society'. He also noted that alumni had a 'conception of the United States that is more sympathetic – or, at least, more objective …'. The Salzburg Seminar also inspired the formation of the European Association for American Studies after the former's 1954 conference of American Civilisation academics. The aim of the European Association for American Studies was to 'continue the work begun by the Seminar-sponsored conference'.[31]

Foundations and public diplomacy since 11 September 2001

The Harvard and Salzburg seminars were targeted at elites among whom support for US foreign policy and society had been challenged or undermined or had otherwise declined in the 1950s and 1960s. A similar problem is said to exist today: numerous voices have declared the inadequacy or hamfistedness of current/ recent efforts to win 'hearts and minds', despite growing global anti-Americanism. Among the foundations, the GMF appears as leading critic as well as sponsor of a range of initiatives designed to undermine opposition to US foreign policy in the war on terror, including American aggression in Iraq. The GMF was originally founded by a West German government grant in 1972 in appreciation of US Marshall Plan assistance. Its headquarters is in Washington, DC, but the foundation also has five offices in Europe – Belgrade, Berlin, Bratislava, Brussels and Paris (GMF 2003). The GMF now has a larger circle of sponsors, including the Ford and Rockefeller philanthropies, the Council on Foreign Relations (CFR), North Atlantic Treaty Organization (NATO), and US Agency for International Development (USAID).[32]

GMF's programmes are essentially focused around two *complementary* goals: promoting trans-Atlantic co-operation and combating anti-Americanism in Europe by building collaborations between US and European elites, including academics, journalists, policy-makers, business leaders, think tanks, and philanthropies. GMF builds partnerships across the Atlantic, with Eastern Europe, and the wider world, by pooling 'intellectual … analytical … [and] financial resources'. Its projects are designed to develop 'innovative solutions' to trans-Atlantic problems, 'an opportunity for American voices to be heard in Europe and for European voices to be heard in America and for both Americans and Europeans to be heard throughout other world regions'. GMF locates itself at the centre of numerous global networks that include universities, mass media, US Congress and Senate, the European Union, industrialists' organizations like the Confederation of Indian Industry, and George Soros' Open Society Institute.[33]

GMF is actively doing – in its own way – what some Americans claim that the US government is not: a long tradition in American philanthropy. The context of the GMF's programmes may be set by its president's most recent writings. In an important article in *The National Interest*, President Craig Kennedy advanced the argument for more powerful, effective and better financed attempts by the US administration to combat anti-Americanism and better to promote the country's image and foreign policies abroad, especially in Europe (Gedmin and Kennedy 2003).

According to Kennedy, the US has a 'public diplomacy crisis' of rising anti-Americanism in Europe and urgently needs a 'serious campaign to open European minds to our positions', drawing on how historically the CIA and the Ford Foundation helped to battle anti-Americanism during the Cold War. In particular, Kennedy focused on the anti-communist CCF which was unfairly portrayed as a 'CIA front', in Kennedy's view – although that is exactly what it was (Scott-Smith 2002). Its principal achievement, despite its failure to stem the tide of European anti-Americanism, was to 'nurture a nucleus of thinkers and activists who were open to American ideas and willing to engage in serious discourse on the major issues of the day' (Gedmin and Kennedy 2003).

Today, in the wake of 11 September 2001 and the Iraq War, it is vital, according to Kennedy, to recognize the correctness of Robert Kagan's views *vis-à-vis* American military strength and European weakness (Kagan 2002; GMF 2003a). While there are differences of opinion and world view, there are also important areas of co-operation and convergence – especially on terrorism and globalization – upon which the US should try to make 'more palatable' US–European differential capabilities 'by building a base of support for active engagement with America'. Kennedy advised that George W. Bush's administration should take four steps to 'advance its strategy of stemming the loss of public support among Europe's elites and common citizenry'. First, use public diplomacy to mobilize public opinion; second, schedule more overseas travel to Europe by administration officials to debate policies and issues; third, allocate more financial resources for public diplomacy information officers – to restore spending to Cold War levels; and finally, ensure that the kind of public diplomacy engaged in is active, explanatory and combative, and not merely an exercise to 're-brand American foreign policy, re-brand diplomacy', as Colin Powell's efforts had tried, in vain, to do (Gedmin and Kennedy 2003).

Recommending a strategy that resembles, and complements, the programmes of the GMF, Kennedy (Gedmin and Kennedy 2003) urges the administration to 'support those European political leaders and intellectuals who are willing to take the increasingly unpopular stand of backing America'. What is needed, he asserts, is to ensure both that the 'good news' gets out about American policy and also 'to knock down slander of the United States in a comprehensive and timely fashion'. As an example of such 'slander', Kennedy points to 'unfounded' allegations of torture and mistreatment of prisoners at Guantánamo Bay. The administration's diplomatic machinery alone, however, is too slow, inflexible, and unskilled to meet current needs.

> *These sorts of challenges require serious intellectual combatants. This means a critical mass of writers, thinkers and diplomats who can engage editorial boards, join the television talk show circuits, participate in internet chat rooms, operate websites – not to mention debate Europe's scholars, business leaders and university students alike. Above all, it means developing a broader, non-partisan network of like-minded individuals on both sides of the Atlantic who are dedicated to the cause of keeping the idea of the West and its ever expanding community of liberal democracies alive. Though times have changed ... institutions like the Congress for Cultural Freedom once worked. Perhaps it is time to consider what additional lessons history can offer.* (Gedmin and Kennedy 2003; emphasis added)

In 2003, GMF engaged in a wide range of activities to build trans-Atlantic co-operation. Critically interested in understanding and acting upon public opinion, GMF financed a survey of Transatlantic Trends across seven European countries plus the United States. In June, GMF organized a symposium of 28 American and European think tanks, shadowing the official US–EU Summit. The symposium analysed diverging attitudes towards the Middle East and on global trade, as well as examining 'the prospects for resolving the tensions' between the power blocs. Presentations of the findings and recommendations were made at the US Capitol by US Congressman, Doug Bereuter; Pat Cox, president of the European Parliament; Marc Grossman, Under-Secretary of State for Political Affairs; and George Papandreou, Greece's Foreign Minister. Continuing the examination of European–American divergent opinion–consideration, as the basis for future consensus building, GMF arranged a special 'Strategic Discussion with Henry Kissinger' for emerging German leaders (GMF 2003a: 1–6).

Finally, GMF launched the Trade and Poverty Forum in February 2003, with the aim of developing US–European and Third World leaders' dialogue on those matters, in order to assist 'the global trading system to better address development challenges'. Its first report, 'Restoring Trust in the WTO: The Challenge for Cancun', is to be followed up by 'attention to how to respond to the breakdown of trade negotiations in Cancun, and how to advance broad development goals ...'. The Trade and Poverty Forum consists of six delegations from the US (headed by Robert Rubin, former Secretary to the Treasury, Carnegie Corporation trustee and Goldman Sachs partner), Japan, India, Brazil, South Africa and Europe. The Trade and Poverty Forum wants to 'focus on rebuilding the confidence of developing countries in the importance of world trade for their economic well-being' and to 'educate the press and public about the importance of US–EU leadership on trade and development matters' (GMF 2003: 7–10).

An important part of GMF's work since 2000 has been its annual meetings of emerging foreign policy leaders, at Hotel Tremezzo, Lake Como, Italy. This programme is conducted in partnership with the Bertelsmann Foundation and the Centre for Applied Policy Research. Over 30 US–EU leaders – 'from a range of professions, from the private sector and media to government and think tanks' – examined the causes of trans-Atlantic division, the Israeli–Palestinian conflict, 'the future of international organizations such as the UN and NATO; economic and financial interdependence; and what steps can be taken to renew and rebuild transatlantic relations' (GMF 2003a: 11).

The GMF has a significant initiative involving research fellowships. In 2003, Mark Leonard was awarded a Fellowship to travel in the United States. Leonard was Director of Prime Minister Tony Blair's think tank, the Foreign Policy Centre, and editor of a book, *Re-ordering the World*, a call for a new 'liberal imperialism' in the wake of 11 September 2001. Leonard asserted that '[Osama] Bin Laden is an aftershock of the mistakes made after 1989' by Presidents George H. W. Bush and Bill Clinton, and by Prime Minister John Major (Leonard 2002). This is an echo of the perspectives shared by George W. Bush's administration and some of its ideological supporters in the neo-conservative Project for the New American Century (Parmar 2005b).

An essay in the same volume by Robert Cooper – a former Blair foreign policy adviser, current serving Foreign Office diplomat and adviser to Javier Solana, the

EU's High Representative for Foreign and Security Policy – argued that the world was divided into three kinds of state: post-modern, modern and pre-modern. In Cooper's view, the EU and US are, more or less, in the post-modern camp and are obliged, for their own security, to co-operate in dealing with Al-Qaeda and other terror bases in pre-modern states (Cooper 2002; Cooper 2003; Parmar 2005c). In so doing, they would need to use any means necessary, including 'force, pre-emptive attack, deception ...', a series of strategies associated with Anglo-American aggression in Iraq, 2003.

Among its past Fellows, the GMF's Transatlantic Fellows Program cites a roster of prominent figures from academic, political and business life, including G. John Ikenberry (Princeton), Christopher Makins (Atlantic Council), Lee Feinstein (CFR), Ellen Bork (Project for the New American Century), Barry Posen (MIT), Cindy Williams (MIT), and John Harris (*Washington Post*).

Conclusions

Taken together, Ford's American Studies and GMF's trans-Atlantic programmes were (and still are) a powerful means by which global elites' 'anti-American' prejudices and concerns were addressed through initiatives that *directly* touched thousands – probably tens of thousands – of men and women. Indirectly, especially through the Congress for Cultural Freedom, Ford's public diplomacy struggle against anti-Americanism affected millions of students, academics and journalists, as well as newspaper and magazine readers.[34] The Kissinger and Salzburg Seminars were integrated, coherent, focused, well-organized and profoundly engaging. They appeared to be authentic educational programmes designed for two-way exchange and learning – and were, thereby, not seen as condescending propaganda or, even, as *any* kind of propaganda.

The programmes at Harvard and Salzburg created enduring nuclei of scholars and other opinion-formers, networked with American institutions and faculty, and with each other, functioning effectively long after the short Seminars were over. The message of the Seminars was not only in the spoken and written word; it was in the very texture of the whole experience: members *lived* Americanism when they criticized and debated race relations or foreign policy. Both Harvard's Kissinger and Salzburg's leaders recognized that the social aspects of the interactions made possible by the Seminars were as vital as the formal programme.

The Harvard and Salzburg seminars were successful for one other reason: they were directed at elites whose national and world orientations were not fundamentally antagonistic to the aims of American power. After all, most Europeans were products of a colonial culture constructed over centuries. As post-colonial powers, their world view transformed into a neo-colonial 'developmentalism' to re-define their relationship with the Third World. Their problems with the United States broadly sprang from resentment at their own nations' fall from global grace alongside America's ascendance, as well as a fear of the consequences of American power in the nuclear age. So overall, despite their scepticism, they were not beyond persuasion by a sophisticated elite diplomacy set in prestigious Harvard Yard or an eighteenth-century castle to lend a patina of antiquity to the United States, and significant gravity to the proceedings. They were susceptible to the exercise of 'soft power' precisely because European elites had a vested interest in the world system, the management of which had passed largely into American hands after World War II.

The GMF's initiatives to build trans-Atlantic unity and combat anti-Americanism are, of course, occurring in a very different historical period, characterised by the rise of non-state actors and citizen groups' power, especially through the proliferation of new communications technologies. Yet, such initiatives merely serve to illustrate the fundamental tendency of East Coast philanthropy in US foreign affairs: to bolster US global hegemony. The effectiveness of the GMF programmes, however, is very difficult to gauge and requires much further research. Nevertheless, its post-11 September 2001 programmes appear to be developing with some sensitivity to US public diplomacy during the Cold War.

The Harvard, Salzburg and GMF programmes supplement(ed) and support(ed) at the level of sub-state and private elite leadership what states are (and were) trying to achieve: alliance-formation as a way to greater US/Western penetration of the world in a period of rising nationalism, anti-Americanism and global struggles against communism/terrorism. Indeed, the programmes were integrated into the objectives of the State Department, which worked with Harvard and Salzburg 'intimately but unofficially' (Whitaker 1974).[35] Ford Foundation and GMF funding helped to construct the infrastructure – the institutional settings, organizations, professional societies, conferences and seminars, alumni networks and publications – that enabled the formation and endurance of elite networks which influenced the climate of intellectual and popular opinion, in eras of both emerging (Cold War) and renewed (post-11 September 2001) American global leadership (Parmar 2004b; Parmar 2002; Coser 1965). Ford and GMF – both inextricably linked with the official makers of US foreign policy, major American corporations and prestigious universities – claimed to be acting non-politically, non-ideologically and independently of the state. In practice, their projects were (and still are) intimately connected with the consolidation of American global power, which, in part at least, faces challenges from an array of opponents – ranging from principled nationalists, democrats, internationalists and anti-capitalists, to those culturally prejudiced against all things American – all of whom are inaccurately, and unhelpfully, labelled as 'anti-American'.

Notes

1 In one letter concerning grant applications to Ford, Kissinger offered to provide supporting references from Allen W. Dulles (CIA Director) and C. D. Jackson, head of the Congress for Cultural Freedom initiative; Kissinger to Don K. Price (Ford Foundation associate director), 10 December 1953; PA53-159, reel 1118; Ford Foundation Archives (FFA), New York.

2 Ford Foundation annual reports; see also, Ford Foundation, *American Studies Abroad*; report 004642, April 1969; in total, Ford Foundation (FF) granted Kissinger over US$390,000; FFA.

3 'Docket Excerpt. Executive Committee meeting September 27, 1956: International Programs: International Affairs: Harvard University International Seminar'; PA 55-9; reel 0492.

4 'Docket excerpt, Executive Committee Mtg. September 27, 1956: International Programs: International Affairs. Harvard University International Seminar'; Grant file PA 55-9; reel 0492; FFA.

5 'Excerpt from Docket: International Affairs: Harvard International Seminar', 29–30 October 1954; Grant file, PA 55-9; reel 0492; Ford Foundation Archives (FFA), New York.

6 'Docket excerpt, Executive Committee Mtg. September 27, 1956: International Programs: International Affairs. Harvard University International Seminar'; Grant file PA 55-9; reel 0492; FFA.

7 'Docket Excerpt September 27, 1956'; Grant File PA 55-9; reel 0492; FFA.

8 Inter-Office Memorandum, Bernard L. Gladieux to Joseph M. McDaniel, 'Harvard International Seminar (-A351 Revised)', 13 August 1952; PA55-9, reel 0492; FFA.

9 'Docket excerpt, Executive Committee Mtg. September 27', 1956.

10 Henry Kissinger, report on 1955 programme; PA 55-9; reel 0492; FFA.

11 'Extracts of letters from past participants', attached to a letter, Kissinger to Harold Swearer (FF), 4 November 1968; PA69-134, reel 2248; FFA.

12 Letter, Kissinger to Harold Swearer (FF), 4 November 1968; PA69-134, reel 2248; FFA.

13 Inter-Office Memorandum, 'Harvard International Seminar', Bernard L. Gladieux to Joseph McDaniel, 13 August 1952; PA 55-9, reel 0942.

14 Inter-office memorandum, Richard C. Sheldon to W. McNeill Lowry, 'American Studies', 5 March 1968, p. 2; PA69-134, reel 2248.

15 Indeed, this was precisely how Kissinger and Elliott contextualized their own efforts; letter, Elliott to Don K. Price (FF), 13 February 1954; PA55-9, reel 0942.

16 David E. Bell and McNeill Lowry, Grant Allocation to Salzburg Seminar in American Studies, Inc., 20 January 1970; p. 3; PA55-216; reel 2081; FFA.

17 Dexter Perkins, 'A Proposal to Strengthen the Salzburg Seminar in American Studies', March 1960; PA55-216, reel 2081; FFA. The Fellows were selected by 'responsible' men in Europe and officers of the US Information Service; many alumni subsequently went on to take up Commonwealth Fund study scholarships in the US, becoming networked in a tightly organised set of US East Coast establishment organizations.

18 Letter, Grayson Kirk to Dexter Perkins (President, Salzburg Seminar), 8 March 1960; PA55-216, reel 2081.

19 All quotes are from: Paul M. Herzog (President, Salzburg Seminar), 'Application to the Ford Foundation for a Grant for the Period 1970–1975', October 1969; PA55-216, reel 2081; FFA.

20 Letter, Grayson Kirk to Dexter Perkins (President, Salzburg Seminar), 8 March 1960; PA55-216, reel 2081.

21 Perkins, 'A Proposal to Strengthen the Salzburg Seminar in American Studies', March 1960; PA55-216, reel 2081; FFA.

22 Cited by Herzog, 'Application to the Ford'; PA55-216, reel 2081.

23 Bell and Lowry, Grant Allocation to Salzburg Seminar, 20 January 1970; PA55-216, reel 2081.

24 Perkins, 'A Proposal to Strengthen the Salzburg Seminar in American Studies', March 1960; PA55-216, reel 2081; FFA.

25 Perkins, 'A Proposal to Strengthen the Salzburg Seminar in American Studies', Exhibit IV; March 1960; PA55-216, reel 2081; FFA.

26 Perkins, 'A Proposal to Strengthen the Salzburg Seminar in American Studies', March 1960; PA55-216, reel 2081; FFA.

27 Bell and Lowry.

28 Perkins, 'A Proposal to Strengthen the Salzburg Seminar in American Studies', Exhibit XIV; March 1960; PA55-216, reel 2081; FFA.

29 Perkins, 'A Proposal to Strengthen the Salzburg Seminar in American Studies', March 1960; PA55-216, reel 2081; FFA.

30 Letter, Daniel Bell to Dexter Perkins, 1 March 1960; PA55-216, reel 2081.

31 Perkins, 'A Proposal to Strengthen the Salzburg Seminar in American Studies', March 1960; PA55-216, reel 2081; FFA.

32 'Partnerships', GMF website at http://www.gmfus.org

33 'Partnerships', GMF website.

34 Ford Foundation, *American Studies Abroad* April 1969; report 004642; FFA.

35 Letter, Elliott to Price, 13 February 1954; PA55-9, reel 0942.

4 In the Line of Fire: US Think Tanks, the War on Terror and Anti-Americanism

Donald E. Abelson

When George W. Bush leaves the Oval Office in 2009, he will certainly be missed by political pundits and late-night comedians who have devoted much of their time in recent years to ridiculing the former Texas governor and 43rd President of the United States. While we may forget some of the more embarrassing moments of Bush's presidency, there are particular images of America's war president that will be difficult to erase from our collective memory: that of a young and untested leader standing amid the ruins of the World Trade Center following the devastating terrorist attacks of 11 September 2001; and months later, that of a brash commander-in-chief proudly declaring from the flight deck of an American aircraft carrier, albeit prematurely, that the brutal regime of former Iraqi leader Saddam Hussein had been defeated handily by the US and its coalition partners.

But, if there is one image that captures the essence of his presidency, it is a depiction of him with his hands cupped over his ears staring into the distance. Spray-painted on a wall in a working-class neighbourhood in Buenos Aires, the image illustrates very clearly how many in the United States and in the international community see him – as a leader who refuses to be diverted from his political agenda. Bush may prefer to insulate himself from his critics as he seeks to redefine America's role in the world. However, he cannot possibly ignore the extent to which his foreign policies have resulted in widespread anti-Americanism, nor can he dismiss how his commitment to fighting the war on terror has contributed to his dismal public approval ratings. Still, when historians and political scientists look back at the Bush years, they will discover that the president was not entirely responsible for the escalation of anti-Americanism. While he must assume responsibility for fuelling anti-American sentiments in much of the developed and developing world, a small but vocal group of think tanks in the United States may also have been responsible for raising the ire of those living beyond America's shores.

In a volume analysing the spread of anti-Americanism and its political conse- quences, it may seem odd to look for the root causes of anti-Americanism in the think tank community. After all, when people congregate in the United States or in foreign countries to express their opposition to American foreign policy, it is the person who occupies the Oval Office and his close circle of advisers, not a group of policy experts researching and writing policy papers and books at the nation's think tanks, who are generally targeted. Indeed, as one might expect, shortly after President Bush ordered the invasion of Iraq, dozens of protests demanding an end to the Bush administration's militaristic posture were held. At the same time, it would be difficult to imagine protesters waving signs and banners condemning scholars at the American Enterprise Institute (AEI), the Heritage Foundation and the Project for the New American Century (PNAC) – think tanks that have largely supported the war effort.

On the surface, this appears to make perfect sense: the president – in consultation with his advisers, the joint chiefs-of-staff and selected cabinet officials – ultimately decides when and under what circumstances to launch a military invasion. This important decision is not made by scholars at think tanks mulling over the advantages and disadvantages of going to war. Why, then, should they bear any responsibility for decisions made by elected officials? They might do so because, as we shall discover in this chapter, while policy experts at think tanks have the luxury of analysing the potential costs of war from their book-lined offices, many have abandoned the security and comfort of their surroundings for the rough-and-tumble world of American politics. By immersing themselves in the debate over the war on terror, think tanks, including those named above, have made a concerted effort to influence public attitudes and beliefs and the policy preferences and choices of leaders. They have not simply circulated publications to journalists, academics and policy-makers in the hope of finding a sympathetic audience. Rather, several think tanks have aggressively sought to frame the parameters of important discussions over national security and, in the process, have attempted to make Bush's war on terror and America's invasion of Iraq more palatable. Scholars at think tanks, unlike policy-makers on Capitol Hill and in the White House, are not in a position to make policy decisions. Nonetheless, their ability to promote and defend ideas in the political arena cannot be ignored. Indeed, by becoming active participants in the war of ideas, several think tanks have played a critical role in marketing America's war effort at home and abroad. In doing so, they, like the Bush administration, have helped to contribute to growing anti-Americanism.

The purpose of this chapter is not to provide a detailed examination of the role of think tanks in US foreign policy, nor is it to suggest that think tanks were responsible for convincing President Bush to wage war on terrorists and the states that nurture them. Rather, the purpose here is to highlight the involvement of a select group of think tanks in the public debate over the war on terror and to discuss their efforts to shape the political discourse surrounding this critically important issue. The chapter begins by discussing the response of some of America's leading foreign and defence policy think tanks to the disturbing and historic events of 11 September 2001. In addition to examining the various ways in which think tanks have attempted to shape the parameters of public discussions about terrorism and US foreign policy, we shall identify some of the many issues that they have highlighted in an effort to educate both policy-makers and the public about this emerging threat in the international community. We shall also consider how think tanks have responded to concerns about the domestic and global implications of America's war on terrorism. Once this has been done, we shall turn our attention to PNAC, the think tank credited and often blamed for laying the groundwork for the Bush doctrine – a doctrine that justifies pre-emptive strikes against adversaries thought to pose an imminent threat to US security.

In the second section, we shall explain why it is important to consider the decision-making styles of presidents in any assessment of think tank influence. As much as some presidents, including Ronald Reagan, were willing to create opportunities for think tank scholars to establish a strong foothold in his administration (Abelson 2006), President Bush's reluctance to expand his small circle of advisers has had the opposite effect. Rather than inviting input from a larger and more diverse group of experts, something Zbigniew Brzezinski (quoted in Abelson 2006) suggested administrations do when their policies go awry, Bush has refused to stray from the path that he and his advisers have followed since 11 September 2001.

Finally, we shall evaluate the contribution of think tanks to the ongoing debate over the war on terror – a debate which, as noted, has contributed to widespread anti-Americanism. By acknowledging that influence can occur at different stages of the policy-making process, it is possible to identify how think tanks have helped to shape and mould this critical policy issue. In doing so, we shall provide a more accurate picture of how and under what circumstances think tanks can make a difference in the political arena. We begin by examining the reaction of the think tank community to the horrific events of 11 September 2001, which, as former Brookings president Michael Armacost predicted (Pillar 2001), have been seared into the national consciousness.

Talking shop and talking heads: think tanks and the war of ideas

For many think tank scholars, the most effective way to communicate their ideas to the public and to policy-makers is through the media. They do this by appearing as guests on the network news and on political talk shows, by providing commentary on various radio programs and by submitting op-ed pieces to dozens of domestic and international newspapers. It is difficult to determine the extent to which heightened media exposure translates into policy influence. Nevertheless, think tanks continue to assign a high priority to enhancing their visibility.

If the war of ideas (not to be confused with the war on terror) were decided solely on the basis of which think tank generated the most exposure on television and in print, the Brookings Institution could easily claim victory. According to Abelson (2006), on virtually every issue ranging from the events of 11 September 2001 to the wars in Afghanistan and Iraq, Brookings scholars are cited more often than their colleagues from any other think tank. But the war of ideas is not limited to the battles that take place between think tank scholars on television and in the op-ed pages. Other important battles are taking place in conferences and seminars organized by think tanks and in legislative hearings where policy experts from America's leading institutes are summoned to advise policy-makers. They are also being waged in the dozens of books and articles that think tanks have generated since 11 September 2001.

The second front: conferences, workshops and seminars

President George W. Bush's war on terror is tailor-made for think tanks looking to find timely, relevant and interesting subjects for conferences, workshops and seminars. Indeed, given the multiple dimensions of terrorism and America's efforts to come to grips with this new and elusive enemy, there is no limit to the range of topics that could be explored. From all accounts, think tanks have made a concerted effort to identify several worthy subjects for discussion. Since 11 September 2001, think tanks specializing in foreign and defence policy have arranged hundreds of conferences and workshops. For example, in 2004, AEI held close to two dozen workshops that included: The Bush Doctrine; An End to Evil: How to Win the War on Terror; Operation Iraqi Freedom; and Intelligence Reform. At the Carnegie Endowment, the workshops and seminars focused on slightly different themes. In that same year, Carnegie scholars looked at: Strategic Asia and the War on Terrorism; Weapons of Mass Destruction in Iraq: Evidence and Implications; and Integrating Democracy Promotion into US Middle East Policy. Other think tanks inside and beyond the Beltway also offered an interesting array of seminars (Abelson 2006).

By organizing conferences, seminars and workshops, think tanks are able not only to discuss timely and relevant policy issues but, more importantly, to provide a forum for scholars, journalists and policy-makers to meet and interact. Rather than staring into a television camera in the hope of reaching millions of viewers, or waiting for feedback on a newspaper article that they may have published, policy experts at conferences can exchange ideas directly with interested participants. This may result in additional meetings, conversations and other opportunities to explore policy options. At the very least, conferences and seminars in which policy-makers and their staff participate can help think tanks to establish closer ties to those in positions of power. And in the process, think tanks may be brought one step closer to achieving policy influence.

For the congressional record: think tanks on Capitol Hill

Experts from the Center for Strategic and International Studies (CSIS), RAND, AEI, Heritage, Brookings and other think tanks have testified before Senate and House committees on several important issues related to national security in the post-11 September 2001 world. Among other things, they have discussed the relationship between civil liberties and national security; reconstruction and rehabilitation in Iraq; combating weapons of mass destruction; the Middle East view of terrorism; terrorism, extremism and regional stability in Central Asia; and the terrorist attacks in Madrid (Abelson 2006). The frequency with which think tank scholars have testified before congressional committees since Osama bin Laden left his calling card in New York and in Washington reflects their willingness to rely on Congress to inject their ideas into the policy-making process. It also reflects the importance that members of Congress assign to the work and scholarship being undertaken at the nation's foreign and defence policy think tanks.

Much of this work has been revealed in the testimonies presented by think tank scholars, but it is also discussed, in considerably more detail, in the books and articles that they have published. In the following section, we shall provide an overview of some of the major works produced by think tank scholars that deal with critical stages in the war on terrorism. Although far from comprehensive, the review will highlight some of the many issues think tank scholars believe are critically important for policy-makers and the public to consider as the government continues to wage war on its adversaries.

Publish and perish: combating global terror

Despite the increase in terrorist activity during the 1980s and 1990s, little was being done in the intelligence community to protect the United States against future attacks – a concern expressed by Stephen Flynn of the Council on Foreign Relations. In an article published in his think tank's flagship journal *Foreign Affairs*, in 2000, Flynn (2005: xi) outlined a scenario whereby bin Laden 'might exploit our perilously exposed transportation system to smuggle and detonate a weapon of mass destruction on our soil'. To Flynn's delight, the article sparked interest in the policy-making community and eventually led to briefings about the vulnerability of America's transportation system. Unfortunately, his fears about terrorism and the unwillingness of policy-makers to take necessary precautions to protect the American homeland were not widely shared. As he points out, 'The common refrain I heard was, "Americans need a crisis to act. Nothing will change until we have a serious act of terrorism on US soil (2005: xii)."'

When terrorists did strike the United States, policy-makers had no alternative – at least no viable alternative – but to react. However, the way in which they reacted, and the effectiveness of their response, has spawned an intense debate in the academic and think tank communities in the United States and abroad. As the initial shock and horror of what occurred on 11 September 2001 began to wear off, scholars in the nation's think tanks and universities took time to reflect on why the attacks had taken place and what the United States had to do to protect its citizens. For policy experts on the left, the story line was clear: Islamic terrorists had made their way to the United States to punish America's leaders for their foreign policy in the Middle East and, in particular, their steadfast support for Israel. Once the United States adopted a more even-handed approach to resolving the Israeli–Palestinian conflict and abandoned its imperialist goals, the threat of terrorism would be significantly reduced (Callinicos 2003; Ross and Ross 2004). If the United States did this, it would no longer have to worry about the bin Ladens of the world. Order, rather than chaos and fear, would come to reflect the state of the international community. As an added bonus, America's strained relations with the United Nations and with much of Western Europe would improve dramatically and the rising tide of anti-Americanism sweeping across the globe would gradually subside.

But for those on the right who believed that this solution could only work in fairy tales, America's response to dealing with terrorism had to convey a very different message. Rather than coddling terrorists and the states that either directly or indirectly support them, what was needed, according to many conservative policy experts, was a clear and forceful demonstration of American resolve. As David Frum and Richard Perle of AEI state in their book:

> The war on terror is not over. In many ways, it has barely begun. Al-Qaeda, Hezbollah, and Hamas still plot murder, and money still flows from donors worldwide to finance them. Mullahs preach jihad from the pulpits of mosques from Bengal to Brooklyn. Iran and North Korea are working frantically to develop nuclear weapons. While our enemies plot, our allies dither and carp and much of our own government remains ominously unready for the fight. We have much to do and scant time in which to do it. (Frum and Perle 2004)

For Frum and Perle, the invasion of Afghanistan in October 2001 was a good start. Among other things, it enabled the United States and its coalition partners to topple the Taliban regime and to destroy bin Laden's terrorist training camps. An even better idea, according to the two AEI residents, was invading Iraq in 2003, a much overdue intervention that allowed the United States to remove another dictator from its roster of enemies. However, they insist that for America to win the war on terror much more has to be done, including removing terrorist mullahs in Iran, ending the terrorist regime in Syria and adopting tighter security measures at home (Frum and Perle 2004) – recommendations that, if adopted, would no doubt lead to new and more virulent waves of anti-Americanism.

Frum and Perle's recipe for defeating terrorism has found strong support among several conservative members of Congress and think tank scholars, including Brooking's Ken Pollack whose book, *The Threatening Storm* (2002), made a strong case for the invasion of Iraq. But, not surprisingly, their recommendations for future interventions have generated considerable controversy in more liberal policy-making circles. The absence of an exit strategy in Iraq (Preble 2004), combined with an escalating body count, has produced little tolerance for additional conflicts. Regardless of how well or poorly Frum and Perle's grand plan for winning the war on terror has been received, their insights help to shed light on the complexity of waging a war that must be fought but may never be won. Their well-publicized views also help to explain why many conservative think tanks should assume some responsibility for creating a political climate that fosters anti-American sentiments.

In their ongoing efforts to dissect the handling of the war on terror by George W. Bush's administration, journalists and scholars will continue to offer different explanations for what motivates American foreign policy. They may also comment on the think tanks that are best positioned and equipped to influence the policies of the incoming administration, and may again succumb to the temptation of assuming that proximity to those in power guarantees policy influence. This was the mistake that several journalists, scholars and pundits made in claiming that the blueprint for the Bush administration's foreign policy was drawn entirely by the Project for the New American Century.

Psst! It's PNAC

By the time George W. Bush entered the Oval Office in 2001, it had become Washington's worst kept secret: a small think tank with modest resources, but powerful connections to key members of the Bush team, was rumoured to have developed a comprehensive foreign policy for the incoming administration. The think tank that had become a favourite topic of discussion for journalists covering Washington politics, and for pundits searching for any clues that would help them to predict Bush's behaviour in his first 100 days in office, was not the Heritage Foundation or AEI, the darlings of the conservative movement. The heir apparent was PNAC, a neo-conservative think tank whose foray into the policy-making community in 1997 sparked considerable interest among, and support from, several high-level policy-makers, including Dick Cheney, Donald Rumsfeld, Paul Wolfowitz, Lewis 'Scooter' Libby and Jeb Bush, former governor of Florida and the president's younger brother.

If there were any doubts about which sources of information would help the president to manage American foreign policy in the post-11 September 2001 world, they were put to rest when the decision was made to invade Iraq. When journalists and scholars skimmed through PNAC's September 2000 study, 'Rebuilding America's Defenses', they thought they had discovered the key to the Holy Grail. In its study, PNAC made several policy recommendations that closely resembled initiatives being pursued by the Bush administration. In fact, the recommendations they made four months before President Bush assumed power (PNAC 2000), such as 'defending the homeland and fight[ing] and win[ning] multiple, simultaneous major theatre wars', may as well have been taken directly from his play book.

Could this have been just a coincidence? Not according to several journalists and scholars who made the connection between PNAC, members of Bush's inner circle and the foreign policy that the United States had embraced. Writing in *The Guardian* in the fall of 2003, Michael Meacher, a British Labour Member of Parliament, stated:

> We now know that a blueprint for the creation of a global Pax Americana was drawn up for Dick Cheney, Donald Rumsfeld, Paul Wolfowitz, Jeb Bush, and Lewis Libby. The document, entitled *Rebuilding America's Defenses*, was written in September 2000 by the neoconservative think tank, Project for the New American Century (PNAC). (Meacher 2003; emphasis added)

The plan shows that Bush's cabinet intended to take military control of the Gulf region whether or not Saddam Hussein was in power. It says, 'while the unresolved conflict with Iraq provides the immediate justification, the need for a substantial American force presence in the Gulf transcends the issue of the regime of Saddam Hussein'. The PNAC blueprint supports an earlier document attributed to Wolfowitz and Libby which said the US must 'discourage advanced industrial nations from challenging our leadership or even aspiring to a larger regional or global role'. Meacher's assessment of PNAC is similar in tone to the one presented by Andrew Austin, who writes:

Not content with waiting for the next Republican administration, Wolfowitz and several other intellectuals formed PNAC, a think tank 'to make the case and rally support for American global leadership.' Top corporate, military, and political figures aligned themselves with PNAC ... Powerful economic interests [also] threw their support behind PNAC. (Austin 2005)

Similar comments about PNAC's origins and its strong ties to the policy-making establishment and to the business community continue to make their way into the academic literature on the neo-conservative network in the United States (Halper and Clarke 2004; Micklethwait and Wooldridge 2004). However, as we shall discuss below, evaluating the extent of PNAC's influence is not as straightforward as Meacher and others maintain.

Peeling away the rhetoric: PNAC's mandate, motives and principles

Gary Schmitt, the president of PNAC, spent years in the academic community and in government before running a think tank. He understood the world of Washington politics and how decisions were made in Congress, in the White House and in the bureaucracy. And he understood and appreciated that the right ideas presented at the right time could make a profound difference.

Founded in 1997 to promote American global leadership, PNAC spent its early years developing a new conservative approach to foreign policy. This approach or strategy was based on the belief that the United States could and should become a 'benevolent global hegemon [sic]'. As William Kristol and Robert Kagan stated:

American hegemony is the only reliable defense against a breakdown of peace and international order. The appropriate goal of American foreign policy, therefore, is to preserve that hegemony as far into the future as possible. To achieve this goal, the United States needs a neo-Reaganite foreign policy of military supremacy and moral confidence. (Kristol and Kagan 1996)

Kristol and Kagan's article struck a responsive chord with several conservative policy-makers and policy experts, who encouraged the authors to create an organization that would promote their vision of American foreign policy. As Schmitt (quoted in Abelson 2006) points out, 'we got approached by a lot of people saying why don't you try to institutionalize this?' After Kristol and Kagan convinced Schmitt to become PNAC's president, they secured sufficient funding to launch the new institute.

Building on the success of their 1996 article, Kagan and Kristol, both project directors at PNAC, published an edited collection in 2000, entitled *Present Dangers*, which further explored the options and opportunities available to the United States as it set out to redefine its role in the international community. Among the many topics addressed by the long and impressive list of contributors were: regime change in Iraq, Israel and the peace process and missile defense, all of which became hot button issues for President Bush. But it was the release of 'Rebuilding America's Defenses' in September 2000, a 76-page document endorsed by several people who would come to occupy senior positions in the Bush administration, that propelled PNAC into the national spotlight.

The report, written by Thomas Donnelly, Donald Kagan (Robert Kagan's brother) and Gary Schmitt, was intended to encourage debate among policy-makers and the public about America's military strength and how it could be harnessed to achieve the country's foreign policy goals. Based on a series of seminars in which participants with specialized areas of expertise were encouraged to exchange ideas about a wide range of defence and foreign policy issues, the document left few stones unturned. But did this document, or blueprint as it is often described, amount to an 'extreme makeover' of US foreign policy, or did it simply propose some minor modifications? Moreover, were PNAC's plans for advancing American national security interests in a world in which the United States could market itself as a 'benevolent global hegemon' the product of original thinking – something think tanks are encouraged to do – or were their ideas recycled from other sources?

The PNAC document, as Schmitt acknowledged, was intended to provide a more coherent conservative vision of American foreign policy:

> We weren't satisfied with what the isolationists and realists were saying about foreign policy [and felt] that they were very much drawing the United States back from the world at large … We thought that even though the Cold War had ended, the principles of conservative foreign policy enunciated during the Reagan years, were still applicable to the world today. In this sense, the PNAC study offered new and innovative ways of promoting American interests in the post cold-war era. Ironically, when the study came out, 'its real impact was on the Clinton folks, not on the Bush people'. (quoted in Abelson 2006)

But when it comes to evaluating the work of his institute, Schmitt, like any responsible policy entrepreneur, can ill afford to be modest:

> I think we do a good job of getting our vision on the table because I think we're very good at what we do … We get a lot of feedback from editorialists and you can tell they read the stuff. If you make a poignant argument and present a case that's well reasoned and brief, you have a lot of impact, or you can at least have some impact. (2004, quoted in Abelson 2006)

Scholars studying PNAC's ascendancy in the political arena cannot possibly overlook the fact that several of the original signatories to its statement of principles received high-level positions in the Bush administration. As Ted Koppel, formerly of NBC, pointed out, you do not have to be a conspiracy theorist to acknowledge the intimate ties between some of Bush's closest advisers and PNAC. However, acknowledging these important connections is a far cry from making the claim that PNAC was the architect of Bush's foreign policy. The president appointed Rumsfeld, Wolfowitz and other foreign policy experts to serve in his administration, but not because they were card-carrying members of PNAC or of any other think tank. They were recruited because they were people whom Bush could trust. Although President Bush appeared to be sympathetic to many of the ideas presented by PNAC, ideas that have helped ignite anti-Americanism, we should not assume that this or any other organization dictated Bush's foreign policy. As Daalder and Lindsay (2003: 2) point out, it is reasonable to conclude that the greatest influence on George W. Bush was George W. Bush.

Knock, knock ... who's there?

Fifty years from now, historians looking back on the presidency of George W. Bush will, in all likelihood, conclude that his demeanour and leadership style changed dramatically after the terrorist attacks of 11 September 2001. The president who entered the Oval Office under a cloud of controversy on 20 January 2001 was very different from the president who surfaced amid the ruins of the World Trade Center. Few – including the future president himself – could have predicted that Bush, ridiculed on the campaign trail as a politician who had gone very far on very little, would see his bid for the presidency result in a nationwide scandal. But it did and Bush assumed his responsibilities as president with the full understanding that the Supreme Court, not the American people, had propelled him into office.

If anyone needed a crash course in international relations, it was George W. Bush. The eldest son of the 41st president of the United States shared his father's love of baseball but showed little interest in world affairs. This was reflected in the limited number of trips that Bush had taken abroad. By the time he became president in 2001, 'Bush's foreign travels [had] been limited to three visits to Mexico, two trips to Israel, a three-day Thanksgiving visit in Rome with one of his daughters in 1998 and a six-week excursion to China with his parents in 1975 when his father was the US envoy to Beijing' (Associated Press, 2000).

What Bush did not learn about foreign policy on his travels or from his advisers, he learned on the job. When terrorists struck the United States on 11 September 2001, millions of Americans prayed that their president was a quick study. To the surprise of many political pundits, including AEI's David Frum (2003), a former speech-writer for President Bush, the president was up to the challenge. Like many world leaders, Bush found his voice in a time of crisis: he had come of age. The inexperienced and untested leader, who months earlier could not answer some basic questions about foreign affairs, had become America's war president, a position that in time he would come to relish. According to Daalder and Lindsay:

> As Air Force One flew over Iraq, Bush could say that he had become an extraordinarily effective foreign policy president. He had dominated the American political scene like few others. He had been the unquestioned master of his own administration. He had gained the confidence of the American people and persuaded them to follow his lead. (2003: 2)

Shortly after Bush's campaign against terrorism went into full swing, his leadership style clearly began to change. The insecurity and sense of vulnerability that had accompanied him to the Oval Office was replaced by a growing confidence and bravado that other commanders-in-chief – including Ronald Reagan, John F. Kennedy, Franklin Roosevelt and Theodore Roosevelt – had exhibited (DeConde 2000). No longer content with assuming the role of student listening diligently to his teachers, Bush began to assert his leadership. Although he continued to rely on the advice of Condoleeza Rice, Donald Rumsfeld and the other 'vulcans', it became clear to those outside the inner sanctum that the president had little interest in expanding his circle of advisers. To put it bluntly, for policy experts residing in think tanks and at universities, the foreign policy-making process at the highest levels of government was, for all intents and purposes, closed. As Daalder observed:

> This is a very, very, very closed system. I think the president does rely on a small group of people [but] I don't think he's listening to the arguments. I think the arguments in and of themselves are being muted more and more. When [Bush] became president, he was always in receiving mode. He'd just sit there and listen. Now he's in broadcasting mode. He spends all his time telling other people what he thinks. Foreign leaders who met with him in his first year thought he was interested in listening to them and now it's all about telling them what he thinks needs to be done. He still listens, but he already knows what he wants. I think he's becoming more confident that he knows what he's doing and he doesn't need anybody's advice. So for these reasons, it is true that the process is not particularly open to outside influence. (quoted in Abelson 2006)

The relatively closed policy-making environment that has come to characterize the Bush White House may have impeded the access of policy experts from outside government, but it does not appear to have undermined Bush's ability to make policy decisions. Rather, limiting the number of participants involved in high-level policy matters has allowed the president to wage the war on terror more effectively. According to Daalder and Lindsay (2003), the president has a clear vision of what he wants to accomplish and will not allow even his closest and most trusted advisers to interfere with his agenda. Moreover, contrary to the assertions of countless journalists and scholars that a small band of neo-conservatives have hijacked the Oval Office, Daalder and Lindsay claim that the president has remained the master of his destiny. As these think tank scholars point out:

> The man from Midland [Texas] was not a figurehead in someone else's revolution. He may have entered the Oval Office not knowing which general ran Pakistan, but during his first thirty months in office he was the puppeteer, not the puppet. He governed as he said he would on the campaign trail. He actively solicited the counsel of seasoned advisers, and he tolerated if not encouraged vigorous disagreement among them. When necessary, he overruled them. George W. Bush led his own revolution. (Daalder and Lindsay 2003)

If President Bush has indeed exercised as much control over foreign policy as the two authors claim, then it stands to reason why think tanks and other non-governmental organizations have had difficulty in gaining access to the highest levels of government. In the final section of this chapter, we shall consider what think tanks have been able to accomplish in this ongoing policy debate and what conclusions can be drawn regarding the extent and nature of their influence.

Winning battles and waging wars: think tanks after 11 September 2001

Think tanks prepared for the debates over the war on terror much like armies prepare for battle. They took stock of their resources, assessed their capabilities, designed a strategy and determined the most effective ways in which it could be executed. Although their efforts may not always have paid off, think tanks have staked out and defended – and continue to stake out and defend – their positions in the war of ideas. Through their publications, conferences and seminars, congressional testimony and ongoing interaction with the media, America's leading defence and foreign policy think tanks have made a significant contribution to shaping the national conversation.

How much of an impact think tanks have had in influencing the substance and direction of the campaign waged by George W. Bush's administration to eradicate terrorism is a question that has yet to produce any definitive answers. In evaluating the extent to which they have made a difference, scholars must, like any competent detective, review what they know and what they do not know about the involvement of think tanks in this controversial policy debate. What is known by scholars who have monitored the debates over various aspects of the war on terror is that several think tanks – including RAND Corporation, CSIS, AEI, Brookings, Heritage, PNAC, the Council on Foreign Relations, the Carnegie Endowment and the Center for Security Policy (CSP) – have relied on multiple channels to convey their ideas to the public and to policy-makers on a wide range of issues. Among other things, think tanks have discussed the problems and prospects of homeland security, the need to overhaul intelligence agencies both at home and abroad, and whether the US needs to mend fences with its European allies. In short, scholars acknowledge that when it comes to ideas about how to fight a successful war against terrorists, think tanks have spoken loudly and clearly.

Several scholars and journalists have also acknowledged that some think tanks have been better positioned than others to capture the attention of policy-makers. Indeed, the consensus is that no think tank has been more effective at communicating its ideas to George W. Bush's White House than has PNAC. In the press and in much of the academic literature that has surfaced since President Bush assumed office, a lot has been made of the strong ties between PNAC and key members of his administration. Even more has been made of how closely the policy recommendations outlined in several of PNAC's publications and letters to policy-makers closely resemble the policies that Bush has pursued since 11 September 2001. But we also know that President Bush has been reluctant to solicit the advice of non-governmental policy experts, preferring instead to surround himself with a small circle of advisers whom he trusts to execute his foreign policy.

By probing more deeply into the relationship between PNAC and the Bush administration, we were able to uncover further information. For instance, we learned that the ideological underpinnings of the Bush doctrine, which among other things helped to justify the war in Iraq, did not originate at PNAC, but were closely linked to recommendations made by several members of his cabinet. As Gary Schmitt (quoted in Abelson 2006) acknowledged, 'It's perfectly obvious that Bush's war on terror was not something we articulated before September the 11th … Bush pulled together a strategic vision based on the advice he received from Cheney, Wolfowitz and Rumsfeld.'

PNAC has been effective at articulating a vision of how the United States can better advance its goals in the international community and, as noted, would dearly like to take credit for being the architect of Bush's foreign policy. Still, this has not prevented the media and some members of the academic community from making allegations that Bush's battle plans for the war on terror originated in a small Washington think tank, nor has it prevented interest groups from filing lawsuits against Bush and Dick Cheney for allegedly implementing PNAC's recommendations.[1] Had journalists and scholars been more diligent in analysing the many sources of influence in the Bush administration, they would have discovered a much longer list. In addition to identifying other think tanks with whom President Bush and his key advisers have had close contact – including AEI, the Council on Foreign Relations and the CSP – they would have considered the potential impact that Bush's father (Renshon 2004) and other individuals close to the president could have had on his thinking.

To suggest that, before he assumed the reins of power, President Bush had given little thought to missile defence, weapons of mass destruction and the potential danger of Iraq and other rogue states to the United States is completely without foundation. His many campaign speeches on foreign policy highlight his thinking on these and other important issues. It is also unreasonable to conclude that it was because of PNAC that issues relating to the war on terror made their way onto President Bush's agenda. If Richard Clarke was unable to convince Condoleeza Rice of the imminent threat that Osama bin Laden and Al-Qaeda posed to the United States, then why would we expect PNAC to have been able to attract attention in the Bush White House? As noted, it was not PNAC that made a difference in the White House. It was a tight-knit group of seasoned foreign policy experts with previous ties to this think tank that left an indelible mark on the president's foreign policy agenda. But despite the presence of several outside influences, in the final analysis, as Daalder and Lindsay remind us, it was the president and the president alone who spearheaded a new revolution in American foreign policy.

The war of the words: think tanks and anti-Americanism

In much the same way as the American Enterprise Institute and the Heritage Foundation helped to pave the way for the Reagan revolution (Edwards 1997), these and other think tanks have played a critical role in setting the stage for Bush to advance his political agenda. By shaping the political climate in which the president has waged his war on terror, think tanks have also contributed both directly and indirectly to the spread of anti-Americanism. Scholars who study think tanks and the role of public intellectuals (Posner 2001; Hitchens 2000) understand probably better than most that ideas have consequences. Therefore, it should not come as a shock that, when policy experts at America's leading think tanks become actively involved in highly contentious public debates – as Frum, Perle and those affiliated with PNAC have – their ideas and the words they use to advance particular arguments can have a lasting impact on the national conversation.

Policy-makers, journalists, intellectuals and members of the attentive public should welcome the free and open exchange of ideas, but they cannot afford to ignore the consequences of engaging in a war of words. In the case of the war on terror, several policy-makers and think tank scholars have made statements about foreign countries, foreign leaders and religious sects that have no doubt fuelled anti-American sentiments. This may be of little concern to those on Capitol Hill, in the White House or in one of the many think tanks located near Washington's Dupont Circle; nonetheless, they might at the very least want to consider how their public statements may advance or undermine America's national interests. If the spread of anti-Americanism does not keep policy-makers and think tank scholars up at night, then they should continue to engage in lively discussions about the benefits of American military supremacy and the eventual destruction of terrorist organizations. On the other hand, if they believe that little can be gained from having more adversaries than allies, then they may want to re-evaluate their strategy. Engaging armies on the battlefield is something that the United States appears prepared to do, but engaging in an ongoing war of words that may lead nowhere is something that policy experts and policy-makers may want to avoid.

Note

1 A lawsuit was filed by Doug Wallace of the Founders Freedom Defense Fund in Reno, Nevada, on 14 January 2005, alleging that the US government had exceeded its constitutional authority by 'implementing a scheme for global dominance called the 'Project for the New American Century'. For more information, go to http://www.wallacevbushlawsuit.com

5 Anti-Americanism and Popular Culture

Toby Miller

Here's the rub: America is at war against people it doesn't know, because they don't appear much on TV.

(Arundhati Roy 2001)

Too bad the terrorists of the 11th of September learned life in Hollywood movies.
(Woody Allen quoted in Augé 2002: 148)

[T]here appears to be no empirical evidence to support the claim that Arabs have a negative view of the US because 'they hate American values'.
(Zogby International 2004: 7)

It's a crude measure but an irresistible one. A visitor to http://google.com who entered 'anti-Americanism' and 'popular culture' as search terms in mid-2004 received no fewer than 21,500 hits. Three years later, the number had increased to 525,000. There has been a flurry of debate recently about the connection of these themes, much of it brought on by the plaintive cry uttered by a woman as she made her ashen way from the falling towers of 11 September 2001: 'Why do they hate us?' Her words were used by George W. Bush in his address to Congress on 20 September of that year, and finding an answer has been a preoccupation ever since.

Some representative US responses include the following:

Former CBS TV news anchor Dan Rather said that the US was attacked 'because they're evil, and because they're jealous of us'. (quoted in Navasky 2002: xv)

Former House of Representatives Speaker Newt Gingrich blamed Hollywood for the country's abject world status, calling for a new public diplomacy that would 'put the world in touch with real Americans, not celluloid Americans'. (Gingrich and Schweizer 2003)

Former Chair of the House of Representatives International Relations Committee Henry Hyde referred to the 'poisonous image' of the US overseas. (Henry Hyde quoted in Augé 2002: 161)

The Council on Foreign Relations maintained that anti-Americanism is partly fuelled by 'the broad sweep of American culture. Hollywood movies, television, advertising, business practices, and fast-food chains from the United States are provoking a backlash.' (Council on Foreign Relations 2003: 24)

Novelist Don DeLillo told readers of *Harper's Magazine* that 'the power of American culture to penetrate every wall, home, life and mind' was the problem. (Don DeLillo 2001)

But the writer Arundhati Roy has powerfully queried the claim that 11 September 2001 was an assault on the US as a symbol of freedom, asking why the Statue of Liberty was left untouched, while symbols of military and economic might were targeted. She suggests that this should encourage us to understand the attack as a brutal critique of power, not of liberty, and that subsequent responses would illustrate much about the US and supposed anti-Americanism (Roy 2001).

The hard data support her claim. A study by the International Federation of Journalists in October 2001 found blanket global coverage of the 11 September attacks, with very favourable discussion of the United States and its travails – even in nations that had suffered terribly from US aggression. Then German Chancellor Gerhard Schroeder announced 'unconditional solidarity', NATO described it as an attack against all members, and *Le Monde* simply stated *'Nous sommes tous américains'* (We are all Americans) (quoted in Council on Foreign Relations 2003: 1). But shortly thereafter, the giant advertising firm McCann-Erickson's evaluation of 37 states saw a huge increase in cynicism about the US media's manipulation of the events (Cozens 2001). The Pew Research Centre for the People and the Press (2002a) study of 42 countries in 2002 found a dramatic fall from favour for the US since that time, while its 2003 follow-up (Pew Research Centre for the People and the Press 2003b) encountered even lower opinions of the US nation, population and policies worldwide than the year before, with specifically diminished support for anti-terrorism, and faith in the UN essentially demolished by US unilateralism and distrust of the Bush regime.

In 2004, the advertising giant Doyle Dane Bernbach (DDB) declared that the US government had ceased to be a 'credible messenger' in the Middle East (quoted in Teinowitz 2004). The Next Generation's Image of Americans project from 2002 interviewed 1200 middle-class teens in a dozen countries, including five that are Muslim. The study found views of US residents as selfish, domineering, violent and immoral. It attributed these views to popular culture (DeFleur and Melvin 2002).

'Which country poses the greatest danger to world peace in 2003?', asked *Time* magazine of 250,000 people across Europe, offering them a choice between Iraq, North Korea, and the United States. Eight per cent selected Iraq, 9 per cent chose

North Korea, and … but you have already done the calculation about the most feared country of all (Pilger 2003).

A British Broadcasting Corporation (BBC) poll in 11 countries in mid-2003 confirmed this. It found sizeable majorities everywhere disapproving of the Bush regime and the invasion of Iraq, especially over civilian casualties (BBC 2003a). Given that Vice-President Dick Cheney had immediately and repeatedly spoken of the need for war against '40 or 50 countries' after 11 September 2001, who could be surprised by such a reaction (quoted in Ahmad 2003: 16)? In the words of the philosopher Leopoldo Zea (2001), this was a shift from *'la Guerra fría a la sucia'* (from the Cold War to the Dirty War). The Council on Foreign Relations' president sorrowfully noted that 'negative opinion of the United States and its policies has metastasized' due to a 'fundamental loss of goodwill and trust from publics around the world' (Gelb 2003: v). No wonder that many Chinese believe the US started Severe Acute Respiratory Syndrome (SARS), and Nigerians are refusing the polio vaccine because it is seen as a Washington plot to infect Muslims with diseases (J. C. Rubin 2004). But comprehensive studies by the Program on International Policy Attitudes and Knowledge Networks (PIPA 2003; PIPA 2004; Kull *et al.* 2003–04) found that a minority of the US population knew that clear majorities all over the world opposed the 2003 invasion, and a significant minority thought the war was supported globally.

During the 1980s, through the height of the second Cold War and then a series of grisly interventions in Latin America, the US was unpopular around the world because of its policies. There was a change under Bill Clinton (though not in most of the Middle East), because of his outlook and style as much as his administration's policies. But the policies of the second Bush group spread anti-Americanism rapidly and profoundly, with Brazil and Russia serving as two striking instances of majorities favouring the US a few years ago before turning into minorities (Kohut 2003). Novelist Kurt Vonnegut quipped that '[i]n case you haven't noticed, we are now almost as feared and hated all over the world as the Nazis were' (2004). After Bush Minor's re-election, a poll across 21 sovereign states found 47 per cent of people opposed to the US in general – not just its government, now, but its population, too – while 58 per cent thought his mandate made life riskier. Longitudinal studies indicated that the big change between the contemporary moment and the last time the US was led by a similarly ideological president, Ronald Reagan, was that while the US government was loathed across the globe at that time for its imperialism, the US population was exempted from responsibility. Now it isn't excused for the violence undertaken in its name (Pew Research Centre for the People and the Press 2005a).

Again and again, US foreign policies in the Middle East feature in the data as sources of anti-Americanism in the region. In June 2004, Zogby International found dramatic reductions across the Middle East in favourable ratings for the US since 2002, especially over Palestine and Iraq (Zogby International 2004). If something about anti-Americanism has really changed since 2001, popular culture can hardly be blamed. But if the attitudes expressed and the policies enacted by the US population and government synchronize with the methods and messages of popular culture, then a proportion of anti-American feeling can be attributed to its influence.

The rich vein of anti-US sentiment relates to four issues, each of which is given considerable attention in most parts of the world: economics, militarism, politics and culture. This chapter is principally concerned with the last category, though as we shall see, it is inseparable from the others. There is continuity on the cultural front since 2001, rather than rupture, because the infrastructure and impact of US popular culture on export were in place before that time. I give some consideration to new diplomatic attempts to influence the country's image abroad. The chapter discusses anti-Americanism, US cultural dominance, the role of the state, and opposition.

Anti-Americanism

Historically, anti-Americanism derives from a quasi-Darwinian belief that the genetically inferior migrants who had left Eastern and Mediterranean Europe for the US would turn it into a physically and mentally degenerate space of ill-mannered brutes (J. C. Rubin 2004). In the 1850s, this had turned into a grudging admiration, and critics now feared 'Americanization', the poet Charles Baudelaire's term for a 'vast cage, a great accounting establishment' (quoted in Grantham 1998: 60), that also came to stand for a new mass populism that might undo hierarchies. This became an ongoing, dual fear – that the US would be a model for the rest of the world, and that it would do so by imposing its will (B. Rubin 2004). Such anxieties were added to by critiques of its racism during the period of mass decolonization and the emergence of Third World blocs, and then the period of its untamed power in the post-Cold War era.

Today there are several distinct, sometimes overlapping types of anti-Americanism. The first two are domestic, the remainder international. Domestic anti-Americanism identifies US history with colonialist expansion elsewhere and favours a more pacific foreign policy. Domestic anxieties about anti-Americanism identify critics of US foreign policy as anti-American *tout court*, and construct loyalty tests for them. Overseas, there is opposition to US cultural domination and the spread of values associated with secular transcendence through money and sex; rivalry with the US over specific economic and cultural markets; bemused and contingent anti-Americanism that is specific to the Bush regime's means of pursuing foreign policy aims; populist anti-Americanism, expressed in violence, demonstrations and elections; leadership anti-Americanism, expressed in public denunciations or private; and separate feelings for US governments and corporations, as opposed to the US populace, although this is changing as the US public becomes identified as a militaristic theocracy – the Middle East increasingly sees distinctions erased between attitudes towards the US government and towards its citizens; rejection of the US based on experience of it as an occupying power; disappointment at the distance between the promises of US capitalism and its realities; identification of the US with unpopular policies of the International Monetary Fund (IMF), World Bank and World Trade Organization (WTO); and reaction to US opposition to international law and its infrastructure. There are also geographical varieties of anti-American discourse. First, Africa, the Middle East and Latin America continue long-standing debates about local democratic participation and control. Second, the major economic powers of Western Europe argue about the need to build pan-Europeanism in contrast to the homogenizing forces of Americanization. Third, the former state socialist polities of Eastern and Central Europe seek to develop independent civil societies with privatized media (Mowlana 1993: 66–7).

Cultural dominance

In 1820, the noted essayist Sydney Smith asked: 'In the four quarters of the globe, who reads an American book? or goes to an American play? or looks at an American picture or statue?' (Smith 1844: 141). Not surprisingly, the US soon became an early-modern exponent of anti-cultural imperialist, pro-nation-building sentiment. Herman Melville, for instance, opposed the US literary establishment's devotion to all things English, questioning the compatibility of this Eurocentrically cringing import culture with efforts to 'carry Republicanism into literature' (Newcomb 1996: 94). At the same time, an identical discourse in opposition to West European imperial and cultural domination was also developing amongst Islamic leaders in the Middle East (Mowlana 2000: 107–8).

Things changed rapidly. By the 1980s, Wim Wenders (1991) said 'Hollywood has colonized our unconscious'. Today, Rupert Murdoch modestly predicts that three companies will soon dominate the world's media – Comcast, Fox and Time Warner (Schulze and Elliott 2004). But there are losses as well as gains for these new maharajahs of the unconscious. For example, the European Audiovisual Observatory (2002) warns that regardless of its cultural messages, Hollywood was 'involved' in the 2001 attacks because of the part it played in an international economy that excluded and dominated most of the world's population, while Standard & Poors' 2002 survey of the industry refers to it as an 'expanding global empire'. How and why these changes happened is discussed in the next section (see also Miller *et al.* 2001 and 2005 for material on sport and film).

In 1996, cultural industry sales (of film, music, television, software, journals and books) became the United States' largest export, ahead of aerospace, defence, cars and farming. Between 1977 and 1996, the US culture industries grew three times as quickly as its overall economy. In 2000, services created one dollar in seven of total world production, and US services exported US$295 billion. The sector generated an US$80 billion surplus in balance of payments, at a time when the country relied on trade to sustain its society and economy, and boasted 86 million private-sector jobs in the area (Miller *et al.* 2005).

US production is adjusting away from a farming and manufacturing base to an ideological one. It now sells feelings, ideas, money, health, laws and risk – niche forms of identity, also known as culture. The significance of this for the country's image elsewhere is, of course, immense, while the domestic correlatives are important in terms of wealth, job creation and ideology. At the same time, cultural identity is turned into a commodity for those in the Third World, with attendant reactions. It is no accident that the push for the Third World to constitute itself as a diverting heritage site and decadent playground for the West has seen the emergence of sex tourism to the South and the transformation of Luxor, Bali and Mombassa into targets for terrorism (Downey and Murdock 2003: 84). This is the point where anti-Americanism meets popular culture – at the site of dominance. For it is claimed that US popular culture attenuates the cultures that it encounters, such that sex, violence, consumption, individualism, gender equality, meritocracy and fun threaten older values (Rehman 2004: 414). As we shall see, the story is more complicated than that might suggest.

In 1998, the major US film studios increased their foreign rentals by one-fifth on 1997; overseas box office of US$6.821 billion virtually equalled the domestic figure of US$6.877 billion. The most popular 39 films across the world in 1998 came from the US, and as that happened, the condition of other major film-making countries was declining: the percentage of the box office taken by indigenous films was down to 10 per cent in Germany, 12 per cent in Britain, 26 per cent in France, 12 per cent in Spain, 2 per cent in Canada, 4 per cent in Australia, and 5 per cent in Brazil – all dramatic decreases, to record low levels in some cases. In Eastern Europe, the story was equally dramatic. Whereas the USSR had released 215 films in 1990, the number was just 82 by 1995, half the number of US imports.

The US proportion of the world market is double what it was in 1990, and the European film industry is one-ninth of its size in 1945. Hollywood's overseas receipts were US$6.6 billion in 1999 and US$6.4 billion in 2000 (the reduction was due to foreign exchange depreciation rather than any drop in admissions). In 2000, most 'star-driven event films' from Hollywood obtained more revenue overseas than domestically, with 18 movies accumulating over US$100 million internationally, figures not attained by even one film from any other national cinema. For 2001 and 2002, all the top 20 films in the world were from the US. Between 1996 and 2002, of the most remunerative 20 films released in Europe, each one was from the US with the exception of *Notting Hill* (1999) and some co-productions that used British studios, such as the James Bond franchise. PriceWaterhouseCoopers estimated that US companies make almost US$11 billion by exporting film, and that Hollywood would receive close to US$14 billion in export revenue in 2004 (Miller *et al.* 2005).

To give an idea of how new this trend is, the past decade has seen a truly foundational change. For example, in 1985, 41 per cent of film tickets bought in Western Europe were for Hollywood fare. In 1995, the proportion was 75 per cent. And 70 per cent of films on European television come from the US. Measured in box office receipts, Europe is Hollywood's most valuable territory. Overall revenue there in 1997 was half the US figure, but twice that of Asia and four times larger than Latin America. In 1999, 65 per cent of US film and tape rental exports were to Western Europe, 17.4 per cent to Asia and the Pacific, 13 per cent to Latin America, and 2.3 per cent to the Middle East and Africa. The majors collected over 60 per cent of their box office revenues from outside the US in the top five European markets, and Hollywood's share of the market in 1996 ranged from 45–55 per cent in France, Italy and Spain, to 70–80 per cent in Germany and the UK. Hollywood's proportion of total video revenues mirrored theatrical box office – between 60 and 80 per cent across Europe (Miller *et al.* 2005).

International Hollywood receipts in theatres attained record levels in 2002 at US$9.64 billion, 20 per cent up on the previous year. Fifty per cent came from Europe/Middle East/Africa, followed by the Asia-Pacific, with 40 per cent, and Latin America, with 10 per cent. Beyond Europe, the percentage of imports from Hollywood has shown astonishing growth: US films accounted for 57.4 per cent of screenings in Barbados in 1970 and 97.8 per cent in 1991; 39.7 per cent in Canada in 1970 and 63.9 per cent in 1990; 59.2 per cent in Costa Rica in 1985 and 95.9 per cent in 1995; 8.9 per cent in Cuba in 1970 and 40.9 per cent in 1993. Africa is the largest proportional importer of Hollywood films, which account for 70 per cent of exhibition in Anglophone nations and 40 per cent in Francophone countries. It is easier today to find an African film screened in Europe or the US than on home territory. Following the hyperinflation of the 1970s and 1980s, which decimated film production in Mexico and Argentina, the percentage of Hollywood films exhibited in Latin America has increased dramatically (Miller *et al.* 2005).

Of course, theatrical exhibition accounts for barely a quarter of Hollywood's global revenues (29 per cent in 1999). Video provides 25 per cent and television 46 per cent. In 1995, 89 per cent of films screened on Brazil's cable channels were US imports, which occupied 61 per cent of time dedicated to cinema on Mexican TV, while in Egypt, the last 20 years have seen Hollywood dominate over Arab national cinemas both theatrically and in video rental (Miller *et al.* 2005). When cable and satellite opened up in the Middle East across the 1990s, there was a scramble both to 'secure access to Western content' and 'Arabize existing Western shows', with US film channels extremely potent contributors, and a special Arab-dedicated Disney channel of dubbed 'family' fare. By 1999, Disney was selling US$100 million a month in the Middle East (Sakr 2001: 93–4) and in 2002 Showtime offered ten new channels through Nilesat.

From its earliest days in the 1960s, Malaysian television relied on US films for content. The trend has never let up and dominates prime time. The same is true in Sri Lanka and the Philippines, where local films are rarely seen on television (Miller *et al.* 2005). Eurodata TV's analysis of films on television in 1999 found that 14 Hollywood pictures drew the highest audiences in 27 nations across all continents. And television drama in 2000 accounted for almost 50 per cent of worldwide television exchange (2000). In 1974, the Soviet Union imported 5 per cent of its programming and in 1984, 8 per cent; but Russia imported 60 per cent of its TV in 1997, much of it from the US. In 1983, the US was estimated to have 60 per cent of global TV sales. By 1999, the US figure had grown to 68 per cent, thanks to 85 per cent of exported children's programming and 81 per cent of TV movies. In 1998, Europe bought US$2 billion a year of US programming. The one failure was the decline of US soap opera in the face of indigenous productions that mimic it, and the loss of a domestic audience in prime time. But even the Latin American internal market in *telenovelas* meant that only 6 per cent of imported television was pan-continental in 1996 – 86 per cent came from the US. US imports could be priced to best local costs very easily (Miller *et al.* 2005).

Role of the state

So where does all this success come from? Rather than being a source of anti-US sentiment, surely the success of these films and TV programs signifies the popularity of the country's culture? Neo-classical economics argues that way, as do mavens of the US industries concerned, based on their contention that US entertainment simply gives people around the world what they want, because its culture industries are demand-driven, *laissez-faire* entities.

This claim about private initiative acting without the restriction of government intervention is a tired old shibboleth. The role of the state in aiding the development and success of US popular culture is venerable, powerful and undimmed. From the mid-nineteenth century, when the first international copyright treaties were being negotiated in Europe, the US refused to protect foreign literary works – a belligerent stance that it would denounce today as piratical. As a net importer of books seeking to develop a national literary patrimony of its own – an 'American Literature' – Washington was not interested in extending protection to foreign works that might hinder its own printers, publishers or authors from making a profit and building a culture industry. This mix of indebtedness and resentment character-izes the relation of import to export cultures, where taste and domination versus market choice and cultural control are graceless antinomies. It also characterizes the dependent relationship of development, a lesson that the US learnt quickly, and used to do unto others as had been done to it. US business and government recognized that commercial empires must make modernity both mundane and extraordinary via control and consent, as per a history that stretched from Dutch art to British fiction (Hozic 2001: 32). The memo-to-self read: practise Import Substitution Industrialization, preach Export-Oriented Industrialization. We have since seen this repeated in film, music and television. This section will focus par-ticularly on film and television drama, as these areas have traditionally provoked the most caustic reactions to US culture.

The US state has a long history of direct participation in film production and control of culture, starting in the silent era with screening Hollywood films on ships bringing migrants through to sending 'films to leper colonies in the Canal Zone and in the Philippines' (Hays 1927: 50) and extending to formal and informal barriers to imports. During World War I, films from the Central Powers were banned across the US. Immediately afterwards, the Department of the Interior recruited the industry to its policy of 'Americanization' of immigrants and Paramount-Famous-Lasky executive Sidney R. Kent proudly referred to films as 'silent propaganda' (1927: 208). In the 1920s and 1930s, Hollywood lobbyists regarded the US Departments of State and Commerce as its 'message boys'. The State Department undertook market research and shared business intelligence and the Commerce Department pressured other countries to permit cinema free access and favourable terms of trade (Miller *et al.* 2005).

In the 1940s, the US opened an Office of the Coordinator of Inter-American Affairs. Its most visible program was the Motion Picture Division, headed by John Hay Whitney, former co-producer of *Gone with the Wind* (1939) and future spy and frontman for the Central Intelligence Agency's news service, Forum World Features. Whitney brought in public relations specialists and noted film-makers like Luis Buñuel to analyse the propaganda value of German and Japanese films. Whitney was especially interested in their construction of ethnic stereotypes. He sought to change Hollywood movies, which were obstacles to gaining solidarity from Latin Americans for the US war efforts, and was responsible for getting Hollywood to distribute *Simón Bolívar* (1942) and produce *Saludos Amigos* (1943) and *The Three Caballeros* (1944). Some production costs were borne by the Office, in exchange for prints being distributed gratis in US embassies and consulates in Latin America. Whitney accompanied Walt Disney and the star of his film, *Donald Duck*, who made a guest appearance in Rio de Janeiro, and the Office had a film re-shot because it showed Mexican children shoeless in the street. The successful integration of Brazilian comic book and cartoon characters into Disney products at this time paved the way for post-war success in opening the Brazilian market to extensive Disney merchandise. At the same moment, the radio network Voice of America was founded, broadcasting US propaganda. It was commissioned to deliver specialist Cold War services promoting US culture after the war, generating Radio Liberty and Radio Free Europe (Miller *et al.* 2005).

During the invasion of Europe in 1944 and 1945, the US military closed Axis films, shuttered their industry, and insisted on the release of US movies. And the *quid pro quo* for the Marshall Plan was the abolition of customs restrictions, among which were limits on film imports. In the case of Japan, the occupation immediately changed the face of cinema. When theatres reopened for the first time after the US dropped its atomic bombs, all films and posters with war themes had been removed, and previously censored Hollywood texts were on screens. The occupying troops immediately established an Information Dissemination Section (soon to become the Civilian Information and Education Section) in its Psychological Warfare Branch, to imbue the local population with guilt and teach US culture through movies (Miller *et al.* 2005).

The Motion Picture Export Association of America referred to itself as 'the little State Department' in the 1940s, so isomorphic were its methods and ideology with US policy and politics. This was also the era when the industry's self-regulating Production Code appended to its bizarre litany of sexual anxieties two items requested by the 'other' State Department: selling the American way of life around the world and, as we have seen, avoiding negative representations of 'a foreign country with which we have cordial relations' (Powdermaker 1950: 36). Producer Walter Wanger (1950) trumpeted the meshing of what he called 'Donald Duck and Diplomacy' as 'a Marshall Plan for ideas ... a veritable celluloid Athens' that meant the state needed Hollywood 'more than ... the H bomb' (444, 446). Motion Picture Association of America head Eric Johnston, fresh from his prior post as Secretary of Commerce, sought to dispatch 'messengers from a free country'. President Harry Truman agreed, referring to movies as 'ambassadors of goodwill' (quoted in

Johnston 1950). Meanwhile, with the Cold War underway, the CIA's Psychological Warfare Workshop clandestinely employed future Watergater E. Howard Hunt to fund the rights purchase and production of *Animal Farm* (1954) and *1984* (1956). On a more routine basis, the United States Information Service, located all over the world as part of Cold War expansion and what we now call public diplomacy, had a lending library of films as a key stratagem (Miller *et al.* 2005).

The Congressional Legislative Research Service prepared a report for the House Committee on Foreign Affairs' Subcommittee on International Organizations and Movements in 1964 with a title that made the point bluntly: 'The US Ideological Effort: Government Agencies and Programs'. It explained that 'the US ideological effort has become more important than ever' because '[t]he Communist movement is working actively to bring ... underdeveloped lands under Communist control'. The report included John F. Kennedy's instruction to the US Information Agency that it use film and television, *inter alia*, to propagandize. It noted that at that moment, the government was paying for 226 film centres in 106 countries with 7541 projectors (1964: 1, 9, 19). Four decades later, union officials soberly intoned that:

> Although the Cold War is no longer a reason to protect cultural identity, today US-produced pictures are still a conduit through which our values, such as democracy and freedom, are promoted. (Ulich and Simmers 2001: 365)

By that point, additional services had been constructed to help sell US culture, such as surrogate radio and sometimes TV broadcasting systems aimed at Cuba, Asia, Iraq and Iran (Miller *et al.* 2005).

Today's culture industries are a private–public amalgam of capitalist innovation, standardized production and state support. They blend Northern Californian technology, Hollywood methods, Wall Street commerce and military funding. The interactivity underpinning this hybrid has evolved through the articulation since the mid-1980s of Southern and Northern California semi-conductor and computer manufacture and systems and software development (a massively military-inflected and military-supported industry until after the Cold War) to Hollywood screen content. Disused aircraft-production hangars were symbolically converted into entertainment sites (Miller *et al.* 2005).

Links continue to be forged. Stephen Spielberg is a recipient of the Defense Department's Medal for Distinguished Public Service, Silicon Graphics feverishly designs material for use by the empire in both its military and cultural aspects, and virtual-reality research veers between soldierly and audience applications, much of it subsidized by the Federal Technology Reinvestment Project and Advanced Technology Program. This has further submerged new weaponry from public scrutiny, even as it surfaces superficially, doubling as Hollywood props (Directors Guild of America 2000; Hozic 2001: 140–1, 148–51). The connection was evident in the way the film industry sprang into militaristic action in concert with Pentagon preferences after 11 September 2001 and became a consultant on possible attacks.

The University of Southern California's Institute for Creative Technologies uses military money and Hollywood directors to test out military technologies and narrative scenarios. And with the National Aeronautics and Space Administration (NASA) struggling to renovate its image, who better to invite to a lunch than Hollywood producers, so they would script new texts featuring the Agency as a benign, exciting entity? There is even a 'White House–Hollywood Committee' to ensure coordination between the nations we engage and the messages we export (Miller *et al.* 2005). Recently departed Motion Picture Association of America head and former presidential apparatchik Jack Valenti (2003) went so far as to argue before Congress that policing ownership of copyrighted films overseas was a key initiative against terrorism, since copying funds transnational extra-political violence.

Opposition

Not surprisingly given these historic links between the US government and popular culture, critical reactions have come from many sources. Although anxieties about stereotypes are often identified with a contemporary liberal sensibility, they have in fact been a long-standing concern, both for domestic conservatives frightened by sex, and other nations objecting to stereotypes. Anti-Americanism based on popular culture has a long lineage.

In 1921, the Great Wall Motion Picture Studio was founded in New York by Chinese expatriates angered by US industry and government neglect of their complaints about representations of Chinese characters. The studio produced films for export home as well as for the US market. In 1922, Mexico placed embargoes on film imports because of the repugnant 'greaser' genre. It was supported by other Latin American countries, Canada, France and Spain (Miller *et al.* 2005). In 1926, the British Cabinet Office issued a paper to participants at the Imperial Economic Conference warning that 'so very large a proportion of the films shown throughout the Empire … present modes of life and forms of conduct which are not typically British'. By the following year, the *Daily Express* newspaper worried that the exposure of British youth to US entertainment was making them 'temporary American citizens' (quoted in de Grazia 1989: 53). French soldiers rioted against their portrayal in *Hot for Paris* (1929). And official complaints over cultural slurs were made during the same decade by Germany, England, France, Italy and Spain. The industry's 1927 list of 'Don'ts and Be Carefuls' instructed producers to 'avoid picturizing in an unfavourable light another country's religion, history, institutions, prominent people, and citizenry'. The British Board of Film Classification of the 1930s insisted that Hollywood films released in imperial possessions follow the rule that 'white men may not be shown in a state of degradation amidst native surroundings'. Belgium's 1945 decision to ban Hollywood film in the Congo came from concerns that it could incite anti-colonial agitation (Miller *et al.* 2005).

The US itself wisely elected not to screen *Gone with the Wind* in Germany after the war, in the light of its racism, and held back *Tobacco Road* (1941) and

The Grapes of Wrath (1940) from foreign release lest they be 'used as propaganda against the United States' in their focus on 'the American dispossessed' which would 'offer considerable embarrassment to our State Department' (Rosten 1947: 119). Franco's Spain enthusiastically embraced the pro-capitalist side to Hollywood, and abjured its pro-worker, anti-fascist and libertarian films. *The Grapes of Wrath, The Great Dictator* (1940), *How Green Was My Valley* (1941), *To Be or Not to Be* (1942), and *Some Like It Hot* (1959) were too dangerous to be seen there until after Franco's death in 1975, while Orson Welles' International Brigade past was excised from *The Lady from Shanghai* (1948). The industry advised against any negative representation of the Fascist Spanish state, even after the war. This was a period when its allies in the State Department supported the Fascists as a bulwark against state socialism. Meanwhile, the tendency of US culture to assume victory in 'just' wars and ignore complicity in others has led to derision and anger. After both World Wars, complaints came from Australia, France, Britain and Canada when Hollywood fictionalized those epic conflicts as exclusively US triumphs (Miller *et al.* 2005).

A papal encyclical letter on improper motion pictures to US bishops offered the following remark:

> We were deeply anguished to note with each passing day the lamentable progress – *magni passus extra viam* – of the motion picture art and industry in the portrayal of sin and vice ...
>
> ... There is no need to point out the fact that millions of people go to the motion pictures every day; that motion picture theatres are being opened in ever increasing number in civilized and semi-civilized countries; that the motion picture has become the most popular form of diversion which is offered for the leisure hours not only of the rich but of all classes of society. (Pius XI 1936)

Countries emerging from colonialism have long had issues with US popular culture. The history of intersections with foreign governments is a particularly complex one in Asia and the Arab world. For decades, Thailand has banned Hollywood's clumsy representations of its monarchy. Conversely, even at the height of the Iranian Revolution, many Hollywood films were still released, despite the opposition they drew. Disney's lucrative 1990s deals in the Middle East were jeopardized by a bizarre exhibit at its Epcot theme park in Orlando that naturalized Jerusalem as Israel's capital, while the company has carefully recalibrated its Latin American stereotypes in order to assist the sale of TV networks there (Miller *et al.* 2005).

In short, the power of Hollywood has long triggered responses from both left and right. European progressives have admired the US for its secular modernity, egalitarianism and change, even as they have deplored its racism, monopoly capitalism, and class exploitation and their corollaries on camera, while the right has been disturbed by the mestizo qualities of African-American and Jewish contributions to the popular. Since World War II, widespread reaction against the discourses of modernization has foregrounded the US capitalist media as crucial components in

the formation of commodities, mass culture and economic and political organization in the Third World. Examples include the export of Hollywood screen products
and infrastructure, as well as US dominance of international communications
technology. Nigeria, for example, was first tied to US television through the supply
of equipment, which was then articulated to the sale of programmes, genres and
formats. Critics claim that the rhetoric of development through commercialism
decelerated economic growth and disenfranchised local culture, with emergent
ruling classes in dependent nations exercising local power, at the cost of relying
on foreign capital and ideology (Miller *et al.* 2005).

This kind of sustained critique assisted in the development of a cultural-
imperialism thesis during the 1960s. It argued that the US, as the world's leading
exporter of culture, was transferring its dominant value system to others, with a corresponding diminution in the vitality and standing of local languages and traditions
that had nurtured national identity. The theory attributed US cultural hegemony
to control of news agencies, advertising, market research, public opinion, screen
trade, technology, propaganda, telecommunications and security. US involvement
in South-East Asian wars during the 1960s led to critiques of its miliary interventions against struggles of national liberation and in turn targeted links between the
military–industrial complex and the media, pointing to the ways in which communications and cultural corporations bolstered US foreign policy and military
strategy and enabled the more general expansion of multinationals, which were
seen as substantial power brokers in their own right (Miller *et al.* 2005).

During the 1960s and 1970s, cultural imperialism discourse found a voice in
the Non-Aligned Movement and UNESCO. In the 1970s, UNESCO set up the
MacBride Commission to investigate cultural and communication issues in North–
South flows and power. At the same time, Third World countries lobbied for a New
International Information Order or New World Information and Communication
Order (NWICO), mirroring calls for a New International Economic Order and a
revised North–South dialogue. The MacBride Commission reported in 1980 on
the need for equal distribution of the electronic spectrum, reduced postal rates for
international texts, protection against satellites crossing borders and an emphasis
on the media as tools of development and democracy rather than commerce. There
continue to be annual Roundtables on the Commission's legacy, but the United
States mounted a successful riposte to NWICO.

UNESCO has ceased to be the critical site for NWICO debate. The US and
the UK withdrew from the Organisation in 1985 on the grounds that it was
illegitimately politicized, as evidenced by its denunciation of Zionism and support
for state intervention against private-press dominance. The past decade has seen
UNESCO distancing themselves from NWICO in the hope of attracting their
critics back to the fold. The UN has also downplayed its prior commitment to
a New Order. Negotiations saw the US arguing officially that the exchange of
entertainment is outside culture, which it defined as the less commodifiable and
governable spheres of religion and language.

In a telling accommodation, the UN began to sponsor large international
conferences in the late 1990s, such as the World Television Forum, to promote

partnerships between commercial media managers, entrepreneurs and investors from the US and Europe and their poorer counterparts from Africa, Asia and Latin America. And while UNESCO is a supporter of the Screens Without Frontiers initiative, which aims to facilitate a 'readjustment movement of North–South information exchanges' within the rubric of quality and public service – i.e. encouraging First World broadcasters to give away non-commodity-oriented programmes – even this project was endorsed provided it was not funded from the UNESCO budget. By 2003, there was talk of a NWICO redux – but this time under US hegemony, with UNESCO and culture displaced as sites and priorities by the WTO and commerce.

Nevertheless, concerns about US cultural influence remain and multiply. At Mondiacult 1982, the Mexico City world conference on cultural production, the French Minister for Culture Jack Lang made the following remark:

> We hope that this conference will be an occasion for peoples, through their governments, to call for genuine cultural resistance, a real crusade against this domination, against – let us call a spade a spade – this financial and intellectual imperialism. (quoted in Mattelart *et al.* 1988: 19–20)

French President François Mitterand's memorable argument of the mid-1990s stressed that cultural struggle over the General Agreement on Tariffs and Trade was not 'the culture of Europe' versus 'the New World'. Rather, it was about the preservation of 'the universality of culture' (quoted in Strode 2000: 67).

While the leftist connotations of this rhetoric are not universally welcome, its moral fervour resonates widely and profoundly, such that all Western European countries now echo it, and the Association of Southeast Asian Nations (ASEAN) issued a statement in the 1990s calling for 'a united response to the phenomenon of cultural globalization in order to protect and advance cherished Asian values and traditions which are being threatened by the proliferation of Western media content' (quoted in Chadha and Kavoori 2000: 417). These states are caught between the desire to police representations and languages along racial and religious lines and financial commitments to internationalism. Since a 1997 WTO decision in favour of the US that denied Canada the right to protect local print media through limiting the importation of split-run magazines, Canadian policy-makers have led efforts to create an international consensus on rules that would allow states to design policies to foster cultural diversity. In 1999, a coalition of Canadian civic organizations prepared the report 'New Strategies for Culture and Trade: Canadian Culture in a Global World'. It recommended the creation of a New International Instrument on Cultural Diversity that would recognize trade exceptions for domestic policies that seek to ensure cultural diversity. In subsequent trade talks, the Canadian government refused to make commitments which would restrict its ability to achieve cultural diversity goals until this international instrument was secured. The Canadians and other culture ministries formed an International Network on Cultural Policy to exchange information regarding diversity initiatives. These and other efforts led UNESCO to create a working group on cultural diversity, which culminated in the adaptation of a Declaration on Cultural Diversity in November 2001. It embodied the anxiety that other nations feel about US popular culture.

Conclusion

Recall Sydney Smith's 1820 rant about the lack of US culture. He knew even then what potential the nation had, provided that it avoided 'the insanity of garrisoning rocks and islands across the world'. Smith asked whether the new nation-state would become 'a powerful enemy or a profitable friend', querying the moral fibre of the US because 'every sixth man is a slave, whom his fellow-creatures may buy and sell and torture' (Smith 1844: 139, 137). Today the United States garrisons over 130 overseas places and its enemy status is blurred.

Clearly, US popular culture has transformed life elsewhere. On the one hand, it represents intense productive discipline; on the other, it promises transcendence through intense commodity consumption. Such links are encapsulated in two famous film scenes involving Clark Gable. In the 1930s, a deputation of Argentine businessmen protested to the US Embassy about *It Happened One Night* (1934) because Gable was seen removing his shirt, revealing no singlet below. This supposedly created an undershirt inventory surplus in their warehouses – overnight! A quarter of a century later, *It Started in Naples* (1960) found Gable showing a local boy how to eat a hamburger, which produced public controversy about compromising Mediterranean cuisine. Thirty years on, the task of tying commodities to films was completed by another kind of envoy, as Disney coordinated the release of *Pocahontas* (1995) with McDonalds' new 'McChief Burger' – early fruit from their 10-year agreement for cross-promotion in 109 countries (Miller *et al.* 2005). At the same time, it is too simplistic to view the protests at this influence as crucial parts of anti-Americanism. They are instead expressions of national sovereignty – and the interests of some state and business executives, of course.

Studies of the image of US film and TV in the Middle East in 2004 reveal that they are almost the only sources of positive feeling in the region engendered by this great, tumultuous force. There is also, of course, massive variation across the region. The US-enabled and US-allied society of Saudi Arabia is much more opposed to US popular culture than are Morocco or Jordan, and everywhere, the much-feared youth of each country are more positive than their elders. The Saudis receive almost no US films or TV drama for public screening, but are the most determined haters, whereas those most-exposed to US TV are the most positive about the country. Across the board, reactions to US imports of entertainment are effectively unrelated to the questions that really make people angry: Washington's policies on Iraq and Palestine (Zogby International 2004).

This should come as no surprise, since:

- popular culture's contents are not clearly and demonstrably key contributors to anti-Americanism;
- the role of the US state in the success of popular culture is vastly greater than is normally recognized;

- the corporate power and foreign and commercial policies of the US, notably its militarism, are key sources of anti-Americanism; and
- the efforts of public diplomacy to eschew popular culture, to counterbalance it, are fated towards a high-culture bias that will not address ordinary people's needs.

6 Culture or Power Politics? Post-Cold War Anti-Americanism in Russia

Skaidra Trilupaityte

Academic discussions about 'anti-Americanism' today often imply that this is not a singular but a plural phenomenon, characteristic of the social, political and cultural encounters of our global world. Many types of anti-Americanism – domestic and Western/Islamic; coming from political right and left; intellectual and popular; Cold War and post-Cold War – are employed in order to explain the different and sometimes non-corresponding historical and psychological factors. This typological variety leads to methodological confusions and may result from attempts to apply this popular catchword to any possible sphere of life, region or period. In each debate, a distinctive type of cultural anti-Americanism is at issue. Some researchers talk about justified responses towards global and excessive US cultural proliferation. Others, in turn, argue that the very essence of anti-Americanism and of the deep-seated prejudices against the US (or, more broadly, against modernity and its representations) derive from cultural predispositions that any American action might bring into play.

Because the debate over the US's image in the world is highly politicized, it becomes hard to make a clear distinction between the above-mentioned references to culture or at least to detach cultural arguments from political and institutional preconditions. Furthermore, exclusive focus on anti-Americanism – an unambiguously negative perception of the US – together with a proclivity to generalize about public opinion ('popular dislike of America') omits the possibilities of various middle-ground views. Recently, the strain of hostile and ideological anti-Americanism often employed to help construct a post-Cold War European identity has been systematically examined; anti-Americanism's affinity to anti-Semitism has also been a subject of interest (Revel 2003a; Berman 2004; Hollander 1995; Markovits 2006). Furthermore, many common arguments transcend boundaries between left and right, in order to give priority to the 'cultural prejudice' definition of anti-Americanism. There are suggestions among liberals that anti-Americanism be interpreted beyond a narrow scope of patriotism and instead in terms of supra-national political dissent against global governance (Ross 2004). Studies in international relations also show that one must not essentialize this phenomenon as a clear system of ideas, since there exist too many global and domestic complexities of anti-Americanism, which is a relational and reactive phenomenon, often existing along with pro-American feelings, and with all its ambiguities and contradictions (Lacorne and Judt 2005; Judt 2005).

By considering the continuing use of Cold War rhetoric in post-Cold War public discourses, one could help broaden the cultural explanation of anti-Americanism; and an investigation of post-totalitarian self-images *vis-à-vis* American power might be fruitfully integrated into studies of the symbolism of America in the European mind (Kuisel 1996; Diner 1996; Ceasar 1997; Berghahn 2001; Pells 1997). Research into contemporary Russian anti-Americanism, which allows the correlation between negative reflections of America and Russia's reaffirmation of its 'great power' status, could become one of the most intriguing endeavours in this field.

After the collapse of the Soviet Union, assessments of Russian transformation rarely reflected specifically on the theme of anti-Americanism, although this phenomenon was recognized in passing. The steep rise of anti-Americanism in Russia during the second half of the 1990s has been frequently noted by those discussing post-Cold War relations between the US and Russia, or those analysing pronouncements of Russian nationalism. Positive and negative Russian images of America have been thoroughly scrutinized in a few profound historical studies, which focus on Soviet and post-Soviet Russian 'Americanization' – governmental and non-governmental aspects of cultural transmissions, or reputations of Western commodities and pop culture (Ripp 1990; Ball 2003; Yurchak 2006: 158–237). A complex historical study undertaken by Eric Shiraev and Vladislav Zubok (2000) stands out as an extremely fruitful phenomenological attempt to understand anti-Americanism in Russia. Additionally, after 11 September 2001, efforts are being made to specify the motivations of Russian anti-Americanism through the use of opinion poll survey data and first-hand experience of Russian politics and media, alongside comparative analyses of different national versions of anti-Americanisms (Connor 2004; Zlobin 2005; Shiraev 2005). Despite this useful literature, we do not yet have sufficiently convincing answers to one of the most stimulating questions: which factors of domestic and global policies regulate the dynamics of anti-Americanism among Russian elites? Or, to put it differently, how and to what extent – if at all – is this phenomenon 'justified' among the disgruntled Russian public?

What follows is a synthetic effort to outline the popular explanations of contemporary Russian anti-Americanism in a field which could broadly be called studies of the Russian transition. It will be shown that anti-Americanism is a contested and ambiguous term with multiple meanings that depend on social and historical context as well as the political and disciplinary purposes of those who employ this language. A nuanced cultural understanding of the dynamics of anti-Americanism is important, yet is often either ignored in the International Relations literature or 'essentialized' as an inherent aspect of Russian culture in popular discussions of the issue. This chapter concludes that cultural explanation of Russian anti-Americanism still proves useful, even against the background of the instrumental use of this ideology by power elites to achieve their political goals. To support this claim, I examine some paradigmatic positive and negative images of

America in Russia, and consider their use in relation to American policies towards processes of Russian transformation. Finally, I shall reflect on anti-Americanism as a component of the new Russian 'great power' identity formation. Most importantly, this chapter is an attempt to better understand the place of cultural politics and analysis in the field of international relations – a theme which itself today has become a topic of debate.

Culture and post-Cold War international relations

Although the Cold War has been over for more than 15 years now, Immanuel Wallerstein has noted that:

> when one listens to some voices in the United States, and some in China or Russia, it doesn't seem to be over for everyone. Such voices seem to take the ideological rhetoric of the Cold War as a continuing marker of how they define the current world reality. Perhaps we should not take them too seriously. Proponents of Realpolitik have always argued that ideology was merely rhetoric that was meant to mask the *raison d'état* of the states, and the ruling strata never paid too much attention to the ideology they officially espoused. (Wallerstein 2003: 127)

Whether one should or should not take the post-Cold War rhetoric seriously, however, is an object of heated political debate. Though overused (Ivie 2000), rhetorical tropes still propel further disputes, in which national interests and the futile ambitions of some politicians merge and the lines between political realism and ideologies become blurred.[1] Today scholars often question the attempts to separate ideology and reality when examining crucial moments in the Cold War. Instead of seeing them as mutually exclusive opposites (which happens whenever the rhetoric is relegated to the field of myths and lies), new studies of the Cold War now generally recognize the rhetorical component of reality (Medhurst 2000). The end of that war is often understood as, first of all, a victory of ideas: 'there were no military defeat or economic crash; but there was a collapse of legitimacy' (Gaddis 1997: 283). Ideological factors also receive much attention in analysis of post-Cold War realities. Because one sees the possibility of fruitful interaction between international-structural-material and domestic-ideational-cultural aspects, critical comparative studies of the Russian transformation should avoid both historical-cultural determinism, and the mistaken approach of the earlier Sovietology which treated revolutionary events and radical social changes as a 'clear break with the past' (English 2000: 239).

One must concede that international realities are continuously framed by the media and by 'power interests' and thus are unavoidably ideological. Knowledge about the external world has always been mediated symbolically. This is even more true today, as various strategies of persuasion in post-Cold War 'soft power' games[2] have replaced the 'hard powers' of the Cold War. Even the continuing imperial urges in the post-Cold War era could hardly be expressed in a traditional military sense, since wars of ideas (and economic arguments) have superseded wars of territory (Cooper 2003: 17). Besides the difficulties in distinguishing diplomatic rhetoric from 'real interests', there also exists a common popular understanding of any US governmental or private and non-governmental organiza- tion's (NGO's) actions as being exemplars of unilateral 'American power', which shape people's beliefs about 'US intentions'. Correspondingly, considerations of elites about America do not always coincide with popular public opinions; while the public broadly defined becomes a target of generalizing surveys or opinion polls, the elites come to signify individual efforts in re-conceptualizing post-Cold War priorities. Nevertheless, the geopolitical symbolism of new post-totalitarian nations most often relates to popular public perceptions that national elites help to crystallize.

Overall, providing cultural explanations of political realities is not an easy undertaking, especially if one tries to find reasonable connections between the ideology of anti-Americanism and relations among states or nations. The concept of 'culture' generally is a tricky one, since it is often employed when no other factors could seemingly explain the differences between societies. Additionally, attribution of differences to culture is unsatisfactory because it cannot smoothly accommodate any generalizing social theory models (Huntington 1996: 478). In international relations, culture has also been a residual category, both unsatisfying and deceptively easy to apply. For example, if one asserts that everything is shaped by power, then all other rhetorical activities become 'background noise', irrelevant in debates on relations among states (Ninkovich 1994). Nevertheless, there were attempts to reconcile theories of culture and power in international relations by conjoining the terms 'state' and 'culture' in different scientific traditions (Steinmetz 1999; Beate 2004; Conze 2004), and by examining cultural components in the processes of post-Soviet transition (Kennedy 2002). After calls to unite the usually distinct fields of American Studies and International Studies (Crockatt 2003: x), one could expect that eventually other fields, such as cultural studies, will also find their relevant place in these disciplinary intersections.

With regard to post-Soviet Russia, cultural explanations of political transition are often represented in opposition to modernization theories that generally treat structural changes as a consequence of economic or political preconditions, not as cultural peculiarities. Cultural theories, with their attempt to explain Russia's 'exclusive' geopolitical situation, have often been criticized for their futile stereotyping and trotting out of rhetoric about exhausted 'Western' attitudes (Spanger 2005). Russia, in these theories, has too often been portrayed as being 'inferior' to the West, or as a country firmly embedded in religious, cultural and historical traditions which reflect subliminal projections of irregularity and European 'Other' (Neumann 1997). While it would be wrong to imagine *a priori* that cultural arguments are generally predisposed around Western hostility, this can occur when, in the name of good intentions, cultural explanations of Russian failures are simplistically described as negative 'Huntingtonian-like' attitudes, from which one is eager to distance oneself (Billington 1998).

An important caveat should be made here. While some cultural theories treat the recent semi-authoritarian power centralization in Russia in terms of an 'authentic' Russian tradition that is favoured by most Russians over 'foreign' models of democracy or civil society (Pipes 2004; Pipes 2005), other seemingly less-culturally based attitudes paradoxically introduce scenarios that are no less pessimistic, precisely because they imply that 'outsiders' are unable to comprehend Russian realities. For example, some say that Western criticism of Russia often does not contrast Russia's recent misfortunes against its own Soviet past (political failures then become only relative, or at least temporal). Alternatively, Western criticism often does not permit sober comparisons of Russia with other 'normal' middle-income non-Western countries; thus at times it could be interpreted as inadequate or even paranoid (Shleifer and Treisman 2004). By disregarding foreigners' criticism because of such interpretations, however, any legitimate anxieties about Russia might conveniently be dismissed as the excessive 'sensationalism' of Western observers (*ibid.*), so the very categorization of 'normalcy' becomes ambiguous. The opposition between the knowledge of 'insiders' and 'outsiders' is precarious, but so is the reduction of arguments about the 'non-Western' particularities of post-Soviet Russia to 'prejudicial' and 'righteous' accounts.

There exists a panoply of research and reasonable explanations about the anti-Westernizing motives of Russian culture, and modern historiography draws on a variety of notions of 'modernizing', 'non-European', 'Oriental', etc. to supply paradigms of Russia's identity (von Hagen 2004). Yet this does not provide an unambiguous and truly comprehensive portrayal of Russia's transition. For example, Svetlana Boym, the supporter of the cultural argument for post-communist countries' development (2001: 349), noticed in the mid-1990s a 'mass perception of the loss of some kind of Soviet communality and of a unified Soviet cultural text' (Boym 1995: 150). Especially during the second half of that decade, nostalgia for Russian goods and the popularity of commodities of Russian origin coincided with nostalgia for Soviet culture (Ball 2003: 237–41). Complaints about the devastation of Russian culture by Western mass-culture products that emerged in Russia across the whole political spectrum – left and right – also served for many as evidence of a new post-Soviet Russian nationalism.

Notably, the links between Russian anti-Americanism and xenophobic Russian nationalism as well as Russia's authoritarian past have been convincingly exposed (Shiraev and Zubok 2000: 82–3). One should, however, be wary of over-generalizations. A 'prototype' case of the former dissident Aleksandr Solzhenitsyn (expelled from the USSR in 1973), whose famous statements during the 1980s formed part of Stephan Haseler's collection of Cold War anti-Americanism texts (Solzhenitsyn 1985), today seems particularly enlightening. Since his return to Russia in the mid-1990s, Solzhenitsyn's conservative, anti-Western, non-liberal albeit openly anti-imperial and, in most cases, anti-Soviet stance has not only distanced him from chauvinistic extremists of the Zyuanov and Zhirinovsky type (Rowley 1997), but has also shown up the multifarious interrelationships between modernizing and anti-modernizing tendencies in the Russian 'search for self'.

Ambiguous approval of Russia's slip towards authoritarianism on the one hand, and declarations about her undeniable transition towards 'normal' democracy (even if it is still to be achieved in the long run) on the other – both being historically 'defensible' for Russia – seem caught in a trap of conceptual dichotomies. After all, 'if Western institutions were inappropriate for Russia, did this amount to Russia's misfortune or blessing?' (Ball 2003: 248). Any answer to this is hard to determine in a political life, since even new proclamations of Russian messianism and 'Russian solutions' continue to be affected by various forms of Western influence, one way or another.

Judgements about 'realities' often become unavoidably motivated by political interests. Disparity between modernization and democracy, or between non-corresponding patterns of development that help distinguish between modernization and Westernization (Huntington 1996), could be valid for overcoming either/or oppositions in deciding what is 'good' or 'bad' for Russia, at least in theory. The question, however, remains whether the vicious circle of 'positive' or 'negative' potentials of Russian anti-Westernization (or, more specifically, anti-Americanism) could be avoided.

Frank Ninkovich, a historian of American international relations, made an important point in demonstrating the difference between culture and ideologies, which complements a common distinction between civilization and culture. Unlike more trendy concepts such as 'discourse' that are detached from institutional realities and, as such, could be easily confused with culture, the term 'ideology' for him clearly relates to power and interest, and indeed is usually explained in terms of interests (Ninkovich 1994: 9). Since ideologies often facilitate understanding of political circumstances, they can be analysed within the framework of 'intercultural dissonance' suggested by the realist tradition. Culture, in this tradition, correlates with the ultimate rationality of power, thus cultural misunderstandings could explain the basic behavioural matrix for political actions. Power is important for safeguarding 'essentially irrational local perspectives'. Therefore 'culture's foreign policy importance can be demonstrated only by connecting it intellectually to power and by integrating it with traditional conceptions of realism' (Ninkovich 1994: 7).

As such, ideology becomes a mediator between culture and power, since it is a cultural product and agent of modern times and so a decisive intellectual factor for spreading civilization. Despite modern cultures being inseparable from ideologies – since it is established that they can only be expressed intelligibly through ideologies (e.g. when US leaders defend the 'American way of life') – there are clear differences between them, too:

> Ideologies provide programs of action while cultures are neutral in that regard. Ideologies can be coherently articulated, whereas it sounds strange to suggest that one can articulate a culture ... Because ideologies travel and cultures do not, ideologies can diffuse as wholes in contrast to the more limited diffusion of isolated cultural traits. (*ibid.*: 13)

Although cultural anti-Americanism has often been defined in terms of modern ideology, the difference between culture and ideology here suggests a distinction between political anti-Americanism and various (latent) images of America. Even if not all images of America are by definition ideological, anti-Americanism certainly fits the bill with its recognizably negative 'essences' and their potential to penetrate various cultural contexts. The lack of complexity makes this ideology (like other modern ideologies) transitory and its stereotypes conveniently adaptable whenever there are political demands for popular uniting images of the 'common enemy'.

Continuing Russian images of the US

During Soviet times, learning the different meanings behind the same words, the tenuous distinctions between official and unofficial thinking, and between the things publicly 'said' and those 'believed', created major methodological problems for those who analysed Russian perceptions of America (Gilbert 1977). In the late 1980s, Vladimir Shlapentokh maintained that Russian attitudes towards the US represented attitudes towards the West in general, for America had been singled out 'to be either a model for imitation or a model for rejection' (Shlapentokh 1988: 158). He talked about the three main ideologies circulating among the intelligentsia of Soviet Russia – official, democratic, and Russophile – all of them upholding distinctive images of the US. Today, Russian attitudes towards America could probably be discussed even without unambiguous distinctions between the Soviet and post-Soviet periods because the above-mentioned dichotomous images (imitation and rejection) reveal the continuing patterns of a love/hate relationship, the interwoven and ambivalent emotions of alliance and rivalry.

Historians of US–Russian relations widely agree that during the late Soviet period, official Soviet anti-American rhetoric notwithstanding, Russian elites and even members of society at large were quite Americanized. Informal fascination with America by elites who could visit the US usually corresponded with dissatisfaction about grim, home-grown realities (Richmond 2003). People venerated 'American goods' (if only available on the black market), and the positive image of the US as the land of prosperity (if at most a fictional one) occupied Russian minds. This image of America permitted associations with prestige and consumer goods of high quality whatever their actual place of origin (Ball 2003: 190).

Yet alongside informal optimistic attitudes, there also existed tendencies of official and unofficial Russian anti-Americanism. One of these intellectual tendencies – largely associated with Russophiles – could be represented as being harshly critical of the Western materialism and, more specifically, of the 'American way of life'. This tendency grew not in binary opposition to, but together with castigation of, the dehumanizing Soviet system which rendered the Russian perception of America such a complex matter. Shiraev and Zubok's (2000) extensive historical research on changing twentieth-century Russian perceptions of America shows that official and unofficial, elite and popular images of America have often involved questioning of supposedly tergiversating American motives. And, predictably, deep mistrust of the West in Russian society was not eliminated with the abolition of official anti-American propaganda.

Typical sources of recent Russian anti-American sentiments – such as residual Soviet mentality, Orthodox Christian national ambition, frustration over lost Cold War power, and disenchantment with the US's post-Cold War intentions towards Russia – stress the unambiguously 'cultural' nature of Russian anti-Americanism (Connor 2004). This is described as 'a unique blend' of cultural European-style superiority, envy that is attributed to a Third World ambivalence towards wealthy nations, and nationalistic resentment rooted in anti-Westernizing historical conditions (ibid.: 233). Those conditions could provisionally be reduced to the 'latent' Russian distrust towards the US, which in turn might be traced back to different periods as well as to different factions of Russian politics and society.

In spite of elites or the intelligentsia in general being widely affected by 'American consumerism' and the quest for American goods, the Soviet official language did not abandon all at once its regular rhetoric of 'American material-ism' and 'American corruption'. During the 27th Communist Party Congress, M. Gorbachev still harshly criticized the US; only since 1987 has it become possible for relatively objective liberal intellectual views on America to appear (Shlapentokh 1988). In the early 1990s, Russian government policies towards the US were described along familiar lines by 'America-centrists', 'America-phobes' and 'idealists' (Israelyan 1993). One could similarly choose other examples – such as radical democrats, 'statist' democrats, 'statist' bureaucrats and passionately (even paranoid) anti-American neo-communists, together with ultranationalists – in order to portray the gamut of Russian political propensities (Pushkov 1993). Since Russian liberals became the main propagators of pro-American attitudes, positive images of America have generally been associated with their political milieu. Pro-American politicians at times were also called 'democrats' and, after the ideas of Western liberalism were discredited in Russia in the mid-1990s, there were attempts at marking a distinction between the old 'Yeltsin-period' liberals and the new 'anti-Western' liberals (Shlapentokh 1998). A more interesting develop-ment to note here, however, is the specific correspondence between the formerly liberal strata and the nationalistic anti-American right that emerged during the second half of the 1990s.

The relationship between anti-American rhetoric and nationalism in this case seems important because prevailing neo-conservative Russian nationalism could hardly be comparable to its more modernizing European counterparts. The lack of modernizing motives of emancipation in Russian nationalism, as opposed to the national liberation movements of anti-Soviet dissent in Eastern and Central Europe, turned it into an expedient instrument in the hands of elites. Berman, who interpreted the autonomous logic of anti-Americanism through the prism of European identity politics, showed that the absence of unappealing forms of nationalism today relates to new possibilities for crusading against the 'American enemy' in which 'politically correct' Europeans could indulge (Berman 2004: 78). Meanwhile, nationalistic Russian anti-Americanism has only a vague resemblance to the recent Western European anti-American hostility. Like the policies of pro-American liberalism, the strategies of Russian nationalism have been largely manipulated by a certain leadership within state institutions. Such nationalisms 'from above' were used during periods of power relocation when various xenophobic cards (anti-Americanism included) were employed in political fights (Gudkov and Dubin 2005). Generally, the Russian Duma (Parliament) has been more eager to pursue domestic anti-Americanism than have Russian presidents, who have persisted with democratic rhetoric on the international front and often maintained good 'personal relationships' with US presidents.

Not coincidently, observers often mention that the social and political 'Westernization' that took place in the 1990s was only 'virtual' democratization. The internationalist liberal identity seemingly crumbled even before it took shape, and the officially promoted correlation of national interest with democratic movements during the second half of 1991 appears accidental, deeply traumatic and in sharp contrast with the 'typical' conservative and defensively anti-Western turn (Gudkov and Dubin 2005; English 2000: 234). While positive images of America in Russia have always rested on a volatile institutional background, the lasting components of Russian 'great power' identity – in which the image of the United States at best plays a referential role of 'constant rival' – today look far more enduring and convincing. This is especially so after 11 September 2001, as it is shown by complex studies of the 'radically swinging pendulum' of Russian attitudes towards the US (Zlobin 2005; Shiraev 2005).

The suspicion of Georgi A. Arbatov, a prominent Soviet Americanologist (who was otherwise in favour of cultural exchanges between the Soviet Union and America), although proclaimed in 1969, could be no less characteristic of recent times:

> Underlying US policy is the so-called 'erosion' of our social system. As a professional student of the United States I feel that this is a basic United States policy line and that it distorts all good proposals, including those regarding contacts. Professor [Zbigniew] Brzezinski speaks of promoting evolutionary changes in the Soviet Union. This is what underlies United States policy of promoting cultural contacts and trade. (quoted in Richmond 2003: 18)

In the early 1990s, a symbolic positioning of Russia *vis-à-vis* American power gave the appearance that Russia was on the way to achieving American standards. However, when policies of 'Westernization' became fully discredited, 'moral equivalence' attitudes enabled people once again to symbolically challenge the former Cold War rival. Since 11 September 2001, American anti-terrorist actions have provided cover for Russian abuses in Chechnya and, whenever concerns have been expressed about human rights violations in Russia, rights abuses worldwide (not excluding the US) have conveniently been signalled.[3] Examples taken from US legislative practice (such as thwarting foreign groups from financing election campaigns under cover of humanitarian activities), even if stripped of historical context, could be used today as expedient comparisons for justifying Russia's centralization of power and expanding governmental control over the public space. Also, criticism of non-profit enterprises – earlier typically coming from the Committee for State Security (KGB)-backed press or, alternatively, from former democrats radically disillusioned with reforms – appears as a kind of common refrain. For example, scathing criticism of the Soros foundations – in the late 1980s (when George Soros came up with his own 'Marshall Plan' for the crumbling Soviet Empire) as well as in post-Soviet Russia – has often been accompanied by vitriolic bashing of US 'secret services' (Kaufman 2002: 227; Shiraev and Zubok 2000: 79). Today, when the activities of international organizations and global networks – or, to put it another way, the 'soft power' of new internationalism – pose a serious challenge to traditional nationalism, the concerns of the Russian president draw on traditional suspicion towards outsiders' intentions:

> The continuing financing of the political activity from abroad should be, I think, in the state's field of vision ... especially if this financing is carried out through the state channels of other countries and these or those organizations functioning in our country and involved in the political activity are, in fact, used as a tool of the foreign policy of other states.[4] (Myers 2005)

America and post-Cold War Russian changes

Besides 'pure' cultural factors, external aspects – such as Russian–US post-Cold War relationships, or the consequences of the totalitarian system's collapse – should be considered for understanding bouts of anti-Americanism in the Russian public arena. During the period of 'romanticized liberal utopia', Yeltsin's foreign policy-makers liked to emphasize that Russia had liberated itself from the totalitarian past just like the rest of the Soviet Union. Moreover, according to the 'twisted logic of Russian liberal reforms, the die-hard anti-Soviet "hawks" during Yeltsin's first years in power turned out to be better allies than American liberals' (Shiraev and Zubok 2000: 37), who were especially supportive of the *détente* doctrine during the Brezhnev years. The defeat of the communist coup in 1991 allowed expression to be given to pro-American sentiments in Russian society, grateful for President George H. Bush's disapproval of conservative Soviet hardliners. The crushing of the coup plotters thus meant a rehabilitation of Russia (and particularly, its White House) in the face of the 'Soviet' Kremlin. One could appreciate that this release of pro-American sentiment, which 'rushed like water through a broken dam' (*ibid.*: 32) during the 1991 events, actually coincided with an optimistic reclamation of Russia's own unique identity in a new era. This new Russia was establishing itself in a multi-polar world without any rivalry between the former Cold War superpowers.

Euphoria about 'the American way' in early 1990s Russia was supported not only by post-1989 liberals and Yeltsin's circle. Additionally, trust in free market achievements was promulgated by American institutions, helpful Western foundations and NGOs which didn't encourage critical assessments of the whole process of 'transition'. Importantly, until early 1992 many expected that Western assistance would provide the same results it had provided for Western Europe after World War II, with the implementation of the Marshall Plan. Thus Western engagement of all sorts and in virtually every sphere of Russian policy was widely encouraged by the Russian leadership (Goldgeier and McFaul 2003: 59). Over-optimism created the naïve belief that, as soon as the Soviet system was totally destroyed and new Western structures became fully operational, living standards would rise to equal those of America.

The crumbling Soviet Union, however, created not only a free but also an economically weak society in which the failures of transition toward the market economy (i.e. the 'shock therapy' implemented by the Russian government), hyperinflation, the gruesome social situation, rapidly rising poverty, crime and corruption soon ruined the euphoria of liberation. Unfulfilled dreams and deep frustration over dashed opportunities conditioned incredulity towards Western models as well as eventual US-bashing on various foreign policy occasions (Pushkov 1993). The search for new scapegoats replaced erstwhile denunciations of communism, and the former optimistic views during the course of events morphed into opposite feelings of resentment. When the vocabulary of 'democratizers' became widely equated with social disorder, suitable solutions for a new Russian identity were proposed by nationalists and communists who, despite their ideological differences, became the first carriers of anti-American sentiments.

After the 'romantic period' of the Yeltsin and Clinton governments, the 'Russian question' came under sharp focus among US policy-makers. Clinton's near-complete neglect of Russia during his election campaign and the first years of his presidency, as well as the lack of clear strategies in the face of new post-Soviet challenges, have often been mentioned. It is frequently alleged that the US administration's ignoring of the anti-government opposition in Russia during the 1990s undermined pluralistic growth and trust in democratic law among regular Russians. Devolution of problem-solving in Russia to American presidential aides, as well as the latter's total inability to facilitate Russia's transformation and unwillingness to prevent corruption among the high ranks of Russian government in obtaining credits from the International Monetary Fund exclusively for Yeltsin's support, have been thoroughly reviewed elsewhere (United States House of Representatives 106th Congress 2000). It was also suggested that Washington's ignoring of – or even support for – Yeltsin's corrupt policies of privatization ('grabatization') helped to reverse the beliefs about 'American help', transforming them into convictions about 'Western conspiracy'. Russians widely understood that America was interested in weakening Russia's independence, while frustration at seeing other nations – primarily those in Central and Eastern Europe that were once under Soviet control – gaining more benefits from their affiliation with Western political structures gave rise to beliefs that America covertly sought to abuse its former Cold War foe. This tendency became apparent from 1993–94, when former expectations of equal partnership with America evaporated and anti-American statements of outspoken Russian personalities demonstrated the sharp turn from post-Cold War euphoria to cynicism.[5]

In these disputes about *who* lost Russia, theories of 'neo-containment' were rivalled by those of the opposite impulse, suggesting that the US should continue engagement with the processes of Russian democratization. These 'classical' calls today do not neatly coincide with the supposed differences between the US 'realists' and 'idealists' (or liberals). For example, it is possible to draw parallels on the one hand between those American and Russian realists and liberals who treat Russia as a weak state and use this image as an excuse for maintaining the status quo and, on the other, those politicians who champion pro-co-operation (or engagement) policies aimed at Russia's change (McFaul 2005). However, the various analyses of the US's 'failure over Russia' have only limited capacity to explain the feelings of disillusionment, disappointment and animosity among Russians generally. 'A mix of pent-up frustration with hard life in general, envy of those who are enjoying an easy life, and wounded pride ignited by the effect of slanted television coverage' (Trenin 2004a) could hardly be fully understood by ignoring significant internal (and cultural) factors.

Proposals for further US engagements in Russia clashed with warnings to stay away from it:

> [When] one school argued that the policy had failed because the United States had pretended for too long that Russia was still a great power ... others countered that the policy failed because the United States did not treat Russia like the great power that it still was. American aid policy was cited as a strategy that negatively (if not deliberately) exacerbated asymmetries in the bilateral relationship. (Goldgeier and McFaul 2003: 238)

Furthermore, contrary to the common myth, the 'American model' of privatization was never adopted in Russia (*ibid.*: 103). Of course, opinions about Clinton's 'loss of Russia' could be balanced, for example, by claims that during his presidency Russia held its first-ever democratic transfer of power. However, having discussed in some detail the American post-Cold War foreign policy impacts on the development of Russia, Goldgeier and McFaul (2003: 336) concluded: 'To suggest that the "American factor" was primary – either as a positive or negative force – is ludicrous.'

As a consequence, competing interpretations of Russian national interests point to external explanations of Russian anti-Americanism. One can stress how the US ignores Russia, or, on the other side, how American idealism and naïvety leads to 'dangerous' attempts to impose Western models on Russia. While some argue that American investment in Russia could help to undercut the appeal of authoritarian nationalism (together with anti-American rhetoric), others would say that the intrinsic Russian predisposition towards 'outsiders' leads to any American involvement in Russian affairs being interpreted at best with incredulity and suspicion. When proponents of Russia's modernization insist that today 'Russia needs Western know-how and access to economic processes and practices at all levels' (Adomeit and Aslund 2005: 9), tacit proponents of realism claim that 'modern Russia is neither capable of integration nor willing to integrate itself into the structures of the expanded West' (Trenin 2004b). Correspondingly, beliefs in Russian willingness and capacity to become a 'European' power are offset by opposite claims that Russians neither dream of integration any more, nor are willing to meet obligatory Western standards. After all, if Russia and America today are 'strategic partners', should not exaggerated Western concern about Russia's own internal reforms be abandoned for the sake of mutual efforts in sustaining global security?

When Americans tried to improve the standards of living in Europe after World War II, many intellectuals felt embarrassed by being forced to accept American charity (Berhahn 2001). American interference in European internal affairs was often viewed as largely profiting American businesses and opening markets for American investment. The implementation of the Marshall Plan, which was considered (especially by French) to be motivated by American self-interest, frequently provoked feelings of resentment (Pells 1997: 56). As opposed to the incredulity of Western European intellectuals, in early 1990s Russia, the attempts by intellectual and power elites to overcome totalitarian legacies consolidated pro-American attitudes and revealed much of the democratic potential among Russians. The expectations, however, brought unreasonable beliefs about the US's abilities to completely transform its former rival. Thus subsequent disillusionment with US assistance was much more distressing, especially considering that a 'Marshall Plan' for Russia never materialized. Hence anti-Americanism is a logical consequence of restoring the pride in one's country by rejecting any 'foreign' models and standards allegedly imposed on Russians from outside.

Double meanings of power

It is important to consider the complex images of the US prevalent in Russia that interact with concrete historical circumstances – this is a far more productive than asserting that Russian culture was unequivocally anti-American. The popularity of American consumer goods in Russia in the mid-1990s still remained high – in opinion polls, the majority of respondents associated America with top standards of living, or rated the country high in other categories, such as 'individual liberties' (Ball 2003: 202). Even when anti-Americanism in politics reached its heights, paradoxically, on the level of consumption, nothing suggested that the predominance of American popular culture had declined, despite the above-mentioned nationalistic rhetoric (ibid.: 269). Yet different polls simultaneously showed a growing inferiority complex and feelings of being abandoned and humiliated by the US. During this period, the new Russian right (or disillusioned liberal democrats of the early 1990s) came up with their own explanation about America's still fighting the Cold War while Russians thought that it was over. The previous Russian partnership with the US was considered a gross mistake, because it allegedly undermined Russian interests and weakened the Russian state. The new identity suggested by neo-conservatives was 'neither Communist nor cosmopolitan; yet it was anti-Western and anti-American' (Shiraev and Zubok 2000: 76).

One of the most popular narratives of this troubled Russian identity implied that the image of Russia was unfairly 'subjugated' to US interests. Eventually interiorized as an indisputable misfortune, the hypothetical Russian loss of the Cold War not only revealed the weaker status of the post-Soviet country but also provoked the need for moral compensation. Some argue that this frustration over collapsed Russian power that is felt today even by some moderate pro-Western politicians should not automatically be tied to any specific political ideology (Connor 2004: 219). Nevertheless, only newly consolidating ideologies helped to articulate the widely touted national humiliation, or the 'sense of wounded dignity' and 'ex-superpower blues' of Russians who felt more comfortable in opposing the US than in acknowledging for themselves a 'junior American ally' status. In this, wealthy elites who are still 'waiting for an opportunity to check Russia's "subjugation" to the United States' (Trenin 2004a) are even more anti-American than Russia's poor who, it could be argued, have more justification for their anti-Western resentment because of dashed opportunities and ruined hopes. Having thoroughly analysed the complexities of Russian attitudes towards US, one could find a direct link between the feeling of national humiliation and anti-Americanism, where Russia's loss of global influence reveals not material but 'geopolitical' jealousy (Zlobin 2005).

The popular search for internal or external enemies reached previously unimaginable scales after the financial crash of 1998, during events in Kosovo and the second war in Chechnya in 1999. Despite the NATO expansion becoming the major issue for disgruntled Russian political elites during the Kosovo campaign, historians today have shown that the growth of animosity towards America was not, in fact, correlated in a straight line with the growth of the Western military alliance (Shiraev and Zubok 2000: 147). Even the bombing of Serbia in 1999, when anti-American hostility seemingly reached its peak among all layers of society,[6] did not directly relate either to special Russian concerns about their Orthodox brethren, or to any particular historical-cultural affection towards Yugoslavia (*ibid.*: 118; English 2000: 239).

Access to different sources of information in Russia during the Kosovo War notwithstanding, common opinions among the public presented the conflict not as a humanitarian campaign and effort to stop genocide, but rather as Clinton's crafty decision to divert media attention from the Lewinski affair. Interpretations of political events reached the highs of Soviet anti-American propaganda in the amount of misinformation. And despite Russians being able to get alternative media sources, they were 'disaffected by what they heard in those broadcasts from overseas' (Shiraev and Zubok 2000: 121). NATO's campaign in Yugoslavia revealed Russia's international impotence, which was an extremely painful reality for Russian power elites to acknowledge (Goldgeier and McFaul 2003: 249). The latter were particularly chagrined because of Russian inability to change the course of events, and it was widely interpreted that America was expanding her sphere of influence in the Balkans because of Russian weakness.

Already in the early 1990s some Russian foreign policy analysts indicated that Russian disillusionment with the US was in large part caused, ironically, by the former Foreign Minister Andrei Kozyrev's pro-Western stances that were subsequently perceived not as authentic policies but rather as Russian kowtows to American interests (Pushkov 1993). The very fact that, after the disintegration of the Soviet Union, the US pursued multiple policies towards all post-totalitarian nations only added to anti-American attitudes in Russia, because any siding by the

US with other countries (as in the case of supporting Lithuanian processes of in-dependence) was immediately understood as American anti-Russian action (*ibid.*: 87). Perceptions of America thus must be understood in relation to the image of a 'strong Russia', and the latter was opposed to the previous 'weak state' tradition propagated by 'Westernizers'. The strong state tradition eventually became part and parcel of the new neo-conservative nationalism, which dwells on the restoration of the 'pride in Soviet Union, stripped of its former ideology' (Jack 2004: 15).

The distinction between democratic vocabulary on the one hand, and the virtual absence of real commitments to democratic structures among Russian politicians on the other, probably should not be interpreted as an inconsistency. Western political observers have often been disenchanted with the 'liberal authoritarianism' of Vladimir Putin and Russia's abandonment of earlier democratic achievements. At the same time, however, a political strategic partnership with Russia in the name of common interests could be perfectly expressed with modernization rhetoric, as often happens in inter-governmental relationships (Spanger 2005).

Many agree that Vladimir Putin proved popular among the Russian people[7] precisely because he does not push reforms or innovations, but, on the contrary, endorses the 'traditional' centralization of power and reconciliation with the Soviet as well as pre-Soviet past. Moreover, the political figure of former President Putin embodies the expectations of contemporary Russians. Thus, after the failures of Russian 'Westernization' policies, the preference towards relative stability under the strong state, which was introduced after a period of anarchic liberalism, seems a logical outcome of transition. Cultural explanations of Russian authoritarianism seemed also reasonably endorsed during the 2000 presidential elections, when Vladimir Putin explained the condition of Russia's super-centralization as 'part of its genetic code, its tradition, the mentality of its people' (Ball 2003: 282). The occasional popularity of some conservative Western leaders in Russia during the 1990s related not coincidently to the supposed respect of those leaders for the strong Russian state (Jack 2004: 275).

Nevertheless, even if one acknowledges that the image of the powerful state still bears supreme importance for Russian self-esteem and self-identification, there is no need to valorize arguments of cultural exceptionalism. Politically constructed 'normalcy' is a protean creation, and so are negative anti-Western projections. Vladimir Putin's brief pro-American turn after the events of 11 September 2001 and his vocal support of the international coalition against terror (even in defiance of the high-rank Russian military leadership) were considered by some as a new historic choice (Jack 2004: 286). That the peak of mass xenophobia corresponded to the greatest popularity of Vladimir Putin in 2002 should not mislead the observer either. Both anti-Americanism as well as different types of chauvinism are significant rhetorical devices only for those who are either competing for power or have lost it (Gudkov and Dubin 2005). But those who have power today are more interested in maintaining the status quo than in pursuing social changes, radical ideologies or phobias.

The Russian government tends to avoid the risk of any rivalry. Thus under-standably, the Kremlin, haunted by the possibility of 'colour revolutions', today endorses pre-emptive political actions in order to forestall excessive activism and new independent forces from national politics, be they foreign NGOs or domestic radicals. Moderate nationalists (Rodina Party) are grouped together with skin-heads and xenophobic right-wingers, or with leftists and their chauvinistic factions (such as National Bolsheviks) in order to discredit the opposition. This shows that the government is also aware that anti-government forces in Russia – which in the cases of Georgia and Ukraine came under the banner of liberal movements – could spring from completely different sources.

Discouragement of 'Western' involvement in Russia, on the basis of its supposedly providing the pretext for new waves of anti-Westernism, should not become a cover for defensive neo-imperial claims imagined as 'indispensable' components of Russian self-esteem. While the eastward expansion of NATO has sometimes, even in the US, been interpreted as undermining the crucial interests of Russia and thus being detrimental to the vitally important US–Russian relationship (Friedman 1999: 337–8), one should also admit that, in gaining Yeltsin's trust by virtue of skilful diplomacy, the Clinton administration smoothed the path for such eastward expansion. This largely favoured the interests of the Central and Eastern European region. Despite the expansion of the Western military organization being explained by many as a cause of anti-Americanism among chagrined Russian elites, the popular criticism of US imperial interests[8] today should not be directly related to 'justified' feelings of victimization among the wider Russian population. For how could one balance the correlation between the disappointment for being neglected by the West, identifications of America as a threat to Russia and the growing need to legitimize Russia's sphere of influence over her own post-colonial 'Others'? Notably, the latter tendency since 1993 has been exemplified by the new concept of Russia's 'near abroad' and, today, for example, by an intensified war of words against the Baltic States.

The 'conventional wisdoms' of *realpolitik* in Russia largely correspond with the goals of traditional *derzhavniks*, but their anti-American ideology is a relative thing. In contrast to contemporary Western anti-Americanism, which tends to express dissatisfaction in political vocabulary (it is 'anti-Bush', 'anti-war', 'anti-US policies'), post-Cold War Russian perceptions of America are often related to narratives of conservative nationalisms in which recognition of Russia as a 'great power' occupies a firm place. Various images could be used for reconfirmation of this tradition, however all traditions are easy to manipulate by those seeking power. Moderate anti-Americanism as a suitable recipe for the new Russian identity in the late 1990s sold well (Shiraev and Zubok 2000: 103), and it correlated smoothly with moderate forms of nationalism. Correspondingly, it seems that whenever the new Russian 'great power' identity is constructed through reconsideration of the Cold War power status, negative perceptions of America as a subversive anti-Russian power are more likely to appear. Russia's official cultural policies often rely on glamorous events that symbolically endorse Russia's pride and power. The ability of elites to embrace dynamic changes and capture different policy choices, however, should not be ignored (Vogel 2005).

To sum up, realist interpretations of Russian anti-Americanism as being inseparable from the 'great power' tradition could provide the most logical explanation for the ups and downs of this modern ideology. On the other hand, anti-Americanism should not be automatically viewed as an intrinsic Russian feature, unchangeable and fixed for ever together with its explicit images of the enemy. By and large correlated with the troubled post-Soviet Russian identity and the search by Russian elites for status, anti-Americanism – a useful tool quickly picked up by all sorts of radicals – has no 'essence' there. The cultural approach towards the Russian transition shows clear correlation between Russia's 'great power' status and inconsistent evaluations of US intentions. Yet such an approach becomes risky whenever it (together with some 'advanced' modernizing approaches) helps to sanction doctrines of neo-imperial interests painted as 'legitimate' national interests. All this, in the end, shows the enduring importance of rhetorical criticism in the fields of post-Cold War cultural policies and international relations.

Notes

1 One could signal that phrases such as 'the new world order' and, even more often, 'the new world disorder' are used today indiscriminately in hundreds of titles promising accounts of exactly the same international system and its events.

2 'Soft power', the term coined by Joseph S. Nye (2004), refers to the power of public diplomacy pursued by state as well as non-state actors.

3 Typical recent commentary about Russia's ostensibly surpassing the US in the fields of media freedom, civil society achievements and other categories (as was declared by the Russian Foreign Minister Sergey Lavrov) could be seen in Америка! Учись у России, 22 September 2005. Available at: http://www.rususa.com/news/news.asp-nid-12590-catid-3

4 Quoted from L. Steven Myers, 'Putin Defends Reining in Private Groups', *The New York Times*, 25 November 2005. Available at: http://www.nytimes.com/2005/11/25/international/europe/25russia.html?ex=1290574800&en=c78ab98f14b486b2&ei=5088&partner=rssnyt&emc=rss

5 According to Shiraev and Zubok (2000: 145), by 1993 anti-American attitudes were shared by 30–40 per cent of Russians.

6 According to Goldgeier and McFaul (2003: 356), polls conducted in December 1999 showed that '55 percent of respondents believed that the United States represented a threat to Russian security'.

7 In contrast to Gorbachev and Yeltsin, who suffer from low popularity today, Putin reached 70–80 per cent approval throughout his term – a 'proof of a necessary solidifying role for Russia ' (Jack 2004: 330).

8 In this popular genre, some opine that inferring any correspondence of American interests with 'progress' or even with the interests of Russia itself is an 'absolutely lunatic assumption' (Lieven 2004b: 69). Still others go as far as to blame the US's post-Cold War international performance for its constant (albeit 'failed') attempts at intentionally eliminating and isolating Russia (Todd 2003: 146).

Part II
Security and Anti-Americanism

7 Fear and Loathing in Brussels: The Political Consequences of European Anti-Americanism

Adam Quinn and Michael Cox

The trans-Atlantic relationship has long resembled a heavy object spotted in the sky: from snapshots alone it is hard to tell if it is airborne – albeit perhaps in descent – or simply plummeting to earth. Recent years have provided no shortage of troubling visions of Euro-American discord, yet it has proven impossible to reach consensus on whether the picture to which they add up shows standard variation in altitude, the beginning of steady decline, or the early stages of a precipitate, disastrous fall (Cox 2006).

The litany of trans-Atlantic fallings-out since the beginning of the twenty-first century has been narrated enough times to require little in the way of repetition here; there are many full and accurate accounts (e.g. Gordon and Shapiro 2004). Without doubt, the arrival of George W. Bush in power changed the mood music in Europe, with early friction over the Kyoto Protocol and National Missile Defense providing much disgruntlement, which, after a brief interlude of 11 September 2001-induced solidarity, segued into a cacophony of diplomatic rancour throughout the planning and execution of the Iraq War. The process was not identical in the case of each major European nation. In some, most notably France and Germany, the government was an agent in courting public hostility to US policy (Forsberg 2005). In others, such as Britain, Spain and Italy, governments were supportive of the Bush administration's policy but pursued this course in the face of substantial, vocal public opposition, in some cases clearly going against a majority of their electorate's wishes. In all cases, however, the common feature was a turning of the attention of political discourse towards the issue of American global power, and the multiplication of public voices expressing a deep distaste for American policy and for the overarching set of political attitudes of which it was perceived as being reflective.

We should not romanticize the period before President Bush's inauguration as a golden age of trans-Atlantic harmony (Cox 2003). Before the 2000 election, with Bill Clinton still shining his charisma upon the process of US diplomacy, there was already serious concern that the European perception of America was sliding into darker shades, nudged in part by such events as the Senate's rejection of the Comprehensive Test Ban Treaty and foot-dragging over Balkan commitments. In France in particular, one senior Congressional Democrat noted, a trend was well underway towards viewing the United States with an element of internal contradiction, both as an imperialist and as a shirker of burdens in its relations with Europe (Biden 2000). It was also clear that American and European attitudes diverged in their assessment of how best to deal with some of the hard cases of international affairs, offering multiple potential flashpoints for a policy clash (Haass 1999).

Nevertheless, the most cited data on the subject seems unequivocal that the arrival of the Bush administration, and the subsequent deluge of policy controversies – the war on terror, Iraq, etc. – brought about a steep decline in regard for US policies, America's leading role in the world, and indeed the American nation itself (Pew Global Attitudes Project reports 2003a, 2004b, 2005a, 2006). Some occasional mild fluctuation aside, it is a trend from which the US image in European eyes has shown little sign of recovering as yet. Such reports having received persistent, widespread media coverage in Europe, it seems likely that this in itself has done something to make negative views of America settle in as part of the landscape in the collective European consciousness (e.g. *The Economist* 2005a, 2005c).

There has been no shortage of articles enquiring into the prospects for change, repair or recovery in the trans-Atlantic relationship (Kupchan 2002; Cox 2005; Asmus 2003; Kissinger and Summers 2004; Risse 2004), and it is not the intention of this article to retread their ground. Rather, it is our purpose, in line with the theme of this edited volume, to examine the increased tendency in Europe towards a kind of blanket negativity directed at America – 'anti-Americanism' in intellectual shorthand – with a view to identifying some of its more serious political consequences.

Before undertaking such observations, it is prudent to make one clarification. To the extent that this contribution to the debate focuses exclusively on European antipathy to America, this merely reflects the purpose of the book in which it appears. An equal amount could easily be written concentrating on overblown American assaults on the European character, from Robert Kagan's derogatory feminisation of Europe in his seminal writings on the subject (2002, 2003), to Jonah Goldberg's Simpsonian railing against 'cheese-eating surrender-monkeys' (2002). This chapter, however, written by two Europeans, is aimed at scrutinising our own 'side', not with the purpose of aiming darts at the other – deserved though a few well-placed ones might be – but in an effort to explain a phenomenon that has already had serious consequences for world politics, and could have more in the coming years.

What problem, whose fault?

The first question is that of definition. To whom and what are we referring when we talk of an 'anti-American' tendency? We know from painful experience that the spectrum of views in European countries extends to include those who would carry out terrorist attacks aimed at bringing death to Americans and their 'collaborators'. This degree of extremism is relatively rare, however. More significant for our purpose is the far more broadly based, mainstream inclination sometimes labelled 'lite anti-Americanism' (Nairn 2003; Fabbrini 2004). This is manifested in disdain for America and its works, but stops short of profound personal engagement with efforts to 'bring down' US society.

Josef Joffe (2006), writing about global anti-Americanism, has identified several of the phenomenon's features. These include: the discussion of America in terms of crude stereotypes; the casual attribution of malign intent and implausible (sometimes conspiratorial) omnipotence to the US government; and the desire to narrow one's own society's contact with 'corrupting' American influence. Europe does not, in its mainstream culture at least, touch the lows of, say, the Arab world in the generation and consumption of black propaganda mining these ideological seams. But only closed ears could fail to recognise some thematic similarities in political comment falling comfortably within the spectrum of European political views generally considered acceptable. At its most brazen, this can be seen in the widespread popularity of conspiratorial trash concerning 11 September 2001 (Meyssan 2002). More insidious, however, is a more moderately intoned discourse of Americanophobia which makes persistent assertions or assumptions as to the ignorance, insularity, materialism, imperialism, violence, greed, disingenuousness and/or profound malevolence of the American nation and its government an acceptable, indeed casual and predictable, currency at political meetings and dinner tables throughout Europe.

Analysts differ as to whether anti-Americanism in Europe is best conceived as a response to particular policies (Applebaum 2005), or as a sort of emotional reaction with its basis not in reason but in the passions (Ajami 2003; Mead 2003; Ceaser 2003). The difference is significant, of course, because if anti-American sentiment is diagnosed simply as the unavoidable by-product of resentment against American power in all its forms, or even a psychological predisposition against all things American, then this removes from the table any consideration of reorienting US policy in order to lessen the problem. Neither interpretation suggests that anti-Americanism is entirely 'un-caused', of course: America's power and actions can still be identified as the trigger for anti-Americanism, even if it does not take the form of a rational dissent citing particular policy disagreements. But to the extent that the phenomenon manifests itself as an emotional and indirect response to what America is or indeed possesses by way of influence in the world, hope for applying logical persuasion as a cure is diminished.

In one of the better known past works on the subject, Paul Hollander (1992) leaned towards the diagnosis of irrationality, presenting anti-Americanism as a form of *a priori* prejudice akin to sexism or racism: 'a particular mindset, an attitude of distaste, aversion, or intense hostility the roots of which may be found in matters unrelated to the material qualities or attributes of American society or the foreign policies of the US' (Hollander 1992: viii). In a vigorous counter-attack on America's critics in Europe, Hollander attributed flourishing anti-Americanism to jealous resentment of US wealth and cultural presence, the emboldening effect on foreigners of anti-American criticism from within America itself, and the low-cost nature of throwing insults at an America lacking the political will to do anything serious in response. Encouraged by these structural factors, certain standard intellectual postures within Europe and elsewhere – such as nationalism, fear of modernity, and defence of tradition – could spiral into a self-sustaining 'irrational dynamic' which used the association between the ideas of 'America' and 'modernity' to explain away the woes of people's lives by reference to the malign influence of a powerful outsider. Others since have continued to pick up on this idea, noting that the mental link between 'globalization', modernity and America across the world has fuelled anti-Americanism among groups on both sides of the political spectrum: insecure workers as well as those who benefit from established hierarchies. Many of the most fervent rebutters of the anti-American perspective are keen on this point, using it to portray America's critics as retrograde in their social outlook and motivated more by fear than understanding (Revel 2003a; Ajami 2003).

Such an approach as Hollander's, which has had subsequent followers, can be buttressed by reference to the history of European thought. If we seek support-ing evidence of bias and misrepresentation, we find no shortage of it in the long recorded history of European intellectual disdain for America, which has been the subject of some renewed scrutiny in recent years (Ceaser 2003; Roger 2005; Mead 2003; O'Connor 2006). From eighteenth-century Continental scientists who por-trayed the New World as a degenerate land stripping man and beast of their better qualities, to twentieth-century fascists and communists decrying the individualist, consumerist hollowness of the American social soul, a thread of Westward-looking contempt has run through some of the most notable traditions of European thought. This trend has been particularly pronounced, as is well known, in France, though the French outlook has not lacked emulation in other nations (Revel 2003a).

In searching for reasons why long-standing, potentially evergreen sentiments should be in such full bloom at this particular moment, many, with good reason, note that George W. Bush's presidency has added a new dimension to old problems (e.g. Judt 2006; Kroes 2006). Equally wisely, however, most partner this with a conclusion that there are deeper factors at work; that there is something about the changed tone of US politics and policy more generally which portends continuing struggles over the American image in the foreign mind's eye (Higley 2006; O'Neil 2006). Some observe that America may be the victim of its own equation of itself with higher values, inviting attacks that judge it more harshly than would seem justified by comparison with other nations (Rae 2006). Attacks based on ideal, rather than comparative, standards are invited, after all, by America's identification of its goals for world order, often overbearing and intrusive from the perspective of other nations, with 'civilization' (Crockatt 2006).

Without exaggerating the intellectual rigour of anti-American critiques, many accounts, including most of those just mentioned, lend themselves to a somewhat more rationalist portrait of anti-Americanism than Hollander's. That is, they accept that much of what is termed 'anti-Americanism' is, at least in part, reasoned opposition to America's conduct in international affairs as opposed to purely emotional enmity unconnected to US behaviour. And if it is correct that American policy choices do in some sense affect the level of anti-American sentiment, then it follows that changed American behaviour might reduce it. There is likely much truth in the idea that in its varied, not altogether ideologically coherent forms, anti-

American sentiment may be generated by US action insofar as the nationalistic features of American grand strategy invite friction with other societies. While anti-Americanism may not be the product of a syllogistically logical critique of US policy – and is often combined with ambivalent admiration for certain features of American society – it could potentially be minimized by an American approach aimed at avoiding irritation of the sore-points of foreign nationalisms (Singh 2006).

From head or heart: three stripes of anti-Americanism

It seems to us that a dichotomous choice between classifying anti-Americanism as either an irrational prejudice or a rational reaction to US policy is unnecessary. It can be one or the other, and sometimes a vexing blend of both.

Europe, as the world, has a plentiful share of those with a loathing for the US based on nothing more than emotional impulse. Americanophobia –associating America and Americans, with no great effort at coherence, with a set of attributes inviting disgust – has only the most tenuous relationship to rational argument or detailed objection to specific policies. More a sensibility than an intellectual position, this form of anti-Americanism is immune to fact, and thus cannot be rebutted any more than can the predispositions of the racist or the homophobe. This is the irrational, or, more neutrally, 'non-rational' strain of anti-Americanism.

In contrast, it is possible to think oneself into a position of the most thoroughgoing anti-Americanism while remaining quite rational, so long as one is prepared to accept the logical conclusions as the price of consistency. Such thinking encompasses objections to specific policies, such as the invasion of Iraq, but moves from the particular to argue that such policies are the external manifestation of the very driving forces which lie at the root of American society itself. To different critics, different forces may be identified. One of the more frequently cited is a potent, uncritical American nationalism convinced that the US has every right to promote its superior values abroad. The essential intellectual structure of this critique is that one should not realistically expect an American government to change the 'bad' policies, because they stem from a social system fixed in place. In intellectual form this is not really so far from the view of many of America's defenders, who often argue that a change of American government can produce only marginal change in policy because of the cultural and structural imperatives at work within the American socio-political system.

Thus one can argue, logically, both that George W. Bush's foreign policy is an abomination, and also that it is the typical, perhaps inevitable, product of a society which operates on the core cultural and political principles of the US. With the use of this argument, one distinction often used to separate 'reasonable' critics from irrational anti-Americans – that of judging whether the critic is attacking merely policies or lashing out at American society as a cultural whole – collapses, as policy is seen as the symptom of a fundamentally flawed society. Such a position is strikingly hard-line – schools of thought which leap to mind being full-blooded anti-capitalists of the old school or perhaps stern religious intellectuals. Indeed, some of the more influential sources of such anti-Americanism have come from within the US itself: consider the extraordinarily popular work of Noam Chomsky, whose intellectually belligerent theory of international relations over several decades has been to trace the problems of the world to the domestic political structure of the US. Despite its ultimate rationality, however, there can be little doubting that such thinking is 'anti-American' in that it condemns precisely what it itself identifies as the defining features of American society. Nor does its rationality necessarily command special regard – many of the uglier ideas in political history have been advanced on grounds of intellectual consistency. It does little good, however, to throw the labels of 'irrationality' and 'prejudice' at positions which are, in truth, better defined as rational extremism. Thus, we have a category of 'rational-extremist anti-Americanism'.

On the middle ground is the largest and slipperiest category: those who mingle reason and hostility, maintaining superficial liberal fairness in their political thinking while nevertheless contriving to end up on the side of the America-bashers in every case. Such critics, based on an instinctive, emotionally founded tendency to believe that America is in the wrong (the non-rational base of their thought), then use the facts and arguments of the field as a pick 'n' mix counter in order to find a combination which supports their desired conclusion: that America is at fault. Reasoned arguments are thus grafted, patchwork, onto a base of pre-existing ill will. As American policy changes, such critics must then change the facts and arguments to which they look in order to explain why America, despite the new circumstances, is still in the wrong. The process continues indefinitely, without prospect of resolution, for the position of the critic is determined not by the failure of America to do that of which he or she approves, but rather a default by the critic into opposition to whatever America happens to be doing at the moment. This approach to political thought mingles a stated commitment to the official goals of the US, phrased in the vaguest terms possible – 'democracy', 'freedom', 'international co-operation' – combined with an unshakeable opposition to concrete American actions.

Though far more moderate than the harder-line anti-Americanism outlined above, this position is on inspection the less intellectually sustainable. The rational anti-American can fall back on a coherent blueprint of die-hard ideology to explain his or her own position. The more butterfly-like critic, based only on the shifting sands of opportunistic critique, has no such option. Though possessed of rational subcomponents – such as a list of arguments why the Iraq War is a poor idea – the back-to-front, conclusions-to-facts nature of many critics' reasoning undermines their claim to rationality and ensures future inconsistencies. Unlike 'non-rational' anti-Americanism (the habit of the unthinking Americanophobe) and 'rational' anti-Americanism (the preserve of the ideological radical) this 'semi-rational/ inconsistent anti-Americanism', combining superficially rational arguments with slippery, shifting commitments on the part of its author, is the form of anti-Americanism most frequently encountered in the European mainstream.

It may, with justice, be noted that it is difficult to see a clear line between what has just been described – apparently non-ideological, issue-specific but nevertheless 'anti-American' criticism of US policy – and the ideal of a balanced, objective approach to evaluating US policy for which opponents of anti-Americanism call. To make the attempt, the best approach is perhaps to take the critic's opus as a whole, and enquire as to the coherence and consistency of the demands it makes of the US. It is surely reasonable to insist that a critic offer clarity as to his or her own position, to which they may then be held when assessing other US policy, past and future. This can then allow for the sort of assessment of their critical track-record which may acquit them of anti-Americanism, or confirm the charge. By avoiding such clear commitments on the part of the critic, semi-rational anti-Americanism exercises the hypocritical freedom to indict the US for its actions without the burden of an intellectual anchor. Actions can be condemned which would be supported if carried out by others, and which the US might well be condemned for failing to carry out if its chosen policy were the opposite. It also leaves the field clear for the critic to continue criticism in the future, on an entirely new tack, if the US should reverse its policy.

These categories are archetypes; one may struggle to file individuals neatly into a single box. Those who subscribe at root to a hard-line rational-extremist anti-Americanism may at times make use of conspiracy theory or emotional rhetoric, clearly undermining their claim to what intellectual legitimacy their internal ideological coherence affords them. Meanwhile those who are at best semi-rational and opportunistic in their attacks on America may appear entirely reasonable within the parameters of the argument they have settled upon at a given time. Only by probing beyond their comfort zone to establish their own convictions and preferred policy alternatives can they be forced to choose between (a) embracing a more all-encompassing, extreme critical perspective, (b) confessing the limits of their rationality and consistency in attacking America, or (c), by far the option most to be hoped for, opting to reconsider their overarching hostility to the US in favour of a more moderate and thought-through neutrality of perspective.

Let us be clear: there is a genuine difference between criticizing American policy and being 'anti-American', but it does not lie straightforwardly in the distinction between reason and prejudice. Rather, it lies in the distinction between four different kinds of criticism. The first is criticizing policies of the US, while admitting the virtue of some of its principles, and holding a consistent position of one's own, thus obliging support for America if and when it acts in line with one's views. This, in the European context, is rational, fair critique of America. The second is to perceive evils so deeply embedded in US society that it simply can do no right. This is rational anti-Americanism. Third, one may possess an underlying emotional prejudice against America which leads one to reason backwards – from conclusions to facts and arguments – with the end goal of arriving at condemnation of the US, consistency and coherence be damned. This is semi-rational/inconsistent anti-Americanism. Finally, one may simply utter abuse aimed at America, without pretence to reason or argument. This is non-rational anti-Americanism.

More discussion of semi-rational/inconsistent anti-Americanism on the part of Europeans follows in the closing section of this chapter. First, however, we might ask why so many Europeans seem inclined to begin their thinking with a disposition hostile to the US, in effect deciding in advance that they will find reasons to condemn.

Full-spectrum uneasiness

During the half-century which followed the end of World War II, what differences there may have been between the US and its European partners needed, ultimately, always to be managed in light of the undeniable dependency of Western Europe on American power to defend it against a clear and present danger (Grosser 1980; Lundestad 1986, 2003). This was the foundation on which NATO stood for its first decades, and the grounds for early American promotion of European integration. With the evaporation of the Soviet threat justifying the American role in Europe, an increase in trans-Atlantic tensions was arguably quite predictable.

Such an argument has evident merit, especially if supplemented with two observations. First, that we should acknowledge the long history of anti-American thought noted in a previous section, meaning that a vibrant stock of Americanophobic ideology already existed, awaiting re-commission. If we limit our historical appreciation of the prior relationship of Europe and America to cheering crowds greeting Woodrow Wilson in Paris and gratitude to Harry Truman for staking the isolationist vampire, we ignore a longer tradition of scepticism towards America and its leaders. Second, perhaps a little less obviously, the Cold War itself played some role in nurturing certain kinds of tension between Europeans and the US. Today we see the release of some of those pent-up frustrations.

During the Cold War, it is true that there was a broad acceptance throughout Western European politics that the US played a necessary role in the Continent's security. However, this acceptance did not stretch to joyous embrace on the part of either the radical left or some sections of the conservative right in Europe. The European left, of course, held deep reservations from the beginning concerning America's global role. Possessed of its own socialistic views on how society should be ordered, the left regarded the US, not inaccurately, as the defender of a more individualistic capitalism, with which they were less than comfortable. In the course of its promotion of that system through proxy battles with the Soviets around the Third World, America also became associated in the mind of the left with a brand of counter-revolutionary zeal, sometimes cynical in the execution, quite antithetical to the sympathies of European leftists who identified with various anti-imperialist movements around the world. While most of the European left was healthily sceptical as to the motives and methods of the totalitarian Soviet Union, it nevertheless also questioned whether the Cold War was entirely a defensive enterprise on America's part, and whether the conflict might not to a significant extent have its causes in the hard-line approach taken by American presidents towards the USSR and other communist movements since Truman.

As might be expected, there was a higher degree of pro-American sentiment and Atlanticist perspective evident on the political right. Nevertheless, the right's political catechism contained principles rather different from those of America's guiding liberalism, and thus its genuflection to America and its causes was far from uncomplicated (Fabbrini 2002). In general, the right was tougher-minded than the left when it came to thinking about communism and the USSR; indeed, it often defined itself in terms of the Soviet 'Other' in such a way as to place itself firmly within the Atlanticist camp. Nevertheless, the nationalistic pride underlying most rightist thinking in Europe sat uncomfortably with an arrangement that entrenched European states' status as mere obedient junior partners under the American defensive umbrella. Necessary though American protection may have been, it brought with it a national emasculation which chafed the psyche of much of the European right throughout the Cold War. It also brought a sense of anxiety that the fates of European nations were now beyond their own control: decisions made in Washington, DC, would decide the future of the Continent; miscalculation or cynicism on America's part could spell catastrophe for the nations obliged to depend upon it. Loss of national standing and autonomy was an unavoidable feature of the European experience of the Cold War, but it was still railed against at times, most spectacularly by Charles de Gaulle, who left a legacy of turbulent, resentful and grudging acceptance of the trans-Atlantic relationship which continues to serve as the ideological touchstone of the French right.

Both the left and right in Europe thus had qualms concerning America, even in the years of greatest collaboration. International circumstances, however, made sure that such worries had to remain in check in the interests of fundamental security. Absent the Soviet threat, we find patterns of thought among European political leaders which are in their fundamentals not dissimilar to those of the Cold War period, but which operate in a context bereft of the same ultimate guarantee of restraint at the governmental level.

One might ask whether today's threats – terrorism, extremism, weapons pro-liferation – might not serve as the same sort of external threat that the Soviets once did, promoting co-operation on the basis of passably common values and interests. It seems, however, that Europeans have too many doubts about present American prescriptions for addressing those threats, and do not feel a sufficiently sharp existential threat to cause them to suppress these for the sake of appearances. Some obvious differences notwithstanding, Europeans and Americans are today as close in terms of values and interests as two separate continents can have any reasonable expectation of finding themselves. Yet it seems that without a press-ing reason for Europeans to doubt their basic security and feel obliged to accept American prescriptions for its preservation, this cannot provide the basis for the sort of self-denying co-ordination of policy to which the Cold War made us accustomed. The reasons why anti-American talk has long been tempting in Europe still apply with full force: for the left, disagreements over economic models, social justice and promotion of capitalism abroad; for the right, worries over national pride and sovereignty. Meanwhile, the reasons it was muted during the Cold War apply with less force.

Visions of things to come

With this sketch of the phenomenon's origins complete, we turn now to the political consequences of a resurgence of anti-American attitudes in Europe. The first that occurs is the likely effect on the tone not just of public discourse, but of political leaders also. European politicians are obliged to operate in an environment where anti-American positions have come to be regarded as statements of commonsense wisdom, while statements of support for the US government are subject to prolonged hostile analysis. There are thus more straightforward political rewards to be reaped from pronouncements needling American positions than from effort to promote collaboration. This means that, without some realignment of public attitudes, policy in European states will in all probability be tilted over time towards a position of reflexive suspicion towards the US, predisposed to be critical of its policies whatever they may be.

There may of course be some leaders, such as Tony Blair and his fleeting 'new Europe' coalition of supporters for the Iraq War, or the ostensibly pro-American new French President Nicolas Sarkozy, who are capable of resisting such a trend in the popular sentiment of their nations and are disposed to do so. It would seem foolhardy, however, to predict that a general movement of public feeling in democracies will not tend to dictate a drift in the thinking of elected representatives towards compatible positions. Hence, one political consequence of rising public anti-Americanism will be increased difficulty for European leaders in sustaining a pro-American stance, or supporting policies identified in the public mind with the US, even if the leaders themselves might by their own instincts be disposed to favour such policies. In short, the political price of visible pro-Americanism appears to have risen substantially, with predictable effects for the number of political actors willing to buy the product.

Second, if domestic political conditions make it more difficult for pro-American politicians, or at least pro-American policy positions, to succeed in Europe, then there will also be an effect on the alignment of the broader international community. The world has been used to seeing the US and leading European nations collaborate closely on the serious issues of international affairs, often to the extent of viewing them as a cohesive Western bloc. While it seems unlikely that the new wave of anti-American sentiment in Europe could produce such an extreme effect as to drive Europe into the arms of any other partner in opposition to America, it does seem plausible that more energy will have to be devoted by the US to shoring up support from Europe, which in the past it has become accustomed to take for granted.

Third, a related consequence of a drift towards resistance to following the 'American course' may be a certain forgetfulness regarding the degree to which European and US interests and values still coincide. Much has been written concerning the differences between Europe and the US: America is a less statist, more individualistic and more religious society than European nations can claim for themselves (Micklethwait and Woolridge 2004). Nevertheless, there are basic principles to which the two adhere with a steadiness which cannot be found so readily in other places. Cold War or no, such values, and the interest in trade and access to resources to which they are coupled, still have enemies in the world. For all their disagreements over the war on terror and the invasion of Iraq, Americans and Europeans have far more uniting them with one another than with the proclaimers of Islamist jihad, vicious pseudo-nationalist autocrats such as the late Saddam Hussein or Stalinist relics like North Korea's Kim Jong-Il. Even more acceptable prospective partners such as China or Russia seem, on due analysis, to be many moons away from having the basis of commonality with either side required to supplant the trans-Atlantic bond.

Their periodic gestures of spectacular lethal nihilism notwithstanding, it seems unlikely that the enemies of the Western social model have the ability to destroy it, though they can certainly visit harm upon its citizens. Still, the throwing of rhetorical stones and the inculcation of a self-conscious 'values gap' between the two continents which provide the supporting pillars of the West cannot but weaken the West. As suggested above, it seems plausible that a more pressingly existential sense of threat to Europe would more likely reinvigorate than destroy the Euro-American partnership. For now, however, in as much as European and American solidarity may be said to aid the defence of their common interests and values, European anti-Americanism (and its reciprocal counterpart in American sentiment) threaten to take eyes off the ball when it comes to pursuing what should be the highest priority, for both sides: the defence of their shared way of life.

Fourth, there is a very real risk that the movement of mainstream political discourse towards anti-Americanism may give comfort to anti-democratic forces in European societies. Within those societies, there will always be a certain amount of extremism, characterized by a powerful hatred of America and subscription to outlandish conspiracy theories concerning its deeds and their context. We are all by now at least partly familiar, through the analysis of terrorist attacks in the UK, successful and foiled, with the processes by which citizens can be led to draw radical religious and political conclusions as a result of exposure to propaganda blaming the US for a global 'crusade' against Islam. It would be unfair if those who levelled more moderate criticisms of the US were to be held responsible for the words and actions of extremists, and these authors certainly would not seek to do so. However, in the same way that the Iraq War can be observed to have provoked an upsurge in terrorist intent without suggesting that the former justifies the latter, so it may be argued to be fact that the culture of intellectual hostility towards US foreign policy which has taken root among the general population of Europe has made fighting the war on terrorism more difficult.

Finally, a sad consequence of anti-Americanism's rise may be the entrenchment of an unedifying mental laziness, likely to enervate the intellectual content of the European debate about international affairs, even as high passions continue to flow. It would no doubt be to romanticize the process of foreign policy-making in democracies to suggest that what emerges is usually the product of dialectics of sweet reason on the part of the general public. Nevertheless, it is to be hoped that, at least on matters of the greatest importance, the public does engage to some degree, and the greater the sophistication and rationality of its analysis the better for the political process. If, however, back-to-front reasoning which assumes the worst concerning agendas associated with America continues to be a feature of European debates; if crass generalizations concerning American culture and politics retain their grip over the mass mindset; if the government of the US continues to be ascribed a malevolence and omnipotence detached from balanced reading of the facts; then the result can only be to infantilize and stunt the public discussion of international affairs in Europe.

Conclusion

The lessons for the well-intentioned observer from the above analysis are not simple. A simplistic response would conclude that if anti-Americanism is (a) an evil, and (b) manifested in criticism of US government policy, then responsible Europeans should refrain from such criticism and discourage it in others. This would be neither wise nor necessary. For many of the reasons that a visceral anti-Americanism is on the whole bad, so an intemperate pro-Americanism would be a vice not a virtue. When such momentous decisions as the declaration of the war on terror or the invasion of Iraq are made, it is the perfect right and absolute duty of Europeans to assess for themselves whether they amount to a programme of international action meriting their support.

One question always hangs over any exhortation of Europeans to turn away from anti-Americanism and towards a fair and rational approach to criticism of American foreign policy: that is, how to tell the difference between the two. Where does biased, unfair criticism stop, and reasonable, commendable criticism begin? It is tempting to conclude that this is a purely political question. However, we might aspire to do better than that. We may do so by returning to the categories of anti-Americanism outlined earlier.

It goes without saying: non-rational anti-Americanism – which amounts to mere slurs and epithets rather than actual arguments – should be shunned. Still, it is simply too easy at the moment for Europeans to disavow anti-Americanism cursorily while churning out a hotchpotch of inconsistent or half-baked criticisms of everything that America actually does. If nothing else, those who criticise the US should be challenged to explain their own position with precision: that is, the values to which they subscribe, the goals they would wish to see pursued in international society, and, beyond the level of generalities, the policies which they would see the US and Europe pursue to advance them.

In a handful of cases such compulsory thinking-through might end up nudging half-baked critics into a full-fledged rational-extremist anti-Americanism. This is hardly to be welcomed, but would at least have the advantage of advancing clarity and intellectual honesty. More often, however, such obligatory thinking-through might force a great many casual anti-Americans to accept that there is considerably more overlap than they presently avow between their own values and those of the US. If such an acceptance were possible, the mainstream of European discourse might be moved away from a fruitless attribution of malevolence, ignorance and cultural parochialism to the US. Few Europeans could retain such positions in such an unsophisticated form if made to think about them harder than they are presently obliged to do. Ideally, it would move towards a more productive discussion of what, in detail, Europeans think they ought to be doing, in co-operation with the US, to advance their largely shared macro-level ambitions for world reform.

Such mature analysis of American policies issue-by-issue, on their merits, could do European societies a power of good in several ways. It would invigorate the political and intellectual culture of their publics by obliging engagement with the complex reality that there is no simple good or bad in US policy in most areas; that in many cases there are no obviously right solutions waiting to be implemented if only the stubborn America would allow it. It would boost their governments' ability to pursue the national interest rationally, by allowing open co-operation with the US on matters of common interest without the fear of political taint through public association. In addition, the spread of moderate, on-the-merits analysis of US policies as a widespread practice within European societies would isolate and alienate the extreme fringe which looks to comprehensive across-the-board anti-Americanism as its guiding narrative of international life.

Many moderate critics of specific policies of the US in Europe may read what has been said here as an effort to group them with a pejoratively labelled anti-American mass. This is not at all our intention; quite the contrary. It is the very integrity of the independent-minded, moderate and intellectually consistent European that we seek to defend. Those who possesses liberal democratic and broadly Atlanticist instincts but who reserve the right to disagree publicly with American policies when they see fit, should consider the fight against anti-Americanism, properly conceived, their own. For in a social environment where casual anti-Americanism has become the norm in the national conversation, it is all too easy for moderates to have their cautious criticisms seized upon as the basis for a far less respectable enterprise of blanket condemnation of America and its works.

The US is not all-powerful, and thus cannot be responsible for all the world's problems (though some of its unwise policy choices clearly make it partly responsible for some of them). Nevertheless, its immense wealth and power clearly afford it some opportunity to pursue what most Europeans would consider positive goals in the world, including economic openness, political liberalisation and the reduction of terrorist organisations. In the messy real world, the pursuit of such goals will involve myriad problems, setbacks and failures; winners and aggrieved losers. Above all, it is certain to involve many mistakes, some very serious, most made in good faith. Only by approaching the matter with this in mind, prepared to meet American policies with measured critique and not blame-dumping or name-calling, can we aspire to arrive at worthwhile conclusions. It might be noted that Americans would do well to subscribe to similar principles in arriving at their own judgements.

As stated earlier, the threats to liberal democratic nations today seem some way off being strong enough to truly endanger their continued prosperous existence. Yet in a world of advancing technology, shifting power balances and newly emergent threats, it would be enlightened for Europeans and Americans to secure the foundations of their partnership. To paraphrase Benjamin Franklin – who did more than his share to promote sympathetic understanding of his nation in the courts of the Old World – Europe and the United States would do well to hang together, for otherwise they may hang separately.

8 Anti-Americanism and International Security: Indications in International Public Opinion

Davis B. Bobrow

The extent and nature of anti-Americanism in international public opinion provides one helpful set of clues to the likely international security stances of governments and movements. When faced with choices about how to respond to US government policy preferences, domestic public opinion provides its political elites with incentives and disincentives to co-operate with, stand aside from through evasion and delay, try to modify, or even resist what Washington seems to want. The opinions of domestic publics also can be used to bargain for side-payments as the price for co-operation and to elicit compliance waivers from Washington. Further, if US officials do not take into account negative or sceptical foreign public opinion about US security policies, they may overestimate the likelihood of foreign support and underestimate the chances that foreign governments will stand aside, make modification attempts or resist.

Accordingly, this chapter examines what polling in the first years of the twenty-first century reveals about the degree of anti-Americanism internationally and its contents. One central matter is the extent to which negative views are specific to particular US policies and a particular American administration (that of George W. Bush) or of a more encompassing nature. The former argues against the rise of the sort of anti-Americanism which would have broad, continuing international security implications; the latter argues for it. Of course, international public opinion need not take either a clearly pro-American or anti-American position. Publics may be less pro-American or anti-American than they are uncertain, divided or ambivalent about the US and its world role.

Consideration of the international security implications of international public opinion needs to go beyond ascertaining distributions of views about specific US policy lines or indeed about the US more generally. Relationships between views of the US and the central security concerns of foreign publics also merit examination. Negative views may feature beliefs that the US acts unconstructively or even counter-productively on agreed-upon threats to security. That is, foreign publics may think that the US has correctly identified threat or opportunity priorities, but is mistaken in kind or degree about the means to pursue them. Alternatively, negative views may feature beliefs that the US has the wrong prioritization of problems and does too much about what is relatively unimportant and too little about what is of critical security importance. Each alternative can both stem from and foster anti-Americanism, but the latter has especially negative implications for security co-operation with America.

As preview, public opinion outside the US has in general been evolving in a direction which makes quick, blanket co-operation less likely. It increasingly suggests a preference for sceptical scrutiny of American proposals and serious consideration of options to delay, divert and modify US government preferences. The burden of proof for compliant co-operation increasingly gets placed on its advocates elsewhere and on the US administration. That, however, does not amount in general to predominant public demands for direct confrontation with the US and withdrawal from co-operative action with it on security matters. In short, there is not so much a desire for less international engagement and activism by the US as for a reorientation of the policy emphases and institutional modalities used by America.

Four categories of international public opinion will be examined.[1] Two deal with broad views of the US, first, in terms of general evaluations of America, the American way or model, and of future US international importance, and, second, general evaluations of American foreign and security policies. Those enable some tentative inferences about anti-Americanism and its broad security implications. The last two focus on views of the US and of security alternatives for two prominent current issues – terrorism, and the invasion, occupation and reconstruction of Iraq in the context of concerns with weapons of mass destruction (WMD). A concluding section integrates these results to arrive at an overall assessment of anti-Americanism in international public opinion and its security implications.

Interpretive approach

Before turning to poll results and their implications, it seems important to clarify the perspective taken on the relevance of international public opinion to the security policy of non-US actors, and on warranted treatment of poll responses as evidence about anti-Americanism and as a source for inferences about security implications. An extreme view of how public opinion affects courses of action pursued by foreign governments and movements has it dictating their policy choices. Political elites act as if they are always expecting a referendum on what they have done and are doing *vis-à-vis* the US and about security. They resemble weathervanes, altering their positions to fit with what they think to be majority views among a public equivalent to a selectorate.

In contrast, the perspective taken here is that international public opinion provides non-US elites with: (1) indicators of likely domestic political risks and rewards from one or another stance toward the US and security issues; (2) clues about how other non-US elites are likely to behave about those matters; (3) instruments useful for bargaining with Washington to extract side-payments for acquiescence; and (4) credible excuses to use with Washington to gain acceptance, even if grudging, of 'more independent' security behaviours. The last use poses at least implicitly to Washington the eventuality of a 'pyrrhic victory' in which a compliant foreign leader will be replaced by a less co-operative one. The bargaining and excuse uses may alter Washington's assessments of the feasibility of security policies which require a substantial, sustained volume of foreign contributions, and of the costs the US will likely have to bear on security or other matters (e.g. foreign economic policies) to get such contributions. The possible uses are realistic if we accept Putnam's (1988) two-level game formulation in which the prospects for international joint action depend on mutually compatible domestic-level and international-level bargains.

How easily such bargains can be struck by foreign and US security policy elites obviously varies widely, but one or more of several sets of circumstances helps. In the first, issues of relationships with the US and of international security have low salience for the pertinent national publics, receive little media attention, and involve little change from past policy actions rather than a 'bold departure'. These characteristics may be inherent in the security issue involved or result from secrecy about it through deliberate steps on the part of a foreign government and that of the US. In the second, some or all of the opposite features are present but in a context of widespread domestic public convictions that the US is a wise, trustworthy, fair, effective, generous and irreplaceable provider of security club or public goods. The absence of either set of characteristics has substantially negative implications for agreement and security co-operation with America. The final set of circumstances involves the political capital of foreign officeholders (individual and political group) and pending needs to draw on it. Incumbent foreign elites with a firm and confident grip on power at home are relatively willing to step outside the zone of 'permissiveness' that the opinions of their public about the US and security suggest. Markers of such a situation include the absence of a competitive opposition (especially one explicitly opposed to US policies), substantial time before a 'mandate renewal' occasion (e.g. a national election), and a high degree of public approval of policy performance on matters other than the US-related issue(s) under consideration. Often some of these conducive circumstances are missing in key foreign polities for the security issues on which the US administration of George W. Bush has most clearly asserted policy preferences. When all three sets are not conducive, the likelihood of security co-operation is especially low.

The evidence to be discussed comes from a secondary analysis of responses to polls conducted in recent years, with occasional reference to responses to similar questions earlier in the post-Cold War years.[2] Because of data access limitations, national publics are the unit of analysis, and all observations are of those aggregates. The ecological fallacy is avoided formally by refraining from inferences to sub-national opinions or combinations of opinions (Langbein and Lichtman 1978). More data are available for advanced industrialized countries than for those of the global South. Data on Southern publics more often than on Northern ones is drawn from only urban or metropolitan area samples rather than from national samples. While important, these limitations on warranted inferences are not severe enough to deny relevance to our central concerns. Northern countries do, after all, predominate in US security alliances, in many regional and global multilateral organizations, and are more likely to have substantial assets which can be contributed to or withheld from US security initiatives. While Southern countries often have large fractions of their populations in rural areas, their urban publics frequently have special political importance.

Space limitations preclude presenting the details of our treatment of poll responses and of the responses themselves.[3] The general rules used to arrive at the summaries in the following pages place more confidence in: (1) responses elicited from many national publics to similar questions with similar alternative answers queried at the same time, and repeated at multiple times; (2) bundles of poll responses to substantively related packages of questions asked of the same public at about the same time and, with regard to opinion stability and change, of the same public at several points in time.[4]

Finally, distributions of responses are considered in terms of crude scores rather than actual percentages for two kinds of reasons. The first has to do with the often recognized problems of margins of error, sensitivity to variations in question and response wording, interview situation, and question order within surveys. All those problems are compounded when drawing on many different surveys asked of many different publics in many different languages. Small percentage differences, even if beyond a poll's margin of error, are thus a shaky basis for inferences.

The second set of reasons has to do with the aim of discerning the political significance of public opinion about the US and security matters. The point is to recognize patterns likely to have different political implications for policy elites in terms of public reactions to current or prospective security co-operation with the US. Accordingly, prior to arriving at the results reported in this chapter, percentage responses were placed on a positive to negative continuum with regard to views of the US or security problem priority. The results reported and used as a basis for inferences are expressed in terms of crude categories on a co-operation with the US continuum: massively supportive/positive; predominantly supportive/positive; supportive/positive; split; rejecting/negative, predominantly rejecting/negative; and massively rejecting/negative.[5] As data availability permits, the scores used are the net calculated by subtracting negative from positive percentages. The larger the number, the more preponderant an opinion. The underlying assumption is that politicians gauge a public's zone of permissiveness on that net result rather than on just positive or negative percentages. Finally, when opinions can be placed in the context of related responses, the rank of the response is used to infer relative emphasis by a particular national public. The higher the rank, the more widely held the opinion in relation to other possibilities probed.

Public opinion patterns

General appraisals of the US, 'the American way' and American importance

Very broad appraisals include evaluations of: America in general; US ways of conducting politics, business, science and technology; and 'soft power' matters of mass culture. This section also includes expectations about the future international prominence of the US, and thus the importance of non-antagonistic relations with it. Anti-Americanism would seem of no more than modest importance if evaluations are positive and judgements of the importance of good relations high; of substantial importance, if evaluations are negative and judgements of importance low. The security implications for following America or standing apart from it are obvious and contrasting. A more complex, indeed conflicted, situation combines negative evaluations and recognition of the continuing importance of the US and getting along with it. Security co-operation seems the only practical course, but only to the minimum extent pragmatically needed to avoid punishment from or disengagement by the US.

In the last decade of the twentieth century most national publics polled had large or modest majorities who responded favourably about their general view of the United States. Positive judgements became less widespread in polls after 2001. Averaging the results of those more recent polls shows that only minorities held such a favourable view in several major Western European countries (France, Germany, Spain), major Latin American states (Argentina, Brazil, Mexico), most states with predominantly Muslim populations (Egypt, Jordan, Lebanon, Morocco, Pakistan, Turkey, Indonesia) and long-time ally South Korea. This shift can be interpreted as evidence for a rising tide of anti-Americanism. Doing so slights continued although often smaller balances on the side of favourability among other Western Europeans (the UK, Italy, the Netherlands), Canada, smaller Latin American states, Israel, Japan and most polled publics in the countries of Central and Eastern Europe that have joined the European Union (EU), and sub-Sahara Africa. In sum, the US seems to retain the political capital of a favourable image among publics in many countries, but less so than in the past, and has moved to a negative favourability balance in a number of countries of regional, and possibly global, importance.

Yet publics in most of the middle power countries at the same time overwhelmingly thought it important to have good relations with the US, that the US was not a declining superpower, and that the US would remain the world's largest economic power (Canada, Mexico, France, the UK, Spain, Russia, Australia, Japan, South Korea).[6] These opinions for the most part argue against support for translating anti-American sentiments into anti-American policy actions.

Even favourable views, however, need not go so far as to welcome emulating major American practices (of politics, business, science and technology, management, ideas and customs) and mass culture. In 2002–04, publics around the world were almost always very positively disposed towards US ways of science and technology, management and mass culture products (music, movies, TV). Negativism averaged across US ways of politics, business, and ideas and customs was, however, far more prevalent than a positive view in major country publics (the UK, France, Germany, Spain, Canada, Brazil, Mexico, Russia, Australia). Exceptions were Italy and Japan. Regionally, positive views were more common in East Europe and sub-Sahara Africa. Middle Eastern publics (with the exceptions of Israel and Kuwait) were massively negative. These crude patterns suggest that many but not all major country publics are selectively 'anti-American' in the sense of negative judgements about US policies seen as altering their domestic societies or, perhaps, those of others. The publics of a set of smaller countries are 'pro-American' about such changes.

General evaluations of America's foreign and security policies

A second set of opinions deals with the extent to which America's world-shaping policies are seen positively or negatively. It includes general views on: whether the US can be relied on to pursue foreign and security policies which take into account the interests of other countries, and whose consequences are positive for them; appraisals of American foreign/security policy in general, and of the US role in several broad aspects of international affairs; and whether problems with US international behaviour follow from specific policies and the second George W. Bush administration or are inherent in the nature of America.

Those bundles of opinions suggest the extent to which generally anti-American foreign and security policy beliefs seem based on conflict of interest grounds, or vary according to issue areas featured in one or another contemporary conception of international security.[7] Further, international public opinion may view the US as simply having a temporarily bad period, or being misguided on some but not all issues. That argues against a verdict of general and lasting anti-Americanism. Such labelling seems far more warranted if negative judgements extend to most at least arguably security policy matters and rest on well-rooted American characteristics. Positive dispositions on the matters in the second set of opinions suggest that publics place a special burden on those who advocate withholding security co-operation from the US; a negative disposition, on those who advocate co-operating. More subtly, the more positive the evaluation in general, the more likely support for and hope about the effectiveness of security policy alternatives for the specific issues viewed negatively that emphasize modifying current US policies through patient persuasion and less than confrontational measures ('a loyal opposition').

We begin with overall appraisals of America's international policies: effects on the respondents' country and similar countries; the extent to which US policy-making takes their interests into account; and the extent to which the US is thought to be a positive influence in the world and on the respondent's country. Few national publics had positive evaluations, and most reported negative ones. The positives were for the most part limited to some countries of Eastern and Southeastern Europe, a number of sub-Saharan African states, several Latin American publics, and countries in some sense protectorates of the US (Israel, Kuwait, Uzbekistan, the Philippines, Taiwan). The publics of major powers tended to see the US as a source of harms, inattentive to how its policies affected others, and, intentionally or not, acting in ways with negative consequences for others. Any coalition of the willing based on public support, the data suggest, will consist for the most part of smaller states and those whose leaders do not feel bound by their public's views of the benefits to their country from co-operating with the US.

The picture that the US as an international actor has what amounts to negative political capital with more, and more important, foreign national publics than those with which it has a positive balance tends to be reinforced by opinions about

American contributions to world peace, environmental quality, and several aspects of the international political economy. Negative views prevailed in most polled publics for US efforts affecting world peace, including an excessive propensity to use force. On environmental quality contributions, Western European members of the EU-15 publics were very strongly negative, while those of the Eastern European countries that joined the EU tended for the most part to be positive. With respect to the world economy, opinions were available on: contributions to growth and to poverty alleviation; globalization in terms of the degree of US influence and the extent to which it was trusted; and whether or not the US posed an economic threat in terms of competition or protectionism. In comparison with the previously discussed opinion bundles in this section and the other world economy contribution probes, the negativism of Western European EU member state publics was less on growth, with many having a positive view, and Eastern Europe country publics having especially positive views. As for poverty alleviation, strongly negative views were almost universally held in all global regions regardless of national levels of economic wealth. A substantial number of positive evaluations appeared only for the accession county publics. Averages of the economic contribution probes were negative with the exception of some Eastern European countries, Kenya and Nigeria.

Foreign leaders will find more public acceptance for co-operating with US policies that apparently hook their countries to the US as a growth locomotive. Negativism about co-operation will be especially strong when it involves US proposed use of force, approaches to global poverty, and globalization strategies. Geographically, foreign leaders in a number of the Eastern European EU member countries, several African states, and scattered US 'protectorates' do have publics whose opinions across most policy areas have been more pro-American than anti-American. Those of most major and middle powers, regional powers and large emerging economies do not, and their leaders may well need to spend their domestic political capital or secure compensatory side-payments in order to pursue sustained co-operation with Washington.

The extent to which Washington begins with the benefit of the doubt from foreign publics with regard to its foreign policies can be crudely gauged by averaging the opinions in this section discussed previously. Doing that finds no national publics massively pro-America in international policy terms. Few are predominantly supportive (Romania, Israel, Kuwait, Thailand) or even supportive (Albania, Croatia, Georgia, Kosovo, Malta, Taiwan, Nigeria). By this composite measure, many of those publics found in the first set of opinions to have prevailingly positive views turn out to be seriously split, including in Western Europe Italy and Ireland, many of the Eastern European countries (including Poland, Hungary, the Czech Republic, the Baltics), smaller Latin American states, many in Africa, and in Asia, India and the Philippines. Among rejectionist publics are those of a number of EU-15 countries, including the UK, and those of Brazil, Mexico, Russia, Australia, China, Japan, South Korea. Predominantly rejectionist publics include major Europeans (France, Germany, Spain), and those of Argentina, Canada, Egypt and Turkey. That is, not only are far more national publics negatively than positively disposed, but those negative publics are from many of the countries most able to provide at the global or regional level major political-military or economic contributions – or resistance – to Washington's international security preferences, including some which are core US security alliance partners.

Other data leave little doubt about the prevalence of international publics' disapproval of the international policies of the second Bush administration. Net majorities in many publics attributed their dissatisfaction with the US to the current presidency and the particular policies and policy style they associated with it. One much criticized aspect of George W. Bush's international practices was their perceived unilateralism, and some European publics and that of South Korea were asked about its posing an important threat from the US in the next decade. Substantial majorities in the UK, France, Germany, the Netherlands, Italy and Poland thought it did, as did half of the public in South Korea. When, however, that perception is placed in the context of how other queried threats were viewed, it was ranked only fourth in South Korea, France and Germany, and much lower in the other Europeans.[8] Concern with American unilateralism, then, may not lead publics to oppose security co-operation with the US on more pressing threats – especially if the US seeks co-operation in a more apparently multilateral rather than unilateral way.

Many of the poll responses discussed to this point were gathered while the US has been seeking acceptance of and contributions to its policies toward international terrorism and Iraq (initially justified by Washington in relation to WMD proliferation and terrorism). International public opinion on those issues sheds light on the nature of security disagreements and agreements with the US that can occur while the publics hold the broader views discussed previously. The robustness of security policy constraints associated with general anti-Americanism seems stronger if simultaneously expressed views of the US on the two specific and stressful issues have been prevailingly negative.

Terrorism

International public opinion may favour or disfavour co-operation with the American war on terrorism for reasons more specific than general attitudes toward the US. Publics giving high priority to counter-terrorism may be more open to accepting that part of a US security agenda. Yet, even for publics for whom terrorism abroad and at home is a high priority problem, negative judgements about the legitimacy and effectiveness of particular means advocated by Washington may lessen support for active co-operation with a US-designed war on terrorism.

In Table 8.1, publics are placed in terms of support for treating terrorism as a major problem and as supporting the US-led response to it. Publics in the upper left section, in effect, tend to support the George W. Bush security priority and its approach; those in the lower right reject both. Those in the lower left disagree on priority with the US but not on its policy response; the opposite is the case for those in the upper right section. The left half of the table has far more placements than the right, suggesting if anything pro-Americanism on counter-terrorism. The lower

Table 8.1 The problem of terrorism and the US response

	The US response						
Terrorism as a problem	Massively supportive	Predominantly supportive	Supportive	Split	Rejectionist	Predominantly rejectionist	Massively rejectionist
Massively supportive	India, Philippines	Hungary, Malta, Romania	Mexico		Bangladesh		
Predominantly supportive	Peru, Czech Rep.	Estonia, Lithuania, Poland, Russia	UK, Italy, Latvia	Slovenia,	Spain	Argentina, Cyprus	
Supportive	Guatemala, Honduras, Venezuela, Bulgaria, Ivory Coast	Denmark, Bolivia, Slovakia, Uganda	Netherlands	France, Germany, Portugal, Brazil			
Split	Uzbekistan	Japan, Angola	Ireland	Belgium, Finland, Luxembourg	Austria, Turkey	Indonesia	Greece, Pakistan
Rejectionist	Kenya	Sweden	South Africa				
Predominantly rejectionist	Ukraine	Vietnam, Ghana	Tanzania			Republic of Korea, Senegal	
Massively rejectionist		Canada				Morocco	Jordan

(Source: Bobrow 2005)

right section has few entries, consisting for the most part of predominantly Islamic publics. When the split publics are considered, it seems clear that the national publics of the EU are divided in terms of predominant sentiment between those whose views seem aligned with US policies and those divided about or negatively disposed toward its broad or narrow aspects.

A small number of European publics were asked (in 2002 and 2004) whether they agreed with the emphasis the US was placing on terrorism. They largely agreed in 2002, but that agreement was much less as of 2004. At the more recent time, Middle Eastern publics disagreed, often massively so. In the last several years, key European publics did massively see an important threat from international terrorism, as did those of Mexico and, to a lesser extent, South Korea. For most of those publics, it was more highly ranked than other possible threats.[9] Terrorism was associated with citizen fear and worry to a predominant or massive extent in all of the EU with the exception of Hungary. That was not the case in Asia, with the exception of India and Malaysia.[10] While EU country publics had very large majorities for making counter-terrorism an EU priority, in only a few (the UK, Italy, Spain, the Czech Republic) did it have top priority.[11] In short, there has been substantial European country demand for attention to terrorism as an international problem, and not simply an American obsession. With a few exceptions, such demand has not been predominant in Asia or the Middle East.

The picture changes when terrorism is posed as a problem in the respondent's country. Most European publics reject it as major problem in their own life space and deny it priority compared to others for their country.[12] High priority or even a split public on importance occurred only in Spain, the UK, Italy, France, Germany, Poland and Russia. Majorities in Latin America did see terrorism at home as a problem, while those in Africa did not. A number of Asian publics attributed importance to an extent substantially greater than the priority given to it in their worries.

In sum, many publics have seen terrorism as pressing in either international or domestic terms, but relatively few view it that way in both. The priority rankings suggest neither ignoring it or a welcoming stance to giving counter-terrorism overriding priority at the expense of all other issues. International public opinion, with the notable general exception of the Islamic Middle East, seems to allow for selective counter-terrorist co-operation with the US but not for counter-terrorism dominating policy agendas.

What, then, would foreign publics support in terms of US leadership in dealing with terrorism? A US-led policy usually was supported, often predominantly or massively, in most publics polled in all regions except the Middle East. There only Israeli and Kuwaiti publics were positive. The publics always opposed were mostly from Islamic majority states (Egypt, Jordan, Lebanon, Morocco, Pakistan, the Palestinian Authority, Bangladesh, Indonesia). Of countries formally US allies, only the South Korean public was predominantly negative, although the Turkish public moved from massively positive to negative. Even the French public with a negative evaluation of the US role did not have majorities rejecting a US-led policy. When asked in 2002–04, publics in the UK, France, Germany and Italy supported a US-led policy, although to a declining extent. That does not seem to fit with most versions of encompassing anti-Americanism, with the exception of the largely Islamic states.

Considerable support for a US-led policy is, however, accompanied by less supportive views (especially in the EU-15) on who bears responsibility for terrorism or on the general and specific contents of the American approach to countering it. UK, French and Polish publics prevailing saw US foreign policy as a cause of terrorism, and German and Italian publics were split on that. Islamic publics predominantly or massively saw American foreign policy as a cause. Islamic publics denied to the US sincerity in its opposition to terrorism, as did those of France and Germany. The view of the US as being just an innocent victim was not prevailingly accepted. Although the general US approach was usually predominantly supported in the Eastern European EU member states, that was not the case in most EU-15 publics. Even supportive ones on that approach were only split on its effectiveness.

What specific kinds of US-desired co-operation have foreign publics supported or rejected? Initially after 11 September 2001, most EU-15 publics supported taking part in counter-terrorist military action with the US, unlike those in other regions except for India. When a few weeks later the questions were specifically about the EU, that support almost always had shrunk among member publics. What those publics did massively support was a civil role against terrorism in its Afghan location. For most EU publics, there also was prevailing support for security-enabling measures (use of bases, intelligence sharing). While they have been selective on means, the willingness of major European publics to support many of them hardly suggests that anti-Americanism or a preference for no participation in defeating terrorism were predominant.

If views of America determine public support for or opposition to counter-terrorist policy measures, then sponsorship by a favourably viewed non-US actor should produce different results for the less well-disposed publics than does sponsorship by the US. If the public inclination is a matter of the particular policy measure, it should not. A 2003 poll posed the problem of 'another country harbouring dangerous international terrorists'. The sponsor alternatives probed were the EU, the US, or both; the policy alternatives, use of force or economic sanctions. All possibilities met with massive or predominant rejection from the publics of the UK, France, Germany, Italy, the Netherlands, Portugal and Poland. That supports a policy content-based interpretation more than one based on views of the US.

Weapons of mass destruction and Iraq

The last set of opinions focuses on weapons of mass destruction and the attempt ostensibly to address that problem through regime change in Iraq by means of US-dominated invasion, occupation and reconstruction. To what extent have views on Iraq reflected a general disagreement with the US on WMD as a threat or instead been a response to the specifics of the Iraq venture? The former suggests differences with Washington about a relatively general international security threat;

Table 8.2 The problem of WMD and the US in Iraq

WMD as a problem	The US in Iraq						
	Massively supportive	Predominantly supportive	Supportive	Split	Rejectionist	Predominantly rejectionist	Massively rejectionist
Massively supportive					Ireland, Portugal, Lithuania	Greece	
Predominantly supportive				Denmark, UK, Italy, Poland	Netherlands, Spain, Sweden	Estonia, Latvia, Turkey, Japan	Luxembourg, Mexico
Supportive							Austria, Belgium
Split				Philippines	France, Germany, Bulgaria, Uganda	Finland, Brazil, Lebanon, Pakistan	
Rejectionist				Bolivia	South Africa	Russia, India, Republic of Korea	Argentina
Predominantly rejectionist					Canada	Jordan	Vietnam
Massively rejectionist				Kenya			Indonesia

(Source: Bobrow 2005)

the latter, about only a specific set of coping measures and their application to a particular case.

Table 8.2 resembles Table 8.1 in placing publics in terms of the importance accorded to a general problem, now the problem of WMD and the US in Iraq. The left-hand side is empty and the lower right-hand section contains many publics from countries of clear international security importance. The same, however, can be said of the upper right-hand section, although with fewer key security countries. Also, publics of some countries often thought to be central to US regional and global security policies are split. In sum, there is an absence of placements suggestive of pro-American security policy attitudes. There are notable cases of disagreement with the US on both broad and narrow issues which can arguably be construed as indicative of anti-Americanism. Those placements are approximately matched by split placements suggestive of neither prevailing pro-American nor anti-American security policy views about WMD or Iraq.

Most publics outside of Latin America and Africa viewed WMD proliferation as an important problem or fear, often massively or predominantly, in general and for two particular proliferators (Iran and North Korea). When WMD priority is examined relative to other often-discussed threats to international well-being, rankings have not placed the WMD problem in first place (with the notable exceptions of Japan and Pakistan), or treated it as being of least importance among the possibilities posed.[13] As with terrorism, most publics do not seem to be rejecting coping measures, but they do not want counter-proliferation emphasized to a degree that reduces attention to ameliorative actions on some other problems.

Recognizing the WMD problem is one thing and taking action against it another. Queries in 2003 explored whether and in what ways sponsorship matters for calls to military action against a North Korea possessing nuclear weapons and an Iran allegedly about to. Four sponsors of military action were posed: the US, the US and allies (a coalition of the willing), NATO, and the United Nations Security Council (UNSC). All four situations inherently involve US support for such actions. Publics were polled in the UK, France, Germany, Italy, the Netherlands, Poland and Portugal. As queries moved from the most unilateral (the US only) to the most multilateral sponsorship (UNSC), public opinion moved in a supportive direction.[14] With UNSC sponsorship, the British public became predominantly positive about taking part, and those of France, the Netherlands and Portugal became split. German and Italian publics' opposition went from predominantly rejectionist to rejectionist.

These results are less suggestive of the blanket opposition to American preferences that simple anti-Americanism implies than of opposition to following unilaterally established US initiatives lacking multilateral sponsorship. There were not massive and reflexively negative dispositions toward military actions against proliferators just because the US might favour such steps. Publics of different EU members did, however, differ in their prevailing view of active military measures – a pattern which casts doubt on the chances of a unified EU position on taking a direct part in military measures whether or not the US operates in a unilateral fashion.

Attitudes on WMD proliferation do not support the possibility that prevailing negativism toward the US's Iraq venture follows from dismissal of the general problems such as weapons and their diffusion pose. Indeed, as of 2002, those few but key country publics polled had substantial prevailing sentiment that Saddam's Iraq was developing WMD, posed a substantial danger, and his removal was necessary. Even in Turkey, opinion was only split rather than rejecting on several of those matters. Yet also present was scepticism about whether the WMD threat was the real motive for the then-proposed US invasion.

Since it was launched, publics have, with very few exceptions, differed only in their prevailing degree of negativism toward America's Iraq venture. Most national publics have found the US invasion unjustified and the war not worth its cost. Many of the negative publics have been massively or predominantly so, and the positive publics not as strongly so. Supportive publics or split ones are found only in a very few major European countries (the UK, Italy, Poland), several small entities in Southeastern Europe, Israel, Kuwait, Australia, the Philippines, and Nigeria. For those publics not extremely negative around the time of the 2003 US invasion, assessments subsequently became more negative.

That verdict has accompanied negative judgements on the security and stability consequences of the venture. Judgements about whether it has reduced terrorism and increased world safety were usually even more negative than those on its justification and overall cost-worthiness. Almost all national publics viewed the United Nations (UN) as damaged. Opinions on the ease with which damage to American alliances could be repaired varied widely, with many publics split. Most of the few international publics polled (France, Germany, Russia, Jordan, Morocco, Pakistan, Turkey) thought the venture showed that the US was less powerful, trustworthy and committed to democracy.[15] Compared with these views, opinions on Middle East regional consequences were considerably less negative in Western Europe, but not elsewhere. That was also true with regard to perceived consequences for the Iraqi population. It is hardly surprising, then, that with few exceptions publics have massively or predominantly rejected military participation in Iraq. In the poll conducted from November 2004 to early January 2005, public opinion was predominantly net negative, even in some of the countries which had troops in Iraq (Italy, Poland, Australia).

The sense of America's invasion and occupation of Iraq as a serious policy mistake seems to have carried over to opinions about subsequent processes of re-construction and regime transformation. International public opinion on roles to be played in the transformation and reconstruction of Iraq has assigned responsibility for financing to the US. All but the publics of countries with military participation in Iraq favoured placing the funding costs of reconstruction solely on the US and its allies there. With regard to a leading role in rebuilding and regime formation, majority preference for those roles has gone to the UN, with only minorities (often small ones) for the US. As for a security guarantor role during reconstruction, the preference was again for the UN, ideally with a multinational peacekeeping force under its direction. There has been, for the most part, only trivial support for that security role to be played by the US alone or with its allies, or by a US-run force wrapped in a UN flag. There has been even more pronounced rejection of the

EU's taking such a leading role. There was, however, in ways echoing supportive stances against terrorism, massive support for the EU playing the role of a helper in civil, humanitarian ways.

Opinions on the Iraq venture seem to provide a strong basis for concluding that massive anti-Americanism exists and has major security implications. Before accepting that conclusion, two other possibilities should be recognized. One is that rejection of US policies stemmed less from anti-Americanism than agreement on the desirability of an American-centred international security order compared to available alternatives. From that perspective, publics might have opposed the Iraq venture precisely because they thought it would undermine that order.

In another possibility, the European Venus as contrasted to the American Mars metaphor, the rejection stemmed from opposition to the use of force *per se*, rather than from anti-Americanism. Some clues about this possibility are provided by mid-2002 polling in Germany, the UK, France, Italy, the Netherlands and Poland. Respondents were posed situations in which Iraqi had WMD, or was providing aid to bin Laden. For each of those, support for military participation was elicited with the additional conditions of the presence or absence of UN approval, as well as with few or many Western casualties. With UN approval and few casualties, the scores were mostly positive, especially for the WMD situation. They were mostly negative without UN approval and with many casualties. With UN approval they did not become predominantly negative for either the WMD or the aid to bin Laden conditions, even with many casualties. There seems to have been neither an allergy to the use of force, nor a blanket rejection at the beginning of the Iraq venture of military action with the US. In short, a preference for clear international organiza- tion authorization and the multilateralism associated with it and the actual presence of major conjectured threats provide at least as persuasive an explanation for the rejection of America's Iraq policy as one emphasizing anti-Americanism.

An integrative perspective

It remains to draw together the various facets of international public opinion in terms of what they suggest about anti-Americanism and its security implications. Since for the most part the same publics appear in both Tables 8.1 (terrorism) and 8.2 (WMD and Iraq), the contrasting pattern of placements argues against widespread prevalence of the sort of anti-Americanism which makes for blanket rejection of security policy co-operation. Rejectionist sentiment clearly prevailed only in Jordan and South Korea. For more countries, public opinion suggests that their governments need especially persuasive arguments to align with US security policies and being willing to risk paying a domestic price. The relevant national publics are those of: Austria, Belgium, Finland, France, Germany, Luxembourg, Greece, Argentina, Brazil, Turkey, Pakistan and Indonesia. In sum, there are a significant number of 'America-sceptic' publics but few clearly anti-American ones across our two stressful issues.

The extent to which these placements should or should not be interpreted as indications of encompassing anti-Americanism also needs to take into account the

Table 8.3 An integrative view of attitudes toward America

US foreign policies	The US as a role model						
	Massively supportive	Predominantly supportive	Supportive	Split	Rejectionist	Predominantly rejectionist	Massively rejectionist
Massively supportive		Philippines					
Predominantly supportive		Nigeria	Israel, Uzbekistan	Kuwait			
Supportive		Ghana, Uganda	Guatemala, Honduras, Venezuela, South Africa	Vietnam, Angola, Mali, Tanzania			
Split	Ivory Coast		**Poland**	**India**			
Rejectionist		Kenya	Bulgaria, *Japan*, Republic of Korea	**UK**, *Italy*, Czech Rep., Indonesia	*Mexico*	Bolivia, **Brazil**	
Predominantly rejectionist			**Ukraine**	Peru, *Russia*, Lebanon, **Morocco**, Senegal	**Canada**, *Australia*	***France***, **Germany**, *Spain*, *Egypt*, **Pakistan**	
Massively rejectionist					Jordan	**Argentina**, *Turkey*	Palestinian Authority

(Source: Bobrow 2005)

Notes
Publics prevailingly viewing their problems with US foreign policies as being not because of basic characteristics of the US are marked as follows: massively not basic publics are shown in ***bold italics***; predominantly not basic publics are shown in **bold**; not basic publics are shown in *italics*.

results found for the first two sets of opinions. Negativism about the US may span perceived features of domestic American ways of life, and thus of their export, and how the US approaches and contributes to international affairs. Even if publics are prevailingly negative on all those counts, it seems at least premature and even exaggerated to label them as anti-American if they attribute their negativism to specific policies and a current US administration rather than to more basic features of the US.

As available data permit, these possibilities are explored in Table 8.3. Opinions on the American way of life as a role model are combined with those on US international policies to identify credible candidate publics for designation as generally anti-American. The logic of those placements is the same as for Tables 8.1 and 8.2. The candidate publics (those in the bottom four rows) are then marked to show their attribution of negativism to the George W. Bush administration and specific US policies or to more basic characteristics of America.[16] If the former prevails, there seems to be less public demand for commitments to alternatives to a US-centred security order and for the sorts of opposition to US security policies that will hinder positive relationships in the future.

The placements in Table 8.3 do not support a view of prevailing worldwide anti-Americanism or pro-Americanism. Also, numerous publics are split in their opinions. Among such publics there is no general prevailing tendency to support their country's co-operating with or separating itself from US security preferences. Their national political elites may well have room to manoeuvre according to the specifics of the security issue at hand and their domestic standing. The entries do, however, suggest prevailingly negative views in a number of countries traditionally thought of as core US allies, in predominantly Islamic countries, and in major states of Latin America. That indicates possible anti-Americanism of a far broader kind among their publics than was shown in the WMD–Iraq table and may somewhat counter the more positive view in the terrorism table. Yet, prevailing public opinion in most of the candidates for anti-American status did not view problems or dissatisfactions with the US as a function of basic American characteristics.

Such beliefs make it easier to accept the need for and feasibility of pragmatic accommodation to, or at least not hostile relations with, a US perceived as a source of rewards or punishments. Those publics have not concluded that it was imperative to give cardinal priority to pursuing a security alternative to one centred on the US, as distinct from tentative explorations of alternatives if America fails to undertake self-correction. That mixed stance seems especially likely as the alternatives involve subordinating security and other issues that the pertinent international publics have with non-Americans, or diverting their national resources from domestic priorities.

The presence of some anti-Americanism in the world surely has been established, but it is far from universal or irreversible. The previous sections report widespread disagreements with and negativism about some (but not all) US policies and its perceived unilateral, selfish style. What anti-Americanism exists seems, however, often to be outweighed by a more complex pattern of opinion. That pattern both calls into question reflexive followership of the US and retains beliefs that the

US is in a 'bad patch' that may pass with political change in America, leading to movement away from the negatively viewed content and style of Washington's security policies.

Why, then, has there been so much talk about anti-Americanism internationally and its posing profound international security implications? Speculatively, the asserted tide of anti-Americanism may have seemed to policy elites abroad useful to drive up the gains that could be extracted from the US for security co-operation, and to limit US pressures on foreign governments to conform openly to its security preferences. They may also have thought it useful for mobilizing pressures within America for foreign and security policy modifications. Inside the US, opponents of George W. Bush's security policies outside of the government, and minority factions within it, may also have seen the alleged tide as a way to mobilize domestic pressures for policy change. At the same time, proponents of Bush policies may have seen potential domestic political gains from characterizing foreign demurs as anti-Americanism. In that framing, foreign doubts and objections lack substantive merit and follow from hostile motives – motives so antagonistic toward the US that just changing policies will not lead to more support from abroad. Instead, policy compromises might weaken what friends the US has in the world and fuel additional rejection of American leadership.

Notes

1 Detailed tables of the poll responses appear in Bobrow 2005.

2 For information on the polls used, when polling took place, and other than national samples, see Bobrow 2005: 47–9.

3 Those specifics are fully reported in Bobrow 2005.

4 The bundling involves an interpretive examination of 'the marginals' approach rather than a statistically established relationship between question responses.

5 Categorization rules for net percentage responses, and for thermometer readings and positive percentages when only those are available, appear in Bobrow 2005: 20.

6 In Canada, Japan and South Korea, publics did, however, tend to view the US as losing international respect.

7 For discussion of those various conceptions, see Bobrow 2001, 1996; Bobrow and Boyer 2005.

8 The other threats posed to Europeans were: US economic competition; Islamic fundamentalism; international terrorism; immigrants; Israel–Arab military conflict; Iranian WMD; and North Korean WMD. Those to South Koreans were: international terrorism; AIDS/the Ebola virus/other potential epidemics; global warming; development of China as a major power; economic competition from low-wage countries; world population growth; North Korea's becoming a nuclear power; the rise of Japanese military power; Sino-Japanese rivalry; a large number of illegal foreign workers; and China–Taiwan tensions.

9 For the Europeans and South Koreans, the possibilities were those listed in Note 8. For the Mexican public, they were: international terrorism; world environmental

problems; development of China as a world power; chemical and biological weapons; US economic competition; drug trafficking; and world economic crises.

10 The other possibilities posed to the EU and publics were: world war; nuclear conflict in Europe; conventional war in Europe; accidental launch of a nuclear missile; a nuclear power station accident; spread of nuclear, biological and chemical weapons of mass destruction; ethnic conflicts in Europe; organized crime; and epidemics. The others posed to publics in Asia and Uzbekistan were: poverty; domestic economic inequality; fair world trade; environmental problems; wars and conflicts; natural disasters; globalization; health issues; domestic economic problems; global recession; crime; human rights; corruption; lack of democracy; illegal drugs and drug addiction; refugee and political asylum problems; unemployment and difficulties getting employment; education; domestic social welfare system; ethics in science; ageing of society; the fast pace of social change and technological improvement; the threat of industry power; religious fundamentalism; overpopulation; and moral decline/spiritual decadence.

11 The other possibilities for EU priority were: enlargement of the EU; implementing the single currency; informing citizens about the EU; fighting poverty and social exclusion; protecting the environment; guaranteeing food quality; protecting consumers; fighting unemployment; reforming EU institutions; fighting organized crime and drug trafficking; asserting EU world importance; maintaining peace and security in Europe; guaranteeing individual rights and respect for democracy in Europe; and fighting illegal immigration.

12 The other possibilities queried were: crime; public transport; the economic situation; rising prices/inflation; taxation; unemployment; defence/foreign affairs; housing; immigration; health care; education; pensions; and environmental protection.

13 The other threats and sources of fear posed were those in Notes 8 and 10; for world dangers, they were: nuclear weapons; religious and ethnic hatred; infectious diseases/AIDS; pollution and environmental problems; and the rich/poor gap.

14 The Polish public was an exception to this pattern.

15 The UK public provided a mixed verdict – perceived military strength increased, trustworthiness decreased, and there was a split on promotion of democracy.

16 Several of the candidates are not marked because of a lack of data.

Part III

Regional and Country Studies

9 A Thermostatic Dynamic? Electoral Outcomes and Anti-Americanism in Canada

Kim Richard Nossal

Anti-Americanism in Canada is unique (Granatstein 1996; Daniels 1998). There is no other country in the world which owes its existence to a conscious act of anti-Americanism: Canada emerged as a separate political community because of the refusal by elites in the other British North American colonies to accept the invitation of the American revolutionaries to join in the new republican experiment. Second, there is no other political community in which anti-Americanism is so deeply established as part of the political culture. At the same time, however, there is no other political community where such deeply entrenched anti-Americanism is generally so bland that Harvey M. Sapolsky (2005) has termed it 'low grade anti-Americanism' – akin to Moisés Naím's argument that there is a 'lite' anti-Americanism that can be contrasted with more virulent forms of this sentiment (Naím 2003). Indeed, for all the deeply rooted and pervasive anti-Americanism in Canada, one would be hard-pressed to find among Canadians the kind of virulent attitudes reported in most contemporary studies of the phenomenon of anti-Americanism (e.g. Hollander 2004; Gibson 2004; Rubin and Rubin 2004; Ross and Ross 2004; Sardar and Davies 2002; Hertsgaard 2002).

There is one further unique quality to anti-Americanism in Canada, however: in no other country can one so consistently see a connection between sentiments about the US and the outcomes of general elections. I will show that over the last half-century, we can see what appears to be a thermostatic dynamic at work in Canadian politics that serves to regulate the impact of the anti-Americanism that is so deeply entrenched in Canadian political culture: if a political party in power pursues policies or exhibits attitudes that distance Canada too far from the US or a particular administration, it will soon find itself out of power, replaced by a party which has campaigned, *inter alia*, on the promise to repair or restore good relations with the US; by the same token, however, if a political party in power pursues policies or exhibits attitudes that align Canada too closely with the US or the policies of a particular administration, it will also soon find itself out of power, replaced by a party which has promised the electorate, *inter alia*, that, if elected, it will see greater distance and independence for Canada.

In this chapter, I will examine this dynamic by surveying the last 50 years of electoral contests when anti-American attitudes towards the US or particular presidents played an important role in electoral outcomes. To do this, however, we need to frame Canadian anti-Americanism more broadly.

Types of Canadian anti-Americanism

As Inderjeet Parmar (2005a: 5–7) has noted, there is little agreement on how to define anti-Americanism; and how one defines it 'is not without consequences' for the ensuing analysis. Thus, for Parmar, anti-Americanism is a 'multifaceted and complex phenomenon', and 'it is important that its varied meanings are explicated'. While much of the literature focuses on the virulent (and murderous) elements of some strands of anti-Americanism (e.g. Joffe 2004: 29), in fact, most definitions in the contemporary literature try to grapple with the obvious multidimensionality of anti-Americanism. In this chapter, I use an ideational definition, borrowed from both James W. Ceaser and Paul Hollander. Ceaser (2003) suggests that 'anti-Americanism rests on the singular idea that something associated with the US, something at the core of American life, is deeply wrong and threatening to the rest of the world'. For his part, Hollander (1992: viii) defined anti-Americanism as 'a particular mind-set, an attitude of distaste, aversion or intense hostility the roots of which may be found in matters unrelated to the actual qualities or attributes of American society or the foreign policies of the US'. In my view, such pithy ideational definitions capture well the essentially multidimensional nature of the phenomenon in Canada while avoiding the necessity of including such intense sentiments as hatred or malevolence in the definition (cf. Rubin and Rubin 2004: ix).

We can also see that anti-Americanism in Canada does not exhibit the same varieties that we see in other places, such as Europe. As Adam Garfinkle (2004: 316–17) has noted, European anti-Americanism comprises three distinct, though interrelated, strands. One is philosophical anti-Americanism, associated with the rejectionism of the nature of the American polity by European thinkers over the two centuries after the American Revolution (Ceaser 1997, 2004). A second type is cultural anti-Americanism, a concern over Americanization of local culture and mores. The third is contingent anti-Americanism, 'stimulated by the dislike of particular policies or personalities in any given US administration' (Garfinkle 2004: 317). Anti-Americanism in Canada has not been grounded in any comparable philosophical critique – perhaps not surprisingly, since the vast majority of people who live in Canada, whether aboriginal peoples or newcomers, English-speaking or French-speaking, are in ideology and culture far more American than they are European. As John W. Holmes (1981: 114) put it archly, 'It is in any case nonsense to talk about Canada being Americanized when it has always been just as much an American nation as the US ... and there is no reason to claim that the US way is any more natively North American than the Canadian.'

Rather, as Granatstein argued, anti-Americanism in Canada has been historically grounded in a unique variety of concerns about Americanization that includes, but goes well beyond, the cultural anti-Americanism outlined by Garfinkle. I argue that the comparable form of anti-Americanism we see in Canada is economic anti-

Americanism – a form of economic nationalism (Nossal 1985) that was driven by the fear that the US, with its vast economy, would absorb its smaller neighbour, and thus bring the British North American community to an end.

Granatstein has argued that Canadian anti-Americanism between the 1770s and 1980s was in large part driven by those in Canada with a vested interest in the particular political outcomes that anti-American sentiments would produce. The ideas that the 'United Empire Loyalists' – those American colonists who remained loyal to Britain and either fled or were expelled from the new republic and came north – brought with them focused on the putative ills of American 'mob' democracy and the supposedly superior qualities of a more conservative monarchical system, suited the oligarchs of British North America well. Likewise, the characterization of Americans as grasping wolves, eager to swallow Canada, served the interests of those elites in Canada whose wealth was dependent on maintaining high tariff barriers and deep opposition to economic integration with the US. The argument is not new: as Granatstein himself notes (Granatstein 1996: 266), the Canadian historian Frank Underhill wrote in 1929 that 'the same interests are preparing to wave the old flag and to make their own private profit, political and economic, by saving us once more from the US'.

The pervasiveness of economic anti-Americanism in Canada can be seen from the number of occasions when Canadians rejected the idea of closer economic integration with the US. The most important occasion came in 1911, when the Liberal government of Prime Minister Wilfrid Laurier negotiated a free trade agreement – the Reciprocity Treaty – with the US. In the general election of that year, the Laurier Liberals were defeated by the Conservatives under Robert Borden. The so-called 'free trade election' of 1911 cast a long shadow in Canadian politics: until the late 1980s, free trade with the US was widely avoided because it was widely assumed that the party advocating free trade would go down to electoral defeat. Thus, for example, when a free trade agreement that had been negotiated between Canadian and American officials after World War II was presented to Prime Minister Mackenzie King, he could not bring himself to sign it. Although he had approved the negotiations, King worried that the agreement would spell the end of Canada, and that he would go down in history as the prime minister who was responsible for the end of the nation (Granatstein 1985). Likewise, when he was campaigning for the leadership of the Progressive Conservative Party in 1983, Brian Mulroney rejected the idea of a free trade agreement with the US: 'That's why free trade was decided on in an election in 1911 ... It affects Canadian sovereignty, and we'll have none of it, not during leadership campaigns, nor at any other times' (quoted in Martin 1993: 44).

However, by the early 1980s, there was a growing elite consensus, reflected in both the private sector and within the state apparatus, that the historical opposition to closer economic integration with the US was obsolete. Changes in behaviour quickly followed. Mulroney led the Progressive Conservatives to a massive parliamentary majority in the general elections of September 1984, and, within a year, changed his mind on free trade (Tomlin 2001). He was persuaded that given the depth of protectionist sentiment in the US Congress, Canada should seek guaranteed access to the American market via a comprehensive free trade agreement. An agreement was negotiated with the administration of Ronald Reagan, and signed in 1987. In 1988, the general election was fought on the issue of the free trade agreement, with the 1911 positions reversed: the Conservatives were proposing free trade, and the Liberals (together with the social democratic party, the New Democratic Party) vociferously opposed the agreement. And whereas in 1911 business interests had lined up squarely against free trade, in 1988, business was very much in favour of free trade, joining with the Conservatives in deriding the opposition of the Liberals and the New Democratic Party as outmoded anti-Americanism. The Conservatives were returned to office, and the Canada–US Free Trade Agreement came into force on 1 January 1989.

More importantly, as the free trade agreements with the US and then Mexico began to have an impact on the huge growth of Canadian wealth in the 1990s (Fagan 2003), economic anti-Americanism within the broader public died almost completely, leaving only contingent anti-Americanism as a force in Canadian politics.

Contingent anti-Americanism in Canadian politics

While we have seen the disappearance of economic anti-Americanism in Canada since the early 1990s, we have not seen the disappearance of the third kind of anti-Americanism identified by Garfinkle, contingent anti-Americanism – in other words, the dislike of particular policies or personalities of any given US administration. This form of anti-Americanism can (and does) co-exist with other forms of anti-Americanism; but it also can (and does) co-exist with essentially positive attitudes towards the US, allowing us to explain, in Canada's case, why anti-Americanism takes the 'low-grade' or 'lite' form it does. While for many years contingent anti-Americanism co-existed with economic anti-Americanism in Canada, it can be argued that with the disappearance of economic anti-Americanism since the late 1980s, this has emerged to be the dominant form.

The contingent nature of Canadian anti-Americanism can perhaps best be illustrated by examining the results of a global poll conducted by the British Broadcasting Corporation (BBC) in the wake of the decision of the US administration of George W. Bush to invade Iraq and overthrow the government of Saddam Hussein. Canadians have generally favourable feelings towards America second only to Americans themselves, and well ahead of the predominantly positive attitudes in other countries that have been traditionally 'friendly' towards the US, such as Britain, Israel and Australia (BBC 2003a, 2003b). But when asked about their feelings towards Bush or the US invasion of Iraq, Canadians responded far less positively. While not demonstrating the degree of antipathy for Bush or the invasion of Iraq evident in France or Jordan, Canadians nonetheless suggested in their responses to the BBC poll that their generally positive sentiments about the US are not automatically reflected in their views of specific American leaders or their policies.

The results of the BBC poll are generally in line with other poll results for

Canadian attitudes towards the US. For example, an Environics Research Group/ Focus Canada (2003) poll revealed that 62 per cent expressed 'very favourable' or 'somewhat favourable' opinions of the US; 35 per cent expressed 'somewhat unfavourable' or 'very unfavourable' opinions. Another poll (Leger Marketing 2003) conducted in April–May 2003 revealed that 50 per cent of Canadians believed that American foreign policy had a negative effect on Canada, with 41 per cent believing that the invasion of Iraq was not justified. A November 2004 poll commissioned by a Canadian advocacy group, Friends of America, revealed similar results. While some of the questions were clearly designed to elicit certain responses ('Deep down, I know that Americans are our closest friends'), the poll nonetheless revealed a basic division between warm feelings for the US and criticism of the foreign policies of the Bush administration ('71 percent Rate US as "Closest Friend,"' *National Post*, 29 November 2004).

In short, the dichotomy evident in the 2003 BBC poll is by no means a new phenomenon. Canadians have always had negative views about particular American presidents and about particular policies of the US. Canadians generally responded very differently to American presidents: Democratic presidents such as Jimmy Carter (1977–81) and Bill Clinton (1993–2001) were viewed more favourably in Canada than Republican presidents, such as Richard M. Nixon (1969–74), Ronald Reagan (1981–89) and George W. Bush (a phenomenon that has led some observers to suggest that if Canadians had the vote in American presidential elections, they would overwhelmingly vote the Democratic ticket). For example, it is instructive to compare the generally unfavourable attitude that Canadians held towards George W. Bush and his policies on Iraq in the mid-2000s with the generally favourable attitudes that Canadians had of his predecessor, Bill Clinton, and Clinton's decision to bomb terrorist targets in Afghanistan and Sudan in August 1998: Canadians gave Clinton a 68 per cent approval rating, with 51 per cent of Canadians approving of the air-strikes and fully 55 per cent agreeing with the question 'If the US launches similar attacks against terrorist facilities in the future would you approve or disapprove of your country's military participating in those attacks?' (Gallup 1998).

Throughout the Cold War and post-Cold War eras, we saw similar displays of contingent anti-Americanism in Canada – primarily in the form of opposition to aspects of American global policy, or US policy towards Canada. This contingent anti-Americanism tended to manifest itself in public anger against an American president and/or some act of commission or omission of the US government, sometimes involving direct Canadian interests, sometimes involving American policy on issues that do not have a direct bearing on Canada or Canadians. Often the flare of public anger or opposition was brief; normally, it did not have a marked impact on the policy of governments in Washington or Ottawa; and rarely did it have an impact on cross-border trade.

There are numerous examples of contingent anti-Americanism in Canada driven by opposition to specific policies or personalities. Some were major events, such as the escalation of the war in Vietnam by President Lyndon B. Johnson in the mid-1960s. The massive opposition to the Vietnam War in the US had major spillover effects in Canada, producing a kind of miniature replica effect: Canadians held similar protests, engaged in similar denunciations, and indeed used the same slogans as their American counterparts. But the war galvanized Canadian anti-Americanism as no other event has, and not simply because of the draft resisters, dodgers, deserters and others who sought to migrate from the US during the conflict.

Some contingent anti-Americanism was prompted by relatively isolated incidents that would flare up, give rise to an expression of anti-American anger in Canada, and disappear, relatively briefly. Among these incidents could be included: the accusations by James G. Endicott, a Canadian missionary and leader of a Soviet front organization, the Canadian Peace Congress, that the US military was using germ warfare during the Korean War;[1] the suicide of Herbert Norman, the Canadian ambassador to Cairo, in April 1957;[2] or the 1971 decision by the US to conduct underground tests of nuclear weapons on the Aleutian island of Amchitka.[3] Likewise, the decision of the Mulroney government to participate in the US-led coalition that expelled Iraq from Kuwait during the Gulf War in 1991 generated a great deal of anti-Americanism (Nossal 1994).

In some cases, a particular administration's policies on a variety of issues galvanized opposition. For example, the administration of Ronald Reagan attracted strong opposition in Canada over the course of the 1980s for its environmental policies – in particular, the issue of acid rain from the US (Munton and Castle 1992); its defence policies (the Strategic Defense Initiative, the decision to test cruise missiles over Canada in 1982); its Arctic policies that challenged Canadian sovereignty (Griffiths 1987); or its use of force against others in the international system (Libya, Grenada, Nicaragua).

Interestingly, the numerous trade disputes that Canadians have with Americans tend not to produce the kind of anti-American sentiments that differences over other policy areas do. Those who have been inclined to demonstrate their anger against the US government for some aspect of American global policy have demonstrated little consciousness of, or sympathy for, their fellow nationals whose livelihoods have been affected by American actions, such as the closure of the border to beef or the imposition of countervails on some product. Likewise, those whose economic interests are affected by American protectionism have not been inclined to demonstrate their anger by protesting outside the American embassy or US consulates. As a result, trade issues, while they produce just as much anger (if not more, since they affect concrete rather than symbolic interests), do not play an important part in anti-Americanism in Canada.

However, because anti-Americanism is so deeply rooted in Canada, some political leaders have found it tempting to try to tap into this sentiment for electoral/political purposes. While most Canadian governments have sought to downplay or minimize contingent anti-Americanism, there are three clear examples of this dynamic at work: under John Diefenbaker, the Progressive Conservative prime minister (1957–63), under Pierre Trudeau and the Liberal government (1980–84), and under the Liberal governments of Jean Chrétien (1993–2003) and Paul Martin (2003–06).

John Diefenbaker was elected as leader of the Progressive Conservatives in December 1956. In the 1957 election campaign, he used the anti-Americanism that had been stirred by the suicide of Herbert Norman to maximum electoral advantage, arguing that the Liberals were too pro-American and that Canada was sure to become 'a virtual 49th state of the American union' (Granatstein 1996: 125). Part of the reason for the Conservative victory in the 1957 election that yielded a minority government, and then the 1958 election that resulted in a Conservative majority, was the appeal to the anti-American sentiment in Canada. But Diefenbaker's anti-Americanism did not fully flower until John F. Kennedy assumed the presidency of the US in January 1961. In 1961–62, a series of deep quarrels divided Diefenbaker and Kennedy over defence policy and policy towards Cuba. The most severe split came over the Cuban Missile Crisis of October 1962. Diefenbaker not only refused to put the Royal Canadian Air Force units of the North American Air Defence Command on high alert, but he also gave a public speech calling for a United Nations investigation into American claims that the Soviet Union was installing missiles in Cuba. Without doubt, Kennedy and other members of the administration were less than amused at having their honesty publicly questioned by the Canadian prime minister (Lyon 1968: 27–64; Robinson 1989, chapter 28). Diefenbaker tried to play the anti-American card in the 1963 election campaign; indeed, as Robinson (*ibid.*: 307) notes, as the 1963 elections approached, Diefenbaker was 'relishing the prospect of an anti-American election campaign'.

A comparable appeal to popular anti-American sentiment was evident in the period of Liberal governments during 1980–84 and 1993–2006. After Pierre Trudeau won the 1980 election, his government enacted a series of economic nationalist policies that targeted the US and American interests. The National Energy Program and the revitalization of the Foreign Investment Review Agency generated considerable opposition in the US (Clarkson 1985) – and because of this were intensely popular in Canada. Compounding these economic quarrels were disputes over the damage in Canada being caused by acid rain emanating from the US and a deepening division between Reagan and Trudeau over the Cold War and American global policy, with Trudeau increasingly willing to disagree publicly with Washington (Granatstein and Bothwell 1991; Bromke and Nossal 1983–84). While Trudeau himself was not anti-American (McCall and Clarkson 1994: 203), there can be little doubt that the obvious disputes with Washington fed and legitimized anti-Americanism in both the Liberal Party and in the country at large.

Jean Chrétien was one of Trudeau's cabinet ministers, and was selected Liberal leader in 1990; the Liberals under Chrétien won the 1993 general elections. During the 1993 campaign, Chrétien promised that he would abandon what he claimed had been the excessively close relationship that the Conservative Prime Minister, Brian Mulroney, had enjoyed with both Reagan and George H. W. Bush. While Chrétien did abandon the annual summit meeting with the president that Mulroney had instituted, and while he did not celebrate his relationship with Bill Clinton in the way that Mulroney had made much of his relations with Reagan and Bush,

Chrétien nonetheless developed a good relationship with Clinton, often playing golf with him and frequently telephoning him over the seven years they were both in office together.

But Chrétien also used anti-Americanism for domestic political purposes. His decision to reinstitute good relations with Cuba (after Canada's relations had been purposely downgraded in the late 1970s as a result of Cuban military adventurism in Africa) was based on his assessment that not only would Cuba be an excellent recipient for Canadian International Development Agency contracts, but that the divergence between Canadian and American positions on Cuba could entrench his own claims to be more distant from Washington. Indeed, Chrétien's attitude towards the political importance of anti-Americanism was revealed inadvertently in July 1997. While attending a NATO summit in July 1997, Chrétien and Jean-Luc Dehane, the prime minister of Belgium, were chatting with one another in French – without realizing that their microphones were open. Chrétien confided to Dehane that he had made defying the US 'my policy. The Cuba affair, I was the first to stand up [unintelligible]. People like that.' But Chrétien also added: 'You have to do it carefully, because they're friends' (*Globe and Mail*, 10 July 1997; *Maclean's*, 21 July 1997).

But with the election of George W. Bush, much of the 'care' was abandoned. On numerous occasions, Chrétien left in little doubt his negative sentiments for the Bush administration and his generally sceptical view of the US in global politics. For example, in a Canadian Broadcasting Corporation (CBC) television documentary broadcast on the first anniversary of the 11 September 2001 terrorist attacks, Chrétien was quoted expressing the view that these events were the result of Western – and particularly American – policy. The West, claimed Chrétien, was 'looked upon as being arrogant, self-satisfied and greedy and with no limits'. He went on to say:

> You know you cannot exercise your powers to the point of humiliation for the others … That is what the Western world – not only the Americans – has to realize. I do think that the Western world is getting too rich in relation to the poor world and this is silly. (BBC News On-line 2002)

These comments were widely interpreted, in Canada and particularly in the US, as arguing that the Americans themselves were responsible for 11 September 2001.

The anti-American pitch increased in the fall and winter of 2002–03 as the Chrétien government's opposition to the emerging war melded with both an antipathy towards George W. Bush and a deep strain of anti-Americanism in the Liberal cabinet and particularly its backbench, sometimes obscuring which was dominant. For example, on 20 November 2002, Chrétien's director of communications, Françoise Ducros, watching Bush speak at the NATO summit in Prague, muttered in front of two reporters: 'What a moron.' But Chrétien did not demand her resignation nor did he condemn the comment. Rather, his response was simply to deny that Bush was a moron: '[He is] a friend of mine. He is not a moron at all.' American talk shows picked up the comment and ran with it for five days before Ducros finally resigned. And even then, Chrétien never rebuked her, but accepted her resignation, commended her for her service and wished her good luck. However, as opposition critics and media commentators noted, the delay in her resignation and the refusal of the prime minister to respond harshly to her characterization left the impression that that view was more widely held within the Chrétien government (CBC News 2002).

If Ducros' comments were more properly anti-Bush than anti-American, the comments of a backbench Liberal Member of Parliament, Carolyn Parrish, were clearly anti-American. On 26 February 2003, while leaving a meeting on Parliament Hill, Parrish was caught by a microphone responding angrily to a question from the media by saying: 'Damn Americans! I hate those bastards.' Although she apologized afterwards – claiming, quite illogically, that the words did not represent her views – she immediately appeared on *The Mike Bullard Show* on the Comedy Network, where the news clip was replayed to the delight of the largely youthful crowd, and Parrish unapologetically claimed that she could not promise not to do it again. Although the opposition called on the prime minister to expel her from the Liberal caucus, Chrétien refused to discipline her, leading Andrew Coyne to comment:

> After so many similar episodes, the conclusion is inescapable: Liberal anti-Americanism is not a problem for Mr Chrétien to manage, but rather an outgrowth of his own attitudes and beliefs. As with its counterparts elsewhere, the Liberal 'street' is less a spontaneous popular phenomenon than the unofficial voice of the regime. She may put it in cruder terms, but by and large, Ms Parrish says what Mr Chrétien thinks. (Coyne 2003)

The antipathy towards Bush – if not towards Americans more broadly – in Chrétien's Ottawa had an impact. Bush cancelled a visit to Ottawa that had been planned for May 2003, and pointedly refused to extend an invitation to the Canadian prime minister to the ranch at Crawford. Relations between the two leaders through much of the remainder of 2003 stayed chilly.

After Paul Martin took over from Chrétien as prime minister in December 2003, he claimed that he was going to make a conscious effort to improve relations with the US. However, he continued the tradition of playing the anti-American card in both the 2004 and 2005–06 general elections. During the 2004 elections, he consistently characterized the opposition Conservatives as proposing an 'American-style' health system and 'American-style' tax cuts (Canadian Television (CTV News) 2004). In the election campaign of December 2005–January 2006, the Liberal Party unabashedly portrayed the Conservatives as pro-American and the Liberals as the upholders of Canadian independence, running a series of attack ads that characterized Harper as Bush's lap-dog. Most importantly, at an international conference on climate change held in Montreal in the middle of the election campaign, Martin sought to score political points by publicly excoriating the US for its stance on the Kyoto Accords, calling on Americans to heed the 'global conscience' on climate change (choosing not to mention the fact that Canada was much further away from meeting its Kyoto obligations than the US was) (*Globe and Mail*, 9 December 2005). And in a move designed to signal to Canadian voters his distance from the Bush administration, Martin also made a point of arranging a special photo opportunity with Bill Clinton, who remains popular in Canada.

Moreover, during his two years in power, Martin made little effort to improve relations with the Bush administration. First, he made no move to squelch the anti-Americanism that continued to be on display among Liberal backbenchers. For example, although Carolyn Parrish continued to express anti-Bush and anti-American views, Martin refused to discipline her. In August 2004, she characterized anyone supporting Ballistic Missile Defense (BMD) as being part of a 'coalition of the idiots', mocking Bush's 'coalition of the willing' (CBC News 2004). After the 2004 presidential elections in the US, she expressed shock at Bush's re-election and claimed that 'Americans were out of touch with the rest of the free world'. Shortly afterwards, she appeared on a satirical CBC programme, *This Hour Has 22 Minutes*, and as a joke stuck voodoo pins in the head of a George W. Bush doll ('where it would do the least damage'), before stomping on it for the cameras (but then also kissed it). None of this was enough to attract prime ministerial discipline. However, when she expressed her anger at Martin's failure to support her bid for re-nomination in her local constituency, declaring that Martin 'could go to hell' and claiming that 'If he loses the next election and has to resign, I wouldn't shed a tear over it', the prime minister expelled her from the Liberal caucus within hours of the story's appearing (Conologue 2005).

Second, on important substantive issues, Martin proved unwilling to challenge anti-American/anti-Bush sentiment in his caucus. For example, although Martin himself was personally in favour of Canada's joining the BMD scheme, and although his government had given the Bush administration some clear signals that Ottawa would join BMD, in the end Martin backed away. A Liberal Member of the Parliament from Québec, mirroring popular views in that province, expressed strong opposition to BMD; while it is unclear whether Québec Liberals threatened to bring the government down over the issue, Martin's behaviour suggested that he was fearful of such an outcome. In February 2005, without warning the US or offering any reasoned justification for its decision, the government abruptly announced that it would not join BMD.

In sum, contingent anti-Americanism remains alive and well in Canada. As the cases of the Conservatives from 1957 to 1963, the Liberals from 1980 to 1984, and the Liberals from 1993 to 2006 show, this contingent anti-Americanism is periodically used for political purposes, just as economic anti-Americanism used to be used by Canadian elites over the two centuries before the 1980s.

A thermostatic dynamic? The political consequences of anti-Americanism

The contingent anti-Americanism so evident in Canadian politics must, however, be put in the context of its essential 'liteness'. The antipathy that many Canadians feel towards some administrations in the US; the anger that many feel about some policies of the US; or the willingness of large numbers of Canadians to indulge in the kind of anti-American sentiments that Brendon O'Connor (2003) has called the 'last respectable prejudice' – all must be put into the context of the essential warmness that the majority of Canadians feel towards the US and things American.

Indeed, it is that paradoxical nature of Canadian attitudes towards the US – at once an essential warmness and an antipathy that is deeply entrenched in Canadian political culture – that may explain why those political leaders who are overtly anti-American, and who seek to play the anti-American card in Canadian politics, find themselves out of power sooner rather than later. If we look at the three cases examined above, we can see that the pursuit of anti-American policies brings the rise of a counter tendency. Diefenbaker's anti-Americanism gave rise to a promise during the 1963 election by the Liberal leader of the opposition, Lester B. Pearson, that, if elected, the Liberals would restore good relations with the US. Likewise, the deterioration of relations between Trudeau and the Reagan administration saw the leader of the Progressive Conservatives, Brian Mulroney, promise that a Progressive Conservative government would 'refurbish' the relationship with the US, as Mulroney put it. And in 2005–06, the Conservative Party of Canada under Stephen Harper promised that, if elected, it would in government abandon the anti-Americanism that had been so much a mark of the Liberal governments of Jean Chrétien and Paul Martin.

It should be noted that a comparable tendency has been observed on the other side, too: that when Canadian governments get too close to the US, or when Canadian prime ministers grow too fond of the American president, a counter-reaction occurs. When the Liberal government of Louis St Laurent grew too close to the US over the course of the early 1950s – encouraging economic integration between Canada and the US; 'abandoning' the 'mother countries' of Britain and France by taking the American side in the Suez crisis of 1956; not standing up to the administration in Washington over the suicide of Herbert Norman – the Conservatives under Diefenbaker arose to push a line in the 1957 election that promised greater independence from Washington. Likewise, when Brian Mulroney forged an exceptionally close and personal relationship with George H. W. Bush between 1989 and 1992 – and openly celebrated that closeness – the Liberals under Jean Chrétien campaigned during the 1993 elections on the promise that, if elected, a Liberal government would pursue a more distant, and more independent, line.

Looking back over a half-century, the dynamic looks quite thermostatic: when a Canadian government moves from a presumed norm that fits the 'comfort' level of Canadians who like distance but not too much distance, it would appear that an electoral corrective comes into play: when a government in Ottawa becomes too anti-American, it is replaced by the political party promising to restore 'good relations'; when a Canadian government becomes too close to the US, it is replaced by a party which comes to power promising more 'distance' and 'independence'.

However, framing the dynamic as thermostatic suggests intent and causality. There is no evidence to suggest that sentiments about the US, whether pro or anti, caused the observed electoral outcome. On the contrary: like most other peoples, Canadians do not appear to base their voting behaviour on a single issue (Clarke *et al.* 1984; Nadeau and Blais 1995), and so it is likely that, if concern over the government's proximity to, or distance from, the US played a role in the calculations of Canadian voters in 1957, 1963, 1984, 1993 or 2006, it was inchoate at best.

Conclusion

I have argued in this chapter that the kind of anti-Americanism that we see in Canada today is neither the philosophical variant so evident in Continental Europe nor the economic anti-Americanism that was so much a part of Canadian political culture for two centuries. As Granatstein has argued, that variant is no longer dominant, having been abandoned by Canada's elites in favour of an integrationist perspective. Rather, the strand that is dominant in Canada today is contingent anti-Americanism, where opposition and antipathy to George W. Bush and his administration's policies co-exist with generalized feelings of friendship, warmth and closeness to Americans and the US. And while we have seen political leaders in Canada – even those who claim to want to improve Canadian–American relations – play the anti-American card, thus oxygenating contingent anti-Americanism, we do not see any shift from those generalized positive feelings.

However, we have seen that there is a dynamic – not a causal dynamic, but an observable one nonetheless – that moderates even the low-grade and ultra-lite contingent anti-Americanism that exists in Canada. Canadians may be anti-American, but if the historical record is any guide, they become concerned when that anti-Americanism translates into sour relations between the governments in Ottawa and Washington. And by the same token, Canadians may feel warmness to the US, but they appear to be discomfited when their government grows too close to the US. In short, the anti-Americanism that is so deeply entrenched in Canadian political culture also appears to be self-correcting to ensure a permanent liteness.

Notes

1 Endicott held a rally at Maple Leaf Gardens, at the time the largest venue in Toronto, on 10 May 1952, attended by a crowd of supporters all but a few of whom (who were quickly hustled out by the organizers) cheered his denunciations of American 'wickedness' (*Toronto Star*, 12 May 1952, 15). His claims were widely rejected at the time, and no evidence has ever been adduced in the five decades since to support his charges. However, as Granatstein (1996: 107–8) notes, 'What was most significant in this whole episode was that, in the middle of a war in which Canadians were fighting and dying, ten thousand people turned out to cheer a man who was spreading stories that only the most credulous could have believed'.

2 Norman had been a student at Cambridge in the 1930s and a member of the Communist Party. He had gone on to join the Canadian Department of External Affairs in 1939 and had been investigated by the US Senate Subcommittee on Internal Security chaired

by Senator Joseph McCarthy in both 1951 and 1952, but had been cleared. His name surfaced again in March 1957. After the subcommittee published its testimony, Norman committed suicide. For reporters, a smiling Robert Morris, the committee's chief counsel, held up a newspaper whose headline read 'Envoy Accused as Red Kills Self'. As Donald Creighton noted (1976: 291), Canadian 'grief and anger were great; and these strong feelings were aroused not merely by the outrage of Norman's death', but also 'by the casual, unconcerned, perfunctory fashion in which both the Canadian and American governments treated it'.

3 The Amchitka test was denounced by church groups and by conservation groups worried about the possibility that the underground explosion would trigger earthquakes or tsunamis. There were large-scale protests held in front of American consulates, and three international bridges were blockaded by protestors. Two Members of Parliament travelled to Washington and picketed the White House. The Liberal government of Pierre Trudeau decided to reflect the growing anger by introducing a resolution in the House of Commons calling on the president to cancel the test; 100 Members of Parliament subsequently sent a last-minute appeal to the White House. Nixon was unperturbed by the protests; the test went ahead on 6 November (Dobell 1985: 400–1).

10 'Allies But Not Friends': Anti-Americanism in Australia

Ann Capling

Anti-Americanism has been a feature of Australian discourse, identity and political life since the nineteenth century. It has been manifested in anxiety about the 'Americanization' of local culture, identity, values and public policies; in stereotypes and ridicule about Americans and American society; and in criticism of US foreign policies and particular administrations. Indeed, anti-American sentiment is commonplace in Australia, and while it sometimes flares up in popular protests and demonstrations, a kind of low-level anti-Americanism can be found easily in day-to-day conversations in classrooms and workplaces; on the airwaves of talk-back radio; in the letters and op-ed pages of newspapers and across the electronic media more generally; and within the public service and government.

On the face of it, anti-Americanism in Australia has much in common with the mild forms of anti-Americanism found in other English-speaking countries such as Great Britain, Canada and New Zealand – especially in contrast to the more deep-seated or virulent forms of anti-Americanism found in some other parts of the world. But Australian anti-Americanism has many distinctive elements that stem from Australia's location and its role and position in the international economy. While geography has predisposed Australia to look to the United States as a protector and an ally, economics has often caused rancour in the relationship. This chapter explores these tensions in the Australia–US relationship as a way of gaining a better understanding of the distinctive nature of Australian anti-Americanism.

Characterising Australian anti-Americanism

There is very little evidence in Australia of the philosophical anti-Americanism that has informed some strands of Western European thought (see for instance Berghahn 2001; Rubin and Rubin 2004). Indeed, during nineteenth-century debates on the development of Australia's political institutions, the American republic was often invoked for its positive qualities. This led the architects of Federation to graft the US bicameral model onto the British parliamentary system, with a House of Representatives for the people and a Senate to represent the states – creating a hybridized 'Washminster' system of government. Moreover, American democratic ideals have resonated deeply in Australian political culture.

However, like the Europeans and Canadians, Australians have expressed concerns about the 'Americanization' of the Australian economy. For instance, the influx of US investment after World War I led Australians to fret about Americanization and question Australia's ability to maintain a separate and distinct identity (Churchward 1979: 108–20). Similar concerns were evident during the high point of Australian economic nationalism in the late 1960s and early 1970s (Bryan 1991: 290–309). Australians have also worried about the influx of American fads, fashions and figures of speech, which are propagated through the import of US music, film and television and digital media products – while simultaneously being among the world's most enthusiastic consumers of these products (O'Connor 2003).

But mostly, anti-Americanism in Australia has tended to be contingent on particular US political administrations and policies. This is especially true in matters where Australia is directly affected by US actions. In the late 1960s and early 1970s, anti-Americanism in Australia was strongly associated with opposition to the Vietnam War and the conscription of Australian servicemen to fight in Vietnam (Murphy 1993: 225). Anti-Americanism surged briefly in 1975 when conspiracy theorists attributed the dismissal of the Whitlam Labor government to the machinations of the CIA.[1]

This kind of contingent anti-Americanism is again prevalent in Australia and is strongly associated with opposition to the foreign policies of George W. Bush's administration, especially in relation to the US invasion of Iraq. The war – and Australia's participation in it – divided the country and it triggered a fierce and ongoing debate about Australian–American relations and the changing role of the US in the world. And as the Australian Treasurer, Peter Costello, observed, Australia's coalition with the US in Iraq has boosted anti-Americanism in Australia.[2]

A headline in *The Sydney Morning Herald*, Australia's largest circulation broadsheet, conveys the depth of anti-Americanism in present-day Australia. Under the heading, 'Our New Nightmare: The United States of America', the article reported the results of a public opinion poll commissioned by the Lowy Institute for International Policy (2005), an independent think tank based in Sydney (Allard and Williams 2005). The Lowy survey revealed a great deal of disquiet among Australians about their relationship with the United States. To begin with, just over half of Australians (58 per cent) viewed the US in positive terms. This low figure is especially striking in comparison with Australians' views about other countries: Australians felt far more positively inclined towards Japan (84 per cent) and China (69 per cent) than they did towards the United States.

The Lowy study also provided strong evidence for the way in which Australian anti-Americanism is closely related to contemporary US foreign policy. Importantly, the survey showed that 57 per cent of Australians feel themselves to be threatened by US foreign policies. This figure is on par with the number of Australians who feel threatened by Islamic extremism – an astonishing result, given that Australians have been the direct and deliberate targets of terrorist attacks by Islamist extremists in Bali and Jakarta.

It is not difficult to explain why Australians feel so anxious about the United

States, and there are strong reasons to be found in relation to Australia's particular position in the global order. As a 'middle power', Australia has had a very strong interest in and commitment to multilateralism and the notion of a rules-based international system. In that context, Australia's interests are best served when the United States plays a constructive role in the global order and when its actions are backed by international consensus (Kelly 2003). Thus, the unilateralist disposition of George W. Bush's administration makes most Australians feel very uncomfortable, and the US foreign policy response to the terrorist attacks of 11 September 2001 is perceived by many to be arrogant and ill-considered. That being said, as this surge of Australian anti-Americanism is closely related to current US foreign policies, it is just as likely to ebb with attendant change in those policies.

The Australia–US security relationship

Australian anti-Americanism has been fairly benign – anti-Americanism 'lite' – and it has been primarily contingent, triggered by specific political leaders, events and policies. This is similar to the sort of anti-Americanism that one finds in Canada – with a very importance difference. Canada was founded as an act of anti-Americanism; Canadians fret endlessly about their relationship with their giant neighbour to the south and fear that they will eventually be engulfed. Indeed, one of the great themes of Canadian history is 'keeping the Yankees out' (Granatstein 1996; Nossal chapter in this volume). By contrast, a central preoccupation of Australian governments is 'keeping the Yankees in' – that is, engaged in the western Pacific region. This impulse stems from Australia's historic feelings of insecurity and the widely held view that it needs a 'great and powerful' friend for protection. In order to understand the unique nature of anti-Americanism in Australia, it is necessary to briefly outline this element of the Australian psyche and the importance to Australians of the alliance with the US.

By dint of its location on the southern fringes of East Asia, Australia has always been preoccupied about potential threats from its neighbours to the north. As Coral Bell describes it, Australia's 'essential strategic dilemma' is derived from its position as a small, Western country 'on the fringe of a society of giants' (Bell 1988: 72–3). This strategic dilemma has led to a strong tendency for Australia to look to its great and powerful friends for protection. Until World War II, Great Britain served in this role, with the Royal Navy its first line of defence. In return, Australia 'paid its dues' by supporting Great Britain in both the Boer War and World War I. However, the experiences of World War II showed that Great Britain could not be relied upon for the defence of Australia, thus forcing Australia to seek a new protector. As a result, the wartime alliance between Australia and the US became the basis for a more enduring security relationship.

This was formalized in the Australia, New Zealand, United States Security Treaty (ANZUS) of 1951. Significantly, it was Australia that pushed hard for the alliance and Washington's grudging agreement was extracted by Canberra in return for the Menzies' government's support for the US objective of negotiating a lenient peace agreement with Japan (which Australian public opinion fiercely opposed). From Australia's perspective though, ANZUS had significant birth defects. Most importantly, unlike the NATO agreement, which treated an attack on any member as an act of war against them all, ANZUS did not bind the US to unconditional military support in the event of an attack on Australia. This crucial omission fed Australia's deep-seated fears of being abandoned and raised considerable doubts about the level of support that Australia could expect should it ever be threatened. To be sure, many analysts reject the abandonment scenario, arguing that the 'ties that bind' Australia and the US are grounded in 'shared values, a common vision of international order and a mutual belief that each other's existence is vital to fulfil this vision ...' (Tow and Albinski 2002: 162–4). Nonetheless, the fear of abandonment remains powerful in the Australian imagination, reinforced by former diplomats (Renouf 1979), among others. Hence, Australia's preoccupation with keeping the US engaged in the region.

The ANZUS alliance has undoubtedly brought many benefits for Australia over the past 50-plus years (Brown and Rayner 2001–02). Its proponents point to the deterrent effect of ANZUS; its role in keeping the US engaged in the western Pacific region; and the means by which the close relationship with the US has allowed Australia to project its influence in the Asia–Pacific region in a way that would be otherwise unwarranted by its size. ANZUS has also contributed to Australia's own defence capabilities and it entitles Australia to high-level intelligence and preferential access to American military equipment and technology. Finally, ANZUS provides Australia with regular access to the senior echelons of the US military and government, although it should be noted that access alone is no guarantee of influence.

But the alliance is not without its downsides and there are political and military costs attached to Australia's close relationship with the United States. In political terms, while the alliance has enabled Australia to play an intermediary role between countries in Southeast Asia and the US, Australia has at times been seen as a 'cat's paw' or a 'deputy sheriff' of the United States. Such an image is counterproductive for Australia and for its desire to maintain an independent foreign policy. Moreover, the alliance carries with it the fear that Australia may be co-opted into conflicts that it would otherwise have avoided. The Howard government's support for the US in Iraq has been seen by many critics in precisely these terms. Similarly, there has been considerable debate about the dilemma that would confront Australia should the United States ever go to war with China, as Australia does not share the US position on Taiwanese independence (Harris 1998). In military terms, the alliance has made Australia highly dependent on the US for key materiel and logistic support. And, the alliance has distorted important decisions about defence purchasing with the result that political considerations have sometimes trumped professional opinion (Kelton 2004).

Despite these disadvantages and problems, Australia's historic sense of insecurity and its fear of abandonment have meant that the alliance has enjoyed high levels of public support in Australia – at least to date. This helps to explain why Australians can feel threatened by US foreign policies (57 per cent) while at the same time believing that the alliance is important for Australia's international security (72 per cent) (Lowy Institute 2005). Australian views about the importance of the alliance command support on both sides of politics as well. On the conservative side of politics, the Liberal and National parties have been strong supporters of the US alliance. In government, they have always been keen to demonstrate Australia's commitment to the security relationship, sending troops to Korea in the 1950s and Vietnam in the 1960s and 1970s, and more recently committing Australian forces to Afghanistan and Iraq. Although the Australian Labor Party (ALP) has tended to place more emphasis on the role of multilateral institutions and the need for United Nations Security Council support for military actions, it has also recognized the importance of the US alliance for Australia's defence and strategic interests. Thus, while the ALP opposed the Howard government's decision to send troops to Iraq in 2003, at the same time it went to great pains to underline its ongoing support for the American alliance.

Anti-Americanism has been a tricky issue for the ALP. In his memoirs, Bob Hawke, former ALP leader and prime minister from 1983 to 1991, wrote of his struggles to shed the party of its ritual anti-Americanism. Indeed, Hawke believed that through the 1950s and 1960s, 'the tag of anti-Americanism had been one of the elements that kept the party from government' (Hawke 1994: 204–6). That Hawke was only partly successful in this became evident during the lead-up to the 2004 federal election, when ALP leader Mark Latham made a number of statements that were openly critical of George W. Bush's administration and its foreign policies. Among Latham's more memorable comments was his description of Bush as 'the most incompetent and dangerous president in living memory' (*Commonwealth of Australia Parliamentary Debates* 2003: 10926).

Latham's comments were designed in part to capitalize on growing domestic opposition to Australia's participation in the Iraq War. But instead they unleashed a storm in Australian politics. Within the ALP, some of Latham's colleagues feared that his anti-Americanism would rebound badly on the party and cause them to lose electoral support (Hywood 2004). Senior party figures sought to distance themselves from Latham's comments and Kim Beazley, former Defence Minister in the Hawke government and a strong and vocal supporter of the Australia–US relationship, was brought back into the shadow cabinet to help to counter the perception that the ALP was anti-American (Oakes 2004). But the damage had been done and the Howard government was able to capitalize on Latham's anti-Americanism to some effect. During the election campaign, government ministers hammered home the notion that the ALP was anti-American and that a Latham government could not be trusted to manage Australia's relations with the United States (Downer in *Commonwealth of Australia Parliamentary Debates* 2004; Abbott 2004). Such sentiments were parroted by many conservative commentators (Albrechtsen 2004; Sheridan 2004).

The Australia–US trade relationship

Australian governments of both stripes have generally sought to manage the domestic politics of the alliance to ensure that periodic bouts of anti-Americanism do not spill over into a more general questioning of the value of the security relationship. An important element of this has been the Australian government's ability to maintain a strong separation between the security and the trade relationships with the US. This has been especially important given the tendency of US trade policy to cause a great deal of difficulty for Australia. Indeed, the economic damage caused by US trade policies has led to frustration and hostility in Australia. Arguably, more than any other aspect of the relationship, it has been US trade policies that have fuelled anti-Americanism in Australia (Albinski 2001: 279; Ravenhill 2001: 249).

There are three fundamental and enduring aspects to Australia's trade relationship with the United States since World War II: asymmetry, imbalance, and the problem of US restrictions on many of Australia's most competitive exports. With respect to asymmetry, the problem is very simple: while the US is one of Australia's most important trade partners, Australia barely registers on its radar. Among US export markets, Australia ranks fourteenth, behind much smaller economies such as Hong Kong and Singapore (Office of the United States Trade Representative 2004a). Australia is even less significant as a source of imports for the US, ranking thirtieth in importance and accounting for a mere 0.5 per cent of US imports (Australia, Department of Foreign Affairs and Trade 2005). As John Ravenhill has observed: 'If power is all about who needs whom most, one need look no further than these figures to understand the essentials of the economic relationship' (Ravenhill 2001: 252–3).

This asymmetry contributes to a second constant – a chronic trade imbalance in favour of the United States, which had blown out to AUD\$12.7 billion in 2004 (Australia, Department of Foreign Affairs and Trade 2005). To be sure, in a multilateral trade system a trade imbalance between two countries does not constitute a problem in itself. And in Australia's case, its trade deficit with the US is offset by trade surpluses with many of its other trade partners in the western Pacific region. Nevertheless, public opinion leans towards a mercantilistic understanding of trade with notions of 'reciprocity' and 'fairness' informing a view that trade relationships should be reasonably balanced. Such a view is widely held among Americans and it was evident during the 1980s when the US adopted a range of aggressive measures to reduce its trade deficit with Japan. The same sort of thinking is prevalent now with respect to the ballooning US trade deficit with China. In a similar fashion, the persistence and magnitude of Australia's trade deficit with the US helps to explain some of the rancour that Australians feel towards American trade policy. This unhappiness is directed especially at very high levels of US agricultural protectionism and its 'unfair' trade policies that impede Australia's ability to expand its agricultural exports to the United States – a third constant in the trade relationship.

Indeed, one of the most vexing areas of the relationship – and of global trade more generally – is the problem of agricultural protectionism. The roots of the problem can be traced back to the 1940s when the Western democracies were negotiating new rules for the establishment of the post-war trade regime. At that time, the US championed the establishment of an open multilateral trade system based on the principles of non-discrimination and trade liberalisation. However, the US also insisted that the new trade rules would apply only to trade in manufactured goods – agricultural products were to be excluded.

The 'agriculture exception' was a severe blow to commodity-exporting countries such as Australia. While providing new rules for the liberalisation of trade in manufactured goods, the General Agreement on Tariffs and Trade (GATT) would do nothing to wind back the use of very high tariff and non-tariff barriers to agricultural trade, nor to curb the use of domestic and export subsidies that allowed the US and Europe to export their farm products well below world prices. Indeed, the resulting imbalance between the interests of industrialized countries and commodity producers in the post-war trade regime served to reinforce Australia's perspective that the US was intent on fossilizing the existing division of labour in favour of the industrialized countries of the northern hemisphere (Capling 2001).

These problems played themselves out in a number of ways between the 1940s and the 1980s, and they became a source of periodic but intense conflict in the bilateral relationship. Of course, the United States was not the only country to make life difficult for Australia's rural producers: European trade policies have been just as damaging to Australia – if not more so. However, it is the behaviour of the US that has been so perplexing and hurtful in the minds of Australians because of the view that allies should treat each other as friends. And at the same time that the two countries were working together to secure reform of agricultural trade during the 1980s, Washington and Canberra were involved in a bitter row over US subsidies for its agricultural exports.

In 1985 the Reagan administration initiated an aggressive programme to subsidise its wheat exports – the Export Enhancement Program (EEP). Although this was a retaliatory measure aimed at the European Community, the export subsidies had a dramatic 'sideswipe effect' on Australia, disrupting its wheat exports to the Soviet Union, China, the Middle East and South Asia and causing a decline in export earnings of nearly AUD$1 billion over two years (Fray 1989; Edwards 1989). Blithe assurances from Washington that the EEP was not aimed at Australia had little effect in Canberra. As Australian Trade Minister Michael Duffy noted at the time, 'If you get caught in the cross-fire, it hurts just as much as if the shot is aimed at you' (quoted in Grattan 1988).

The EEP caused enormous anger and frustration among rural constituencies and within the Hawke Labor government itself. Even the conservative opposition parties, which would normally be reluctant to criticize a Republican administration, expressed their strong condemnation of the US subsidy practices (Summers 1986). Australia's position was summed up by Foreign Minister Bill Hayden during a visit to the US for talks on the ANZUS alliance. These talks took place in August 1986 at a time when the US was suspending its alliance with New Zealand (as a result of Wellington's refusal to allow US nuclear submarines to access New Zealand ports), and was thus telling New Zealand that it was a 'friend' but no longer an 'ally'. Hayden noted that through its trade policies, which inflicted terrible damage on Australia, the US was telling Australia that it was 'an ally but not a friend' (quoted in Higgott 1989: 149).

The subsidy row reinforced Australian views about the hypocrisy of American trade policy that championed free trade – but only in areas where US producers were competitive. And it rebounded into Australian domestic politics as well: during this period the Labor government was driving an ambitious programme of economic reform that involved dramatic trade liberalization and painful industry adjustment. American trade policies provided plenty of ammunition for the ALP's critics who demanded to know why Australia should try to 'level the playing field' when countries like the US did not play fair themselves. But perhaps the most damaging aspect of this dispute was the way in which it heightened perceptions of the asymmetry in the bilateral relationship and Australia's lack of influence in Washington, as was evident in its inability to secure any from the EEP or from other aspects of American agricultural protectionism.

This sense of powerlessness fuelled a robust public debate about whether the bilateral defence relationship should be used as a bargaining chip to secure improvements in the trade relationship. Within the ALP government, Treasurer Paul Keating, Foreign Minister Bill Hayden and Trade Minister Michael Duffy each raised the prospect of using US defence installations in Australia[3] as a bargaining chip in trade negotiations (Shires and Sargent 1986; Dunn 1987). While the prime minister was quick to hose down such suggestions, declaring that the joint facilities were inviolable, he did warn the Americans that other aspects of the relationship should not be taken for granted. In a special address to the US Congress in June 1988, Hawke told the Americans: 'Australians must not be given reason to believe that while we are first-class allies, we are, in trade, second-class friends. Trade issues must not be allowed to fester, or to erode our wider friendships or alliance' (Hawke 1994: 425–6).

During the subsidy war, the opposition parties distanced themselves from any suggestion that the defence relationship could be used to leverage the trade relationship. However, when confronting the same frustrations from the government benches a decade later, they found themselves invoking precisely the same linkage (Kelton 2004: 76–9). This was rhetoric borne of deep frustration and anger, but at no time have Australian governments of either political complexion made good on these suggestions. Indeed, they have been strongly of the view of the need to quarantine the military alliance with the United States in order to prevent Australian anger at US trade policies from undermining the security relationship. Such a view has been widely shared among Australia's trade, foreign policy and defence experts as well (Bell 1991; Tow 2001; Kunkel 2002; Wood 2002).

This also reflected Washington's own preference for keeping trade and defence interests in separate boxes. However, the Republican victory in the presidential elections of 2000 heralded significant change in US trade and foreign policy. The first substantial change related to a shift in emphasis away from non-discrimination and the multilateral trade system in favour of discriminatory, bilateral trade agreements (which are more commonly known as free trade agreements (FTAs)).

The second major shift, prompted by the 11 September 2001 attacks, was the decision by the Bush administration to use trade policy in the pursuit of other foreign policy objectives, such as the securing of allies in the 'war on terror'. This new approach to trade policy envisioned the use of free trade agreements as instruments that combined economic, political and strategic objectives which had hitherto been kept separate. Trade agreements were seen as part of a strategy to shore up security relations and alliances. And they came with clear expectations on Washington's part: US Trade Representative Robert Zoellick (2003) declared that any country seeking a free trade agreement with the US must also offer its co-operation 'or better – on foreign policy and security issues'.

The Australia–US Free Trade Agreement

The Bush–Zoellick policy of using FTAs in the pursuit of broader foreign policy and strategic interests aligned closely with the Howard government's desire to shore up Australia's relations with the US which, by the late 1990s, were in considerable disrepair. There were significant problems on a number of fronts. In the trade relationship, the Howard government had become increasingly concerned about the blow-out in Australia's chronic trade imbalance with the US. The burgeoning trade deficit served to reinforce Australia's long-standing complaints about US barriers to its exports and it was exacerbated by a number of protectionist measures undertaken by the Clinton administration, the most notable of which involved the imposition of US import restrictions on Australian and New Zealand lamb in 1999. Australia and New Zealand took their case to the World Trade Organization (WTO), which subsequently ruled in their favour. Although the Australian lamb industry suffered no lasting damage as a result of the dispute, the US had once again behaved as a bully and a hypocrite in the eyes of Australians (Capling 2001: 176–7).

While the lamb dispute had soured the trade relationship, the events surrounding the East Timor crisis created deep strains in the security relationship. One of Australia's roles in ANZUS is to act as a window into Southeast Asia and especially to 'interpret Indonesia' for US intelligence. However, the Howard government mangled this task badly in the events leading up to Timor's referendum on independence in September 1999. In the months preceding the ballot, Australia held back important intelligence material from Washington (an event that contributed to the suicide of an Australian diplomat, Merv Jenkins) and rejected US interest in playing a greater role in the referendum process. The US was subsequently highly critical of Australia's failure to keep Washington fully informed in the lead-up to the referendum and its logistical and diplomatic responses to the violence that followed (Shanahan 1999).

The souring of the relationship led the Howard government to consider ways of lifting Australia's profile in Washington and repairing the damage. The Bush–Zoellick strategy of combining economic, security and foreign policy objectives in the form of free trade agreements closely aligned with Howard's own policy preferences for bilateral trade agreements and closer relations with the United

States. Hence, the Howard government's decision to pursue a free trade agreement with the United States.

Bilateral trade agreements have become politically attractive in Washington for a couple of reasons. First, they are relatively quick to negotiate, especially when compared to the glacial pace of multilateral negotiations within the WTO. Better still, bilateral trade agreements enable the US to achieve many of its own trade and investment objectives without suffering much domestic political pain; as the dominant partner in a bilateral negotiation, the United States has found it very easy to dodge awkward demands for the liberalization of its own highly protected sectors. And this was very much the case when it came to the negotiation of an FTA with Australia.

A comparison of each government's account of the agreement revealed what Australia's trade experts had predicted: the deal was heavily lopsided in favour of the US. According to the office of the US Trade Representative (USTR), most of Washington's objectives had been achieved (Office of the USTR 2004b). All US agricultural exports and 99 per cent of its manufactured exports to Australia would be admitted duty-free. By contrast, the deal was 'sensitive to concerns that have been expressed by some members of Congress and some US farm sectors', which meant minimal liberalization of barriers against Australian beef and dairy products, and no change at all in Australia's sugar quota.

The USTR noted major achievements in other areas, especially in respect to many aspects of Australia's domestic regulatory framework. For instance, US drug companies would benefit from changes to the Pharmaceutical Benefit Scheme. The US film and television industry would gain from 'important and unprecedented provisions to improve market access' in new media formats (for more on state support to the US film industry, see Miller's chapter in this volume). Australia would further strengthen its intellectual property rules, adopting US standards in areas such as copyright. American services suppliers would be accorded 'substantial access' to the Australian market, and American companies would have the right to bid for Australian government contracts. And henceforth, American investment in Australia would be completely exempted from screening by the Foreign Investment Review Board.

In contrast to the USTR's announcement, the Australian government was decidedly more subdued in its statements. Naturally the prime minister praised the agreement as a 'once-in-a-generation opportunity' that linked Australia to the 'biggest economy in the world' (quoted in Allard and Wilkinson 2004). But his words masked considerable dismay and disappointment within the government, as the agreement has fallen well short of Australia's expectations. In a candid moment, Trade Minister Mark Vaile admitted that the deal was 'a disappointment', and suggested that its benefits would be measured in millions, rather than billions, of dollars.[4]

The biggest disappointment related to agriculture. Throughout the negotiation, the Howard government had emphasized the importance of getting a good deal for Australian farmers. A bilateral trade deal could not address the worst barriers and distortions in the US agricultural sector – that is, the billions of dollars of domestic and export subsidies that prop up farmers each year. Nonetheless Canberra expected to secure substantial improvements in Australia's access to the US domestic market for sugar and beef. In the words of Foreign Minister Alexander Downer, a deal without free trade in farm products would be unacceptable (quoted in Eccleston 2001) – a point underlined by deputy Prime Minister John Anderson, who declared that it would be 'un-Australian' to accept a deal without sugar (quoted in American Broadcasting Company (ABC) News Online Report 2004). As it turned out, the provisions for beef were disappointing, sugar was excluded completely, and the cuts to agricultural tariffs achieved in the Australia–US agreement were slower and smaller than those in the free trade agreements that the US has with seven other countries, including other significant agricultural producers such as Canada (Allard and Wilkinson 2004).

While the business lobby that pushed for the agreement endorsed it, many other Australian companies and business organizations were more muted in their support, seeing only modest benefits in the agreement. And for many Australians, the benefits to the business community were dwarfed by the costs of the agreement to Australia's social programmes and to its capacity to regulate in areas such as culture and health. For instance, there was widespread criticism of the inclusion of the Pharmaceutical Benefit Scheme in the agreement, with medical professional associations, research institutions, non-government organizations and independent experts all raising concerns about the impact of Australia–United States Free Trade Agreement (AUSFTA) on drug affordability in Australia (Capling 2005). A year after the dust had settled, only 34 per cent of Australians thought the AUSFTA would be good for Australia (Lowy Institute 2005: 21).

The poor outcomes in the FTA reinforced the perception that Australians are viewed by the United States as 'allies but not friends'. This has become especially problematic given the way that both the Australian and US governments have sought to intertwine the trade and security relationships in recent times. After 11 September 2001, both governments explicitly framed the quest for a trade agreement in the context of the strengthening the alliance more generally (Downer 2002; Zoellick 2002; Vaile quoted in Colebatch and Wilkinson 2004).

This new linking of trade and security runs counter to a cardinal rule of Australian foreign policy that trade and security interests should remain separate. An important part of managing the Australia–US alliance has been keeping a strong separation between the defence relationship and the economic/trade relationship, and this has been especially important given US trade policy and its tendency to cause a great deal of difficulty for Australia. However, by explicitly linking trade and security concerns in the context of the FTA, the Howard government may have unintentionally created a situation in which the anti-American sentiment that is generated by trade conflicts could spill over into the alliance (Garnaut 2002).

The political consequences of Australian anti-Americanism

Anti-Americanism is typically regarded as a problem for the US. But globalization means that many of the problems that confront the United States can only be managed or resolved through close co-operation with other governments. And, while American military and economic power is unrivalled, even hegemonic powers need allies and friends. In that sense, anti-Americanism is also a problem for the allies and friends of the United States, including Australia. Indeed, it could be argued that anti-Americanism in Australia poses as great a challenge for the Australian government as it does for the US, especially to the extent that it has the potential to erode public support for the alliance.

This chapter has argued that an important element of alliance management has been the quarantining of the trade matters from other aspects of the Australia–US relationship. This has been especially important given the propensity for US trade policy to damage Australia's economic interests, thus generating considerable anti-Americanism. But the Australia–US trade agreement and the unprecedented linking of trade and security interests could yet produce unexpected consequences. When future trade conflicts occur – as they most surely will – it will be far more difficult to isolate them from the security relationship. Thus anti-Americanism in the trade arena could, for the first time, have the potential to weaken Australian support for the alliance itself.

Notes

1 In her analysis of the crisis in Australian–American strategic relationship during this period, Coral Bell (1994) concludes that the dismissal was the result of domestic political issues, not foreign intervention. However, she also notes that the former Head of the CIA, William Colby, included Australia, alongside Chile and Vietnam, on his list of 'crisis areas' in the 1972–75, leaving the door slightly ajar to the possibility of CIA involvement.

2 Costello's speech reported in 'Taking Issue with Growing Anti-American Attitudes', *The Australian*, 22 August 2005.

3 The US bases in Australia were at Nurrungar in South Australia, North-West Cape in Western Australia and Pine Gap in the Northern Territory. Of these, only Pine Gap remains operational today.

4 It is impossible to predict with any certainty the potential economic costs and benefits of the agreement, as was evident in the results of economic modelling exercises done after the deal was completed. The government-commissioned study, by the Centre for International Economics (2004), predicted gains to Australia of AUD$6 billion a year but economists and trade experts were highly critical of this study and its assumptions. A second study (Dee 2004), commissioned by the Australian Senate inquiry into the trade agreement, predicted annual gains to Australia in the realm of about AUD$53 million a year, much closer to Vaile's initial estimations.

11 Anti-Americanism and Regionalism in East Asia

Heribert Dieter

The past decade has been characterised by tremendous change in Asia in general and in East Asia in particular. Probably no other phase since World War II has seen so many fundamental transformations in the region: the decline of Japan as the most dynamic economy in the region; the emergence of China as a leader and an economic centre of gravity; and the unforeseen Asian crisis, with its severe impact on both the economic and the political systems in the region. In recent years, a tendency towards closer economic integration in East Asia and an increasing unwillingness of Asian leaders to follow the leadership of the US has been observed. What is the relationship of these developments? Is East Asian regionalism being driven by anti-Americanism or are other forces at work?

First, the meaning of 'anti-Americanism' has to be defined. What does that term stand for? Anti-Americanism does not signify the universal rejection of values that are universal to Western societies, including the United States. These are the importance of civil liberties, human rights, the acceptance of a capitalist mode of production, as well as democracy as the only accepted form of political organization. In East Asia, there certainly is no uniform position on those general issues. The Chinese government has a different approach than, say, the South Korean government. However, there is no fundamental divergence of positions between East Asian governments and the US. There are different emphases; the US stresses individual liberties, whereas East Asian governments put greater stress on the economic and social rights of citizens. But in some aspects, the gap between Europe on the one hand and East Asia and America on the other is greater than that between Asia and the West. The death penalty is the prime example; in the European Union, the death penalty is no longer applied, while countries like China and the US continue to use this archaic form of punishment. Out of those 80 countries that have officially abandoned the death penalty, not a single East Asian country can be counted but most European countries can. Consequently, it seems fair to say that with regard to human rights, one cannot identify a fundamental divergence between East Asia and the US.

The mode of production is similarly not fundamentally divergent in the economies of Asia and the US. By and large, all of these economies are characterized by private ownership of the means of production. One could argue that this is not the case for some sectors of the Chinese and Vietnamese economies, but rapid change in these countries is bringing them into convergence with partners of the Organisation for Economic Co-operation and Development (OECD). Again, the differences between some countries in the West are as significant as those between East Asia and the US. The influence of 'economic guidance' is greater in East Asia, but even there it is decreasing and these changes do not permit the establishment of a fundamental rift that results in anti-American attitudes.

So what about cultural values and religion? Here, two things should be considered. First, in many East Asian countries religion does not play a prominent role in the political arena. Unlike the US, there is no significant religious force in any major East Asian country that displays a strong aspiration for influence. At the risk of generalization, religion in Asia appears to be much more of a private affair than in America, where the attendance of Sunday masses is far greater than in most other OECD countries. In the US, 44 per cent of the population went to church at least once a week in the late 1990s. The Philippines – a former Spanish and subsequently American colony – shows greater church attendance, but other countries in the region show a much more limited influence of churches: only 3 per cent of the Japanese, 9 per cent of the Chinese and 14 per cent of the South Korean population go to church at least once a month.[1] Religious beliefs, therefore, can hardly be the source of anti-American feelings in Asia.

Second, American culture continues to be popular throughout East Asia. Whether music or film, there is very limited rejection of these expressions of American culture. The two American icons of the food industry, McDonald's and Coca Cola, similarly continue to be popular throughout the region.

Having looked at the important issues of human rights, the economic regime as well as religion and culture, it appears difficult to identify an area in which anti-American feelings are fuelled in East Asia. At the same time, one cannot overlook a tendency of reduced attractiveness of the US as both an economic model as well as a coalition partner. But the source of these significantly more critical approaches to the US are not to be found in anti-American feelings. Rather, American foreign policy, including foreign economic policy, has been the cause of this development. The US has drifted away from its traditional allies in East Asia, not the other way round. American policies have caused great irritation and frustration in East Asia, and the reaction to these policies is driving regionalism. East Asia is looking to its own abilities and resources because American policy has forced them to do so. Regionalism in East Asia is externally induced, but the driving factors have been policies of the Clinton and Bush administrations, not a general disdain for America.

This chapter looks at the externally and internally induced drivers of Asian regionalism in turn. In the next section, the Asian crisis and its legacy will be examined. Another reason for Asian regionalism is the declining attractiveness of the American economy, which will be analysed in section three, followed by the study of the new role of China for and in the region. In section five I shall look at the unfortunate diplomacy of George W. Bush. The last section will contain a description of the steps taken towards regionalism in Asia, with regard to both trade and to finance.

The lasting legacy of the Asian crisis

The Asian crisis was a turning point for regionalism in East Asia. That crisis was not limited to one economy but affected an entire region. Furthermore, there were virtually no warnings of it. Both this inability to forecast and the dimension of the biggest economic crisis since World War II have caused concern. Considering the enormous influence that the International Monetary Fund (IMF) had, and taking into account the severe mistakes of the IMF in the recent financial crises, it is no surprise that many observers are asking for a substantial improvement of the Fund's performance. Perhaps the most serious addition to the choir of IMF-critics is Joseph Stiglitz, who published vitriolic attacks on the work of the Fund (Stiglitz 2000, 2001, 2002a).[2]

There are several reasons for criticizing the Fund; the economic consequences of the IMF's work are too frequently negative. In particular, in the Asian crisis the Fund has probably done more harm than good. Instead of helping to overcome the crisis, the IMF in fact deepened it (see Dieter 1998; Stiglitz 2002a). The insistence of the IMF on austerity measures, especially the tightening of fiscal and monetary policy, was ill-designed for the affected Asian economies. The Fund simply used the recipes of the 1980s for the 1990s, and the results were intolerable. Indonesia, a country which had enjoyed remarkable economic growth since the early 1970s, is still suffering from the IMF-designed crisis management. The Fund's dogmatic condemnation of capital controls made an alternative crisis management impossible. Malaysia's strategy – using temporary capital controls – has worked remarkably well: by fixing the exchange rate and lowering inter rates, both investment and consumption levels in Malaysia quickly recovered (Kaplan and Rodrik 2000).

Although the IMF had been criticizing governments in developing countries for the lack of transparency in their economies, the Fund itself was characterized by an extreme lack of transparency during the Asian crisis. The IMF was a 'secretive institution', according to Jeffrey Sachs (1997). The agreements of the Fund with its member countries were not published. The decision-making processes were obscure. Discussions in the executive board were also not published.

Furthermore, the interests of creditors dominated the work of the Fund. The main purpose of IMF programmes was to ensure repayment of loans and bonds (Stiglitz 2001: 14). The IMF has been a creditor cartel that did not give enough consideration to the needs of its weaker and less powerful member countries. The conditionality of the Fund's programmes was excessive. The countries hit by a financial crisis had to implement too many and too detailed conditions. The former Managing Director of the IMF, Horst Köhler, has taken a very critical position on conditionality.[3] Whether his successors will take a similar position remains to be seen.

Following some intensive debate after the Asian crisis, the discussion today is somewhat less polarized. Very few observers now ask for the closure of the Fund. Also the other extreme, the creation of some sort of a global central bank, is not often proposed any more. There has been significant progress with regard to the IMF's transparency; today both the Fund's programmes as well as its internal discussions can be followed on its homepage. However, as the heated discussion following the publication of one Joseph Stiglitz' books shows, there are still enough issues that need further analysis and there is much room for improvement in the work of the Fund.[4]

The events in 1997 and 1998 have contributed to the evolution of a new type of regionalism in Asia. The existing regional integration projects of the ASEAN Free Trade Area (AFTA) and Asia–Pacific Economic Co-operation (APEC) have had a diminished role in this period. Indeed, the limits of the Association of Southeast Asian Nations (ASEAN) underlined the inability of conventional, trade-based integration systems to avoid the emergence of financial crises and to limit their intensity. Although ASEAN is one of the oldest regional integration projects, and was in operation for three decades, it had nothing to offer in 1997. Neither liquidity nor even good advice were provided. Instead, two ASEAN countries, Thailand and Indonesia, had to call the IMF to the rescue. ASEAN emerged damaged from the crisis and its vision – the establishment of a free trade area and the continuation of its low-key approach to regional integration – looked problematic. Although regional policy-makers would not state it, it seems in many quarters that the benefits from this type of inter-governmental regionalism are deemed too limited to warrant other than minimum effort. Successful exporters to world markets can expect very few advantages from the creation of a free trade area in their region.

If more effective crisis management might have been expected from APEC, such expectations were disappointed. The failure of APEC to provide any meaningful response to the biggest economic crisis in the Asia–Pacific region since 1945 made this project seem less important, if not irrelevant, for many Asian members. The two APEC Summits which could have proposed solutions to the crisis – the 1997 meeting in Vancouver and the 1998 meeting in Kuala Lumpur – were unable to provide even the hint of an alternative rescue package for the affected countries.

The legacy of the Asian crisis for Asian countries therefore is threefold. First, Asian countries have no desire to return to the IMF in the event of a repetition of a financial crisis. This is mainly so because the Clinton administration forced the IMF to implement policies which were good for the American financial sector but bad for Asian recipients. Second, the Asian crisis has shown that weak institutions have no role to play in the event of a crisis. Therefore, the search for improved co-operation is accompanied by the willingness to engage in a process which will require the partial loss of sovereignty. Unlike before the crisis, Asian countries have learnt that non-co-operation can result in greater loss of sovereignty than co-operation. Third, many Asian governments have lost confidence in their partnership with the US. Since Washington exploited the situation rather than providing help, Asian governments have developed wariness towards dependence on America. Beyond that, the US is becoming less attractive with regard to its own economic performance.

The declining attractiveness of the American economy

In the 1990s, many observers were assuming that the American economy had finally returned to its earlier strengths and had once again become the world's leading economic power. This, however, was a misreading of the economic development in the US. Although America did enjoy a remarkable economic boom, the important point is that the foundations of that economic miracle have been rather wobbly. At the beginning of the twenty-first century, the American economy is characterized by the aftermath of the greatest speculative bubble in the stock exchange, an equally unsustainable boom in the property market, high and rapidly rising foreign debt, and high indebtedness of private households as well as of the government. These imbalances will have to be corrected at same stage, as Robert Gilpin pointed out:

> America's unprecedented good economic fortune will one day run out, and when it does, the United States must confront its low personal savings rate, deteriorating education system, and accumulated foreign debt, and it must adjust to a rapidly changing global economy characterised by intensifying competition, exclusive regional arrangements, and an unsustainable financial system. (Gilpin 2000: 7)

For many observers the boom of the 1990s was quite a surprising development. In the early years of that decade, few Americans were as confident in their economy as they were towards the end. The memory of the crash in the stock exchange of 1987 was still quite alive, and the country slid into recession in 1991. Furthermore, many Americans were concerned about the lack of competitiveness of their companies. Both Japanese and European companies seemed to be so much better and more efficient producers. Some authors were concerned about the growing rift between rich and poor in Ronald Reagan's America of the 1980s (Davis 1986). America seemed to be destined to lose its hegemonic position in the international system (Kennedy 1989).

The event that changed the American perception was the first Gulf War, which began on 16 January 1991. That military operation was the largest since the Vietnam War, and this time it was a successful operation. Increasingly, Americans noted the economic difficulties of their competitors, in particular the inability of the Japanese to overcome their economic problems. The crisis of the Asian economies in 1997 swept away any remaining doubt on the supremacy of the American economic model.

Unfortunately, the boom of the 1990s was as much the result of psychological factors at play as it was the result of productivity improvements and other factors. Consequently, a hard landing continues to be a distinct possibility for America, with severe repercussions for the global economy. The American economy slowed down significantly after 2000 (OECD 2004). This is not surprising after a long phase of high growth. What is remarkable, however, is that the account deficit continued to rise despite slower growth. Two factors are primarily responsible for that. First, the Bush administration turned budget surpluses into significant budget deficits. Second, the American consumer continued to indulge in a spending spree and thereby functioned as the global economy's consumer of last resort. These two factors, combined with the extremely low savings rate in America, resulted in the need to import capital on a large scale. The US also benefited from financial crisis in Asia and Latin America: capital was searching for investment opportunities, and America seemed attractive (Altvater and Mahnkopf 2002: 227).

The United States encouraged these inflows with a specific tax policy; since 1984, foreigners do not have to pay taxes on interest earned in the US. The unequal treatment of American nationals, who pay tax on interest earned, and foreigners, is an unfair tax regime for the countries were the capital originates (see Williamson *et al.* 2003: 10). It encourages tax evasion in developing economies and is an obstacle to the development of financial markets in these countries. This does not provide (potentially useful) tax competition either, because Americans are having to pay these taxes.[5]

It is important to understand that the decisions of foreigners contribute to the stability of the American economy. First, capital inflows – both foreign direct investment and portfolio inflows – can be the source of current account deficits. Second, whatever the cause, persistent inflows increase the vulnerability of an economy, because those holding claims will one day ask for a return on their capital, reduce their engagement and thereby force the capital-importing economy to adjust. The experience of many countries throughout the twentieth century has shown that it is difficult to say what precise level of capital inflows is unsustainable but, as a rule of thumb, inflows of around 5 per cent of gross domestic product (GDP) cannot be sustained for longer periods of time without a financial crisis (Hesse 1990: 45f).

Today, America's ever-increasing appetite for capital is threatening not only the well-being of the American economy but also that of the global economy. These fears are expressed not only by academic observers, but also by a former finance minister and former president of Harvard University. Larry Summers points out the rising risks:

> Globalization has been a boon to the US economy, but America's spending addiction now threatens to undermine that virtuous global economic circle. The country that is now more economically central than is has been in decades is borrowing more than any other country in the world ... Unless it is brought under control, the US savings crisis will soon be the world's problem. (L. Summers 2004: 47)

The current account clearly demonstrates the change in the American balance of payments in the last decade or so. In 1991, the United States recorded for the last time a surplus in the current account. Even that was not a genuine surplus, but rather the result of high transfer payments by Germany, Japan and Saudi Arabia to finance the cost of the first Gulf War.[6] Ever since, the American current account deficit has been growing. It was relatively modest until 1997, but thereafter the import of capital grew exponentially (OECD 2004).

There is a correlation between the rising current account deficit and the declining savings rate in America. A current account deficit occurs when an economy spends more than it saves. The difference is the balance on capital account, i.e. an inflow of capital. A surplus of spending over saving can happen for a number of reasons: purchases of imports, investment in infrastructure or companies, but also because of a government deficit. The analysis of current account crises in other countries clearly shows that a decisive factor is the use of the capital that flows into an economy. If that capital inflow is used for investment in factors that produce goods which are sold on world markets, then current account deficits are less worrying. If, however, capital inflows are used to finance consumption or non-productive investment, for instance in real estate, then a current account deficit is less acceptable.

In the US, both the composition of capital inflows and the type of investors have changed in the past few years. Up to 2001, foreign direct investment – the least volatile type of capital inflows – dominated. However, due to relatively low real returns in the US, inflows for foreign direct investment (FDI) shrank. Whereas in 2001 America recorded FDI inflows of US$144 billion, one year later that figure dropped to a mere US$30 billion. In 2002, Germany attracted more FDI than the US. Even the Netherlands – with US$29 billion – attracted almost as much FDI as did America.[7] Since 2002 this trend has increased. Between July 2003 and June 2004 the balance of FDI was around US$150 billion. Americans invested much more abroad than did foreigners in the US. This is not surprising; *The Economist* has pointed out that FDI in America is not attractive. In the first quarter of 2004, FDI in America generated an average return of 5.5 per cent, compared to a return of 11.7 per cent for American FDI abroad.[8]

This leads to the question of the composition of capital inflows. Who lends to America? Since foreign direct investment has ceased to be an important source of capital inflows, portfolio inflows have replaced them. Today Asian governments or their central banks are accumulating claims on America. Asian countries today hold around US$4000 billion in foreign reserves, most of them in US dollars. In principle, the capital flows to America can be characterized as suppliers' credit: Japan and China buy American Treasury bonds, and American consumers use the borrowed money to buy Asian products.

This is surprising; a country that puts such effort into being independent from other countries in security affairs needs the continuing goodwill of the Chinese and other Asian governments if it wants to avoid a sudden shock. It is odd to realize that the self-declared world's greatest power is also the world's greatest debtor. Those countries which hold such large claims on America have quite a powerful tool in their accounts; they can wreck American financial markets at the click of a mouse. Surely they have no obvious incentive to do so. But if they wanted, they could dump their holdings of American treasuries on financial markets, which would probably cause a crash there; in the absence of buyers, interest rates would skyrocket. It is a new form of mutually assured destruction that has quietly emerged over the last few years (L. Summers 2004: 48).

Larry Summers has pointed out that Americans should be uncomfortable because foreign governments hold high claims on America. And it is not difficult to construct an unpleasant situation for Washington. Let's assume that there might one day be a severe conflict between China and America over the Taiwan issue. The island's government could be tempted to formally declare independence, which would almost inevitably result in military action from the mainland Chinese. An American government intending to intervene could be blackmailed by Beijing; any help for Taiwan would result in the dumping of Chinese reserves. And China is not Japan; it neither has American troops on its territory nor does it have that specific, asymmetric relationship that has characterized American–Japanese relations since 1945. China needs no books to demonstrate that it can say no.[9] The bottom line is clear; Asia policy-makers have observed that the American economy is in decline. This makes America less attractive as a partner, while increasing the appeal of co-operation in the region. The key here is the remarkable return of China to the centre stage.

The rising power: China as a hub for regionalism in East Asia

During the last decade, China has become much more attractive as a partner for its neighbours. In November 2004, ASEAN countries and China agreed on the establishment of a free trade agreement until 2010. This development would have been inconceivable before the Asian crisis, let alone in the 1980s or early 1990s. China today is no longer predominantly perceived as a threat, but rather as an opportunity by many of its neighbouring countries.

China is providing the region with a vision of a future in harmony and prosperity, a role traditionally played by America. But George W. Bush's fight against terror has resulted in the perception that the future will not be bright and prosperous. Compare that with China; President Hu travels through the Asia–Pacific region and – in stark contrast to the past – is giving press conferences that are characterized by charm and joy. Although the leadership in Beijing is too smart to challenge the US militarily, it does challenge America's leadership in the economic, political and psychological arena.

While the US wanted to play the role as a hub for regionalism, China is the country that is achieving this goal (see below, the section titled: Steps towards regionalism in Asia). The US has not yet successfully concluded an FTA with any major player in the region apart from Singapore, while China already has an FTA with Thailand and the agreement with ASEAN. US Senator Max Baucus has publicly expressed concern about America's exclusion from integration processes in Asia and has termed the US trade policy *vis-à-vis* Asia as foolish (Baucus 2004).

In the early twenty-first century, China is returning to the centre stage. Two hundred years earlier, China was contributing one-third to global GDP, a percentage that shrank to 5 per cent in 1978. In 2002, calculated with purchasing power parities, China had become the world's second largest economy and was contributing 12 per cent to global GDP (*Financial Times* 2003). Within the foreseeable future, i.e. the next 20 years, China will become the world's largest economy, overtaking

Japan and perhaps the US as well. Without doubt, the continuation of the growth experience of the past two decades will be difficult. But so far China has mastered quite a few difficult junctures, so there is no need to be overly pessimistic on China's account.

The weak financial sector in China has to be seen in the context of extremely high foreign reserves of over US$1500 billion, and the trade policy is significantly more appealing to the neighbouring countries than that of the competing regional power, Japan. In 2003, China imported for the first time more than Japan. Imports represent 30 per cent of China's GDP, but only 8 per cent of Japan's. Whereas Japan has frequently tried to portray itself as the region's leading country, it has not done much to increase its attractiveness. By contrast, China has been successfully creating a network of mutual dependencies. It imports from and exports to the region, and this creates increasingly robust political ties. China's neighbours today are no longer hedging their bets against China, rather they are hedging with China. Although it is true to say that the actual economic might of China is still smaller than that of Japan, perception matters; as China rises, so Japan and America decline.

The influence of George W. Bush's non-diplomacy on Asian regionalism

The post-World War II order was widely accepted as being functionally necessary and ideologically legitimate, at least by the major allies of the US, as well as by those in Asia – namely Japan, South Korea, Thailand and the Philippines. However, the events of the early twenty-first century have demonstrated that there are plainly limits to even the US's capacity to impose itself militarily and a preoccupation with material or strategic assets. In recent years, US diplomacy towards Asia has been unfortunate, to say the least. Washington has continued to emphasize bilateral security treaties with a range of countries in Asia, but this has not enabled them to solve problems such as the nuclear threat originating from North Korea, the tension between China and Taiwan, or Islamist terrorism in parts of Southeast Asia. George W. Bush's administration has yet to present a coherent strategy to address several new developments in the region, some of which have been outlined in the previous sections.

After George W. Bush's first term in office, Washington was isolated in Asia in unprecedented ways, as Francis Fukuyama pointed out (*International Herald Tribune* 2004). At the moment, the US has chosen to take an obstructionist role towards Asian regionalism, but that leads to both a loss of American influence on the shape of regionalism in Asia as well as a strengthening of the supporters of regionalism in Asia. Again, there is no anti-Americanism at work, but rather opposition against American policies.

It was the administration of George W. Bush's father, George H. W. Bush, that opposed the first attempt to create an Asian regional integration project, the 'East Asian Economic Caucus', suggested by Malaysia's then Prime Minister Mahathir Mohamad in 1990. America was successful in halting that initiative, as it was seven years later when Japan suggested the creation of an Asian Monetary Fund, in September 1997. The trouble is that America was much less successful in constructing an integration process in East Asia that would give America a seat at the table.

The forum to consider is APEC. When it was started in 1989, APEC had the potential to create a community that included all important players of Southeast and East Asia as well as the US. But again, Washington preferred to obstruct the integration process by insisting on enlargement of APEC to include – which was probably was the single biggest problem – the Russian Federation. By doing that, Washington achieved a short-term political goal – the hindrance of an Asian integration project – but paid a price for it; in the long term, the integration will take place without America. Today, the message is nicely summed up by *The Economist*: 'Yankee stay home'. However, that attitude is the consequence of bad American policies, not of hostility towards the American nation or values.[10]

To the contrary; it is not Asian nationalism that drives Asian regionalism, but rather the assessment by Asian policy-makers that the US approach to foreign policy is undergoing a structural change. Nationalism is now a much stronger and little understood factor underwriting US policy in the contemporary era. It is so powerful that it actually competes with, indeed seems to over-rule, the liberal reading of hegemony in US foreign policy. As Lieven noted:

> Nationalism risks undermining precisely those American values that make America most admired in the world, and that in the end provide both a pillar for present American global power and the assurance that future ages will look back on America as a benign and positive leader of humanity. (Lieven 2004b)

The point made here is that the roots of contemporary American foreign policy are national. Indeed, the country's foreign policy has always been mediated by American domestic interests and priorities, rather than simply reflecting the logic of the international system itself. It is certainly important to acknowledge that scholars working in a traditional realist framework have some important insights to offer, especially given the desire and willingness of George W. Bush's administration to employ its material assets in pursuit of unilaterally defined goals. However, this sort of analysis cannot capture the complexity of either the domestic influences on foreign policy, or the wider international environment within which it unfolds.

The policy of George W. Bush, characterized by his go-it-alone attitude, is worrying staunch allies of the US such as Japan and South Korea. Politicians in both countries claim that confidence has been severely damaged in recent years. Bush's policies are perceived as lacking consideration for the specific historic context in East Asia. For instance, Bush's undercutting of South Korea's 'sunshine policy' towards the North of the country is not well understood in Korea[11] (*International Herald Tribune* 2002). The inability or unwillingness of Washington to explain the motives for its foreign policy causes resentment. After all, branding North Korea as a member of the 'axis of evil' is not helping South Korea, which finds itself once again in the frontline – this time in the fight not against communism but against evil itself.

Steps towards regionalism in Asia

Today, East Asia places a greater stress on multilateral and regional co-operation than at any other moment of history since World War II, although here, too, there may be a marked disconnect between theory and rhetoric on the one hand and application and practice in the region on the other. But we live in an era of the 'new regionalism' in East Asia that has progressed apace since the financial crises of the latter part of the 1990s.

The key elements of the new regionalism have been enhanced regional economic dialogue and interaction, both among the states of Northeast Asia (China, Japan and South Korea) and between these states and the states of Southeast Asia through the development of the ASEAN + Three process. In 2003, trade between the Northeast Asian states grew by nearly one-third. At US$224.5 billion, the region provided 15 per cent of total world exports and 20 per cent of global GDP (*Financial Times* 2004). To be sure, and notwithstanding such growth, the regional co-operative dialogues remain rudimentary when contrasted with the level of integration to be found in Europe, but these dialogues have been spurred on in the last decade by the perceived limitations of the multilateral system and the changing relationships of the major regional actors to the US.

For example, the active dialogues on regional monetary co-operation, post the 2001 Chiang Mai agreement, developed out of a growing disillusion with the role of the IMF and US policy during, and since, the financial crises of the closing years of the twentieth century (Dieter and Higgott 2003). The renewed interest in regional trade arrangements – especially the purposeful development of AFTA, the ASEAN–China FTA proposal and other FTA discussions (beyond the spate of bilaterals with the US) – have been spurred on, in part at least, by the limitations of the World Trade Organization (Dieter 2003).

Asian countries today are the most active players with regard to the creation of bilateral and multilateral trade agreements. In contrast to the 1990s, when very few countries from Asia engaged in bilateralism, in the twenty-first century Asia is seeking bilateral trade agreements. Again, there is no evidence that anti-Americanism is the driving force for those developments. Rather, the fear of being excluded in the event of a collapse of the global trade regime appears to be the most important factor.

Monetary regionalism

By the end of 1999, when the worst impact of the Asian crisis was over, East Asian policy circles once again addressed the topic of more intensive regional monetary co-operation. The regular ASEAN Summits were expanded by the participation of Japan, China and South Korea, the new body being called ASEAN + Three (or APT). Since then, some steps in the search for a new monetary regionalism have been undertaken. In December 1997, the first 'East Asian Summit' took place in Kuala Lumpur. Not surprisingly, monetary issues were discussed (Rüland 2000: 433).

Second, during the APT meeting in Manila in November 1999, the scope for regionalism in Southeast and East Asia was discussed. The summit chair, then Philippines President Joseph Estrada, told the news media that the goals were a common market, monetary union and an East Asian Community. In addition, increasing numbers of Japanese observers advocate monetary co-operation in Asia. Eisuke Sakakibara, former State Secretary of the Japanese Finance Ministry, spoke out for a co-operative monetary regime in East Asia. At the beginning of May 2000, Japan suggested a plan for a network of currency swaps, in effect a regional liquidity fund, to Asian finance ministers attending the annual meeting of the Asian Development Bank in Thailand. The idea was that Asian countries should be able to borrow from each other via short-term swaps of currency reserves. The finance ministers of the ASEAN countries, China, Japan and South Korea reached an agreement in Chiang Mai.

During the 2000 APT meeting in Singapore, the Chiang Mai Initiative was reaffirmed. At the same time, the Chinese Prime Minister Zhu Rongji made a proposal for a free trade area between China and ASEAN, excluding Japan. In January 2001, France and Japan tabled a joint paper during the Asia Europe Meeting (ASEM) Finance Minister Conference in Kobe. The paper suggested that stable exchange rates and financial flows were attainable at a regional level. In May 2001, the Chiang Mai Initiative was clarified during the annual meeting of the Asian Development Bank in Honolulu. The network of bilateral swap agreements was more precisely defined. Japan pledged to lend up to US$3 billion to South Korea, up to US$2 billion to Thailand and up to US$1 billion to Malaysia. However, it was decided that only 10 per cent of these sums would be available automatically. For sums above the 10 per cent level, the approval of the IMF would be required.

The president of the Asian Development Bank, Tadao Chino, at the occasion of the ASEAN + Three Finance Minister Conference in South Korea highlighted the three pillars of monetary regionalism in Asia: first, improved exchange of data; second, the pooling of currency reserves; and third, the development of an Asian bond market. Chino suggested replacing the bilateral swap agreements with a regional liquidity pool within three to five years.[12] These activities do not guarantee that monetary regionalism will be implemented successfully in the region. They do, however, demonstrate that the region is in search of greater independence, mainly from institutions and policies heavily influenced by the US.

Conclusions: US policy is the key to understanding Asian regionalism

Anti-Americanism is not the driving force behind regionalism in Asia, as I have tried to demonstrate in this chapter. Governments in Asia are increasingly disillusioned with American leadership, but that does not imply that they are distancing themselves from values and norms that are characteristic for America; democracy, the respect for human rights, and the organisation of the economy in a market-oriented manner are, by and large, shared by Asians.

Nevertheless, Asians have become significantly more critical of the US in recent years. The main factor has been the Asian crisis; Asians felt both put up and let down by America. They had followed American advice, and that cost them dearly. The IMF – heavily influenced by the American Treasury – abused the situation and forced Asian countries into so-called 'adjustment programmes' which were hardly disguised measures for permitting American companies to benefit from distress sales.

At the same time, three other factors have nurtured regionalism in East Asia: the decline of the American economy; the rise of China; and the lack of diplomatic skills from George W. Bush's administration. These three factors are each important on their own account, but in combination they are producing a potent cocktail which has reduced America's importance for the region in an unprecedented way.

The bottom line is quite simple: Asia has not changed as much as America has changed. The policies of the US have been a key factor in driving Asian regionalism, but the blame for that ought to stay in Washington. This development mirrors quite similar ones in other parts of the world, whether it is Western Europe, Latin America or even the US's next-door neighbour, Canada. Increasingly, people see the US as a potential problem, not a solution. Asia is not drifting away from the US; rather, America is drifting away from the rest of the world.

Notes

1 See a study of the University of Michigan, http://www.umich.edu/~newsinfo/
   Releases/1997/Dec97/r121097a.html
2 Martin Wolf has supported some of the criticism in the Stiglitz book. Both the IMF
   standard policy of raising interest rates and the big bailouts orchestrated by the IMF also
   meet with Wolf's disagreement. He argues that the bottom line in the evaluation of the
   Fund's work is not the quality of the rhetoric of IMF officials, but the economic success.
   And there the record is not looking good (*Financial Times*, 10 July 2002, p. 19).
3 In a speech delivered to three parliamentary committees of the German Bundestag
   in April 2001, Köhler identified the reform of conditionality as one of the greatest
   challenges to the Fund.
4 The Chief Economist of the IMF, Kenneth Rogoff, chastised Stiglitz bitterly for his
   book. In an open letter, Stiglitz was decried for, among other things, his criticism of the
   former Deputy Managing Director of the IMF, Stanley Fischer (www.imf.org/external/
   np/vc/2002/070202.htm).
5 Other OECD countries are applying a similar regime. However, no OECD country has
   recorded capital inflows of the same magnitude.
6 In 1991, Fred Bergsten stated that America had given the term 'collective leadership'
   a new meaning: the US leads, and the US collects.
7 Handelsblatt, *'Weltweit sinken die Direktinvestitionen'*, 5 September 2003, p. 10.

8 *The Economist*, 'Keep an eye on it; The dollar', 10 July 2004a, p. 66.
9 In 1989, Shintaro Ishihara together with Sony Chairman Akio Morita published a book on 'A Japan that can say no'. Regrettably, when Japan had a chance to lead East Asia and could have provided an Asian Monetary Fund in 1997, the Japanese government once again accepted the decision taken in Washington: no AMF, please.
10 *The Economist*, 'Yankee stay home; East Asia diplomacy', 11 December 2004b, p. 50.
11 *International Herald Tribune*, 23 July 2002, p. 1.
12 Speech on 15 May 2004, http://www.adb.org/AnnualMeeting/2004/ Speeches/chino_asean+3_statement.html

12 US–Latin American Trade Relations: Path to the Future or Dead End Street?

Cintia Quiliconi[1]

Latin America has a complex relationship with the US. On its own, the region includes over half a billion people and a gross national income of US$2 trillion, making it the wealthiest region of the developing world. Historically and currently, Latin America as a region of the developing world is the one with which the US has the strongest relationship: the 33 million Latinos in the US are now that nation's largest and fastest growing non-Anglo group, and US trade with Latin America represents 58 per cent of its trade with developing countries. This relationship is also far more intense when viewed from a different perspective; an absolute majority of all Latin American trade is with the US, and US military forces have intervened in Latin America on at least 50 separate occasions during the last hundred years. However, the hemisphere has usually been given short shrift by Washington.

George W. Bush's administration stated during the first presidential campaign that Latin America was going to be one of its highest foreign policy priorities and that the long-neglected region would occupy a central place in US foreign policy strategy. In the first months of his presidency, Bush broke with tradition and visited Mexico instead of Canada on his first trip abroad. But in the wake of 11 September 2001, Latin America has suddenly, again, found itself relegated to the wings of the world stage.

During the Cold War years, the US saw Bretton Woods institutions and multilateralism as being favourable to its interests. By defining these interests broadly and in an inclusive manner, Bretton Woods institutions were able to include other countries which were keen to sign on to a vision that stressed a system governed by rules. Since the end of the Cold War, US policy towards international institutions has hardened and economic policy has become much more explicitly linked to security policy (Higgott 2004b). In this vein, the US's continued rhetorical commitment to multilateralism has been replaced with a new strategy of signing preferential trade agreements (PTAs) with regional partners and allies.

Robert Zoellick, former US Trade Representative, has explained clearly what, from the US's point of view, the country seeks through expanding its range of bilateral trade negotiations. In Zoellick's view, PTAs will trigger competitive liberalization as an alternative route to global free trade that cannot be reached in other forums. Facing a lack of progress in the Free Trade Area of the Americas (FTAA) and multilateral negotiations, the US has turned to bilateralism – often as a means of favouring loyal allies and punishing indecisive friends. These PTAs have generated some adverse reactions in the Western Hemisphere.

Anti-Americanism in the region is understood in this chapter as the prevalence of a negative image of the US in Latin American countries, followed by the rejection of the economic policies that the US has tried to impose in the region by different civil society groups. The target of this rejection is mainly American foreign policy, and particularly American foreign economic policy. However, the anti-American sentiment entails neither the rejection of core values such as democracy or human rights, nor a lack of popularity for American culture whether in music or film or other main industries.

The intended aim of this chapter is to show that anti-Americanism in Latin America has experienced a cycle based on different issues and has had different degrees of intensity. During the 1960s, 1970s and the early 1980s, anti-Americanism in the region was related mainly to security issues and violations of human rights and sovereignty. The debt crisis in the 1980s, together with the end of the Cold War, introduced economic reform in Latin America as an imperative issue and shifted the main focus of the US–Latin America agenda; during the 1980s, the goal of US intervention in the region became controlling democratization during transition. As in the 1960s and 1970s, mass popular pressure against the US was controlled through the support of dictatorships; conversely, the reconstruction of democracy was accompanied by a shift in control of political society to control of civil society. Democratization and free market policies during the 1990s appeared as the most effective means to ensure stability.

These processes were controlled through the US penetration of the local elite in civil society. This penetration, along with the shock of the economic crisis of the 1980s and the exhaustion of the Import Substitution Industrialization (ISI) model, served to soften anti-American sentiment and resistance to US policies in the region. The failure of the so-called 'Washington consensus' policies served to revive anti-American sentiment against foreign economic policy in the region. In addition, American foreign policy after 11 September 2001, followed by the Iraq War and the political and economic instability that appeared in Latin America, ended in widespread rejection of the US's policies and the revival of anti-American sentiment.

Taking into account the cycle of anti-Americanism described above, the general consensus is that anti-Americanism in Latin America was first related to security issues and, after the failure of the Washington consensus policies, this sentiment became rooted mainly in economic issues. Nonetheless, if we take into account that economic policy became much more explicitly linked to security policy (Higgott 2004b), it can be said that it is not that anti-Americanism has changed its target, but rather that security issues have become intertwined with economic issues and the US is exerting soft power through economic relations with security aims.

This chapter is divided into four sections. The first section analyses how trade structures shape the different Latin American positions regarding the US and particularly the FTAA. The second section discusses the change in economic policies that led to the implementation of the Washington consensus. The third section addresses when and how anti-Americanism re-appeared in Latin America during the 1990s. The final section concludes the chapter.

Washington consensus

Since the 1980s trade liberalization and democratization processes in Latin American countries have advanced hand in hand. This trend gathered momentum as most of the developing countries embraced this 'rush to free trade' and integrated their economies into a global one. At the same time, an important number of them were experiencing the process of democratization.

The debt crisis in the 1980s introduced economic reform as an imperative issue in Latin America. During the 1990s, most policy-makers of the international financial institutions (IFIs) argued that the process of opening up to free market trade was an integral part of the whole economic reform. In the early 1990s, the economic reform recipes applied in most of developing countries had a mix of three main ingredients: stabilization, liberalization and privatization. One of the most important consequences of the debt crisis in Latin America was a radical change in the economic philosophy:

> In contrast to the external shocks and crisis of the 1930s, which had led to a switch away from *laissez-faire* towards a strategy of import substitution, and provided for a greatly enlarged role for the state, the shocks and crisis of the 1980s led to exactly the reverse movement, towards an outward-oriented development strategy based on deregulation, liberalization, and privatization. (UNCTAD 1995: 73)

The Washington consensus led most of the countries in Latin America to adopt similar outward-oriented policies, which replaced the inward-oriented policies that had been promoted by the Economic Commission for Latin America and the Caribbean (ECLAC) in previous decades.

Anti-Americanism and resistance to the implementation of neo-liberal policies among Latin American countries almost disappeared during the 1990s due to a combination of three different causes. First, the financial crisis of the 1980s, accompanied by the exhaustion of the ISI strategy, empowered the liberalizing winds and weakened the domestic opposition to reforms. Second, there was important pressure from the IFIs, mainly influenced by US concerns, that encouraged Latin American countries to implement the Washington consensus reforms. At the same time the new direction of foreign direct investment flows, which were previously focused in Organisation for Economic Co-operation and Development countries, played a crucial role by encouraging and legitimizing the new policies. Third, there were a series of changes in the ideological approaches of the administrations in Latin America, with most of them embracing in varying degrees neo-liberal policies and unilateral liberalization.

These structural shifts in Latin American economies and polities altered the traditional aversion in the region to integration with the US. Public opinion came little by little towards supporting democratic, market-oriented, open and competitive policies, with the hope of obtaining important economic and welfare benefits. Thus, the wave of economic reforms that swept through Latin America in the 1990s reflected not so much ideological conversion but the exhaustion of other means of redressing prior policy failures.

Today, the rules and institutions of the democratic regime in Latin America are similar to those in the more mature democratic countries, but its societies are completely different from them. In Latin America, democracy exists in a context of widespread poverty and inequality. For the first time, a developing region with a deep level of inequality is entirely organized under democratic regimes. The tension between economic and political reforms is a key characteristic in Latin America during recent decades (UNDP 2004). The reform strategy that has promised to bring prosperity has failed. It has not brought spectacular growth to the region; moreover, in some parts of the region it has in fact brought increased inequality and poverty (see Stiglitz 2002b).

The critics of the reform have pointed out that growth was not sustainable and it also exposed countries to new sources of volatility, which was, in turn, associated with an increase in poverty. The poorest typically bear the brunt of increases in unemployment; unskilled workers are usually the most affected and have no savings to turn to (Stiglitz 2002b). Even though the standard neo-classical theory predicts convergence between the less developed countries and the more developed countries, as the former will grow faster than the latter, the Latin American performance in relation to the US during the 1990s does not support that theory. Even in the earlier part of the 1990s, when reforms were supposed to be successful, per capita income in the US grew more rapidly than that in Latin America (see Stiglitz 2002b).

Trade structure and the FTAA

For Latin America, the FTAA that aims to achieve a free trade agreement among the 34 countries in the hemisphere brings the promise of access to the large US market and to US capital and technology. However, the process itself is different from previous experiences of integration as it seeks to integrate sub-regional blocs and very asymmetric countries. The forms of the sub-regional and hemispheric negotiations are dependent both on internal, domestic political calculations and on external, structural factors. As Phillips (2003) pointed out, the relationship between sub-regionalism in Latin America and the FTAA negotiations varies not only across sub-regions but also across the individual member states of those sub-regions.

Liberalism in Latin America took place under a confluence of external and internal conditions and factors. On the external side, industrialized capitalism, with the promise of bringing technology and capital, induced the unilateral opening up to trade and investments and promoted stabilization policies through complementary political measures. Pressure to implement reforms was exerted through the renegotiation of foreign debt and the promise of providing better access to markets.

From the internal perspective, the debt crisis and the imperative need of substituting the obsolete ISI 'development' model that had prevailed for many years also put pressure on leaders to accept the IFIs' recipes. This situation had conditioned and softened the receptive attitude of local elites that became more prone to accepting and establishing a new association with transnational capital.

The FTAA can be understood as an attempt to entrench these neo-liberal reforms. As is widely known, these reforms provided a road map for policy-makers, focusing on a fairly narrow set of economic indicators – a sort of macroeconomic template that could be employed with the endorsement of multilateral institutions and lenders, foreign governments and export-oriented business sectors. Domestic agriculture and industry faced intense external competition, labour unions were weakened and the traditional circuits of political power were disarticulated and weakened also (Stark 2001).

The trade patterns in the hemisphere after a decade of liberalization and implementation of neo-liberal policies mainly showed the following characteristics. On the one hand, high-tech equipment and industrial goods characterize US exports to Latin America – particularly motor vehicles, parts and accessories, computers, telecommunications, electronics, electrical machinery and electrical power generation industries.

On the other hand, there are two main Latin American exports to the US trade: petroleum products and semi-manufactured and manufactured goods. In petroleum products, the historical major producers (Mexico, Venezuela and Ecuador) are now accompanied by newer producers (Colombia and Argentina). Trade in manufactured and semi-manufactured goods represents around 30 per cent of Latin American exports to the US and they are heavily concentrated in the big three economies of the region – Mexico (the one most favoured by the North American Free Trade Agreement), Brazil and Argentina.

According to ECLAC (2003), in the last decade three trends of export specialization can be identified in the Latin American region. First, there has been an increase in the north–south trade of manufactured goods mainly oriented to the US market, for instance from Mexico and some Central American and Caribbean countries. This trend of export is characterized by the maquila industry (maquila industry applies to companies that process or assemble components imported into Mexico that are then re-exported), mainly in Mexico. Second, there has been integration of South American countries in the south–south trade. These countries also have a more diversified trade in terms of export markets that include their own regional markets and China. Even though the exports of basic products have been reduced in terms of their importance in the total of regional trade, the situation differs in Mercosur (the Regional Trade Agreement between Brazil, Argentina, Uruguay and Paraguay, founded in 1991) and the Andean Community countries, where the exports of basic products and manufactured goods based on natural resources still represent a high percentage of the total external sales (58 per cent Mercosur, 86 per cent Andean Community). Third, in some Caribbean countries and Panama, the export of services – particularly tourism, finance and transportation – is becoming very important. Even though this is a simplistic classification of export specialization, it sheds light on the potential interests of countries in the FTAA.

The hemispheric initiative played a mixed role for Latin American countries. As was pointed out, the economic structure of Latin American countries is very asymmetric. Mexico and some Central American and Caribbean countries – the countries geographically nearest to the US – are highly dependent on the US market for exports, particularly, as signalled, in maquila industry products. Mexico has no problem in terms of access because it is part of the North American Free Trade Agreement (NAFTA), but the other Central American countries see the FTAA as the guarantee of preferential market access to the US.

In terms of imports, Latin America is highly dependent on the US; the US has responded to the Latin American need for new capital goods, and its multinational corporations in the region have supported the demand for intermediate goods. In terms of exports, it is important to highlight the way in which the US has maintained its primacy as a destination for Latin American exports despite the changes in the composition of these goods and services. As was pointed out, in various Latin American countries the export of raw materials has now been replaced by the export of manufactured goods and services, but regardless the US continues to be the main market for new and traditional exports alike. Conversely, Latin American exports to the European Union and China are still dominated by primary products supplied mainly by Mercosur countries (Bulmer-Thomas 1998).

The diversity of products and trade explains why, after more than ten years of painstaking discussion and public shouting matches, the US and Latin American countries have not even agreed on what issues to include in the FTAA negotiating agenda, and negotiations have reached a deadlock. Brazil, which leads the South American group in the negotiations, wants the US to open its markets to Latin American agricultural goods. The US, in turn, wants Latin America to open its markets to US computer goods, to respect intellectual property rights and to allow US companies to participate freely in investment, services and government procurement. These are the two extremes of the spectrum, while trapped in the middle are Central American, Caribbean and some Andean countries with a different agenda.

Rather than aiming at the region-wide and comprehensive free trade deal that was envisioned at the 1994 Summit of the Americas in Miami, the ministers of trade agreed in Miami in November 2003 to produce a two-tiered process, leading to an anorexic FTAA. Moreover, the Summit of the Americas held in Mar del Plata, Argentina, in November 2005 concluded without a clear agreement on when and how to resume stalled talks aimed at achieving the FTAA. In essence, Mercosur countries plus Venezuela, which did not see much benefit for themselves in the US trade offer, argued that the conditions for achieving the free trade agreement were not symmetrical. What Latin American governments consistently asked for were changes in US farm policy that would lower barriers to the region's food and fibre exports. In particular, they wanted cuts in US subsidies to agricultural products and reductions of tariffs and quotas on key commodities.

These changes would revive negotiations toward the FTAA and open the way to more secure access to US trade, investment and technology – precisely what the region desires from the US. Such reforms would relieve disputes with Brazil and Argentina, the region's largest agricultural exporters. George W. Bush's administration basically supports this agenda and has taken the lead in the Doha Round of multilateral trade negotiations to push for an accord that would require Europe, Japan and other governments, as well as the US, to lower subsidies and other barriers. But powerful US agricultural producers and their representatives in Congress make it impossible for the United States to change its farm policy on its own (Hakim 2006).

Meanwhile, enthusiastic countries such as Colombia and Peru are negotiating more comprehensive, bilateral deals like the one signed between the US and the Central American Countries plus the Dominican Republic, known as the US–Central American Free Trade Agreement (CAFTA). Each bilateral agreement is an effort by the Latin American countries concerned to gain preferential treatment for their trade, and, viewed in this way, these agreements amount to a sort of beggar-thy-neighbour policy, as was used in the 1930s. Coalition-building is not present in the bilateral negotiations that are currently the focus of the US drive. Rather, the agreements are driven by the US's offensive interests and seem to be accepted by Caribbean, Central American and Andean countries – faced with the overwhelming resources and the sheer economic might of the US – in order to protect previous unbound and non-reciprocal preferential access. This is especially the case for the CAFTA, which essentially guarantees the access granted under the Caribbean Basin Initiative, and the free trade areas under negotiation with the Andean countries, which will replace the Andean Trade Preference Act. Much of this preferential access was concentrated in the textile sector.

Tussie and Quiliconi (2005) argued that this trend is coetaneous to the expiry of the elaborate quota system that has regulated the trade of textiles and garments since the early 1960s and has existed under several guises since then. This expiry means that the textile sector in many Latin American countries will have to compete both at home and abroad with previously controlled and restricted suppliers. In this sense, the race by Latin America towards PTAs with the US is driven by the fear of erosion of previous agreements and has focused on securing their foothold by using bilateral agreements. Hence the drive is mainly from microeconomic sectors and its strength depends on how the value chain is globally integrated. This usually implies an exchange of lower effective protection for key exports of Latin American countries for domestic regulatory reform, which may seem a high price in terms of 'plus' agreements from the World Trade Organization (WTO-plus).

Bilateral and hemispheric negotiations are driven by two opposite but, in the end, complementary forces. On the one hand, from the developing countries' perspective, the opportunity of gaining access to textile and foodstuff markets, on the other hand, from the US's perspective, the opportunity of obtaining a WTO-plus regulatory setting for intellectual property rights, investments and service provision. Hakim (2006) points out another new element that has appeared on the horizon, namely China's growing presence in Latin America. In fact, some members of the US Congress view China as the most serious challenge to US interests in the region. They cite as potential threats to US policy in the hemisphere the huge financial resources that China is promising to bring to Latin America, China's growing military-to-military relations in the region and its clear political ambitions. Moreover, China's interest in Latin America is expanding, since the region has become a vital source to it for raw materials and foodstuffs. In the past six years, Chinese imports from Latin America have grown more than six fold, or by nearly 60 per cent a year.

Anti-Americanism in the region

So far, the analysis has looked at the ways in which governments have reacted to the US hegemony in a government-led forum. In this section we shall shift the focus to civil society's opposition to US dominance. The heightened impact of trade negotiations in the post-import substitution era has sown the seeds of domestic discontent and opposition. The anti-globalization movement consolidated these new forms of participation and protest, which were subsequently fuelled by fresh levels of anti-American sentiment as positions hardened in the context of the war on terrorism following the events of 11 September 2001 and the rising risks of a full-scale US-led war in the Middle East.

The 2003 Latin American poll taken by Zogby International showed that there was almost universal dislike of President George W. Bush in the region. In turn, a 2003 *Latinobarómetro* poll showed that 87 per cent of Latin America rated Bush negatively. Moreover, the percentage of Latin Americans who held a negative image of the US had more than doubled, from 14 per cent in 2000 to 31 per cent in 2003. Sixty per cent of Latin Americans still held a positive view of the US, but that percentage had been 71 per cent in 2000. In key countries such as Mexico, the level of anti-Americanism was high (58 per cent had a negative image of the US in 2003, raised from 22 per cent in 2000). In other Latin American countries, the percentage of people with a negative view of the US reached 62 per cent in Argentina, 42 per cent in Brazil and 37 per cent in Chile in 2003 (Latinobarómetro 2003).[2]

However, the *Latinobarómetro* poll carried out in 2005 shows that almost everywhere, opinions towards the US were thawing, though they are yet to reach the warmth of the late 1990s. There are two exceptions. One is Venezuela, where President Chávez accused the US of planning to invade his country. The other is Uruguay, where a left-wing government took power. The most anti-American country remains Argentina. In many other countries, respondents thought that relations with the US were becoming closer. That may be due to the fact that the memory of the Iraq War, which was very unpopular in the region, is fading. Central America, with which the US enacted a free-trade agreement, is the most pro-American part of the region (*The Economist* 2005d).

The exhaustion of the neo-liberal model in Latin America has shown mixed characteristics. The decline of the model since the second half of the 1990s reversed the strong influence of neo-liberal policies in the region, and put into question the strong influence that the US has been exercising in Latin America.

The 'spectacular' failure of the model in its best student, Argentina, has played a key role in this sense. In this scenario, some of the region's leaders have turned to populist and anti-American rhetoric to win supporters and votes.

Argentina, along with Brazil and Venezuela, has become the centre of resistance to the US. Kirchner has imposed a hard negotiation style with the US and the IFIs, resisting US pressure to negotiate better pay-outs for holders of the country's defaulted bonds. Meanwhile, Lula da Silva is determined to be a counterweight to the US in trade issues, especially in the FTAA negotiations. Argentina and Brazil, in a very political gesture, have decided to repay IMF debt in order to gain room to manoeuvre in their economic policies. Chávez, in turn, has openly challenged the US and even accused it of helping his opponents to attempt to oust him from power. All these developments have been reinforced by the election of left-wing Indian leader Evo Morales in Bolivia.

Most leftist parties and social movements in the region celebrated Chávez's victory in Venezuela's referendum and Morales' triumph in the Bolivian elections as the prelude to an upcoming chain reaction of anti-American and anti-free trade 'revolutions' in Latin America. Venezuela and the US have clashed repeatedly, for example at the fourth Summit of the Americas in Mar del Plata, where violent anti-American demonstrators filled the streets. Chávez was the only head of state to join the protests (although Bolivian presidential candidate at that time, Morales, also joined him). His raging polemics fired up the crowds and revealed once again his political reach and popularity in the region. However, a quick look at Venezuela's neighbouring governments shows that the Venezuelan anti-capitalist strategy is highly unlikely to be adopted by others in the region. The widespread level of protests related to the FTAA showed that trade relations between the US and Latin America have become a primary force in generating anti-Americanism in the region along with the opposition to American economic foreign policy.

There is a peculiar situation currently in most Latin American countries: a weakness and even rejection of the neo-liberal ideology supported by the US in the spheres of public and political awareness, yet at the same time, a certain persistence of the neo-liberal ideology in the policy-makers (particularly in the ministries of finance and economy, presidents of the central banks and political leadership) which is sometimes hidden by a more populist-sounding speech (Borón 2004). The US war on terrorism and Washington's regime change in Iraq have fanned even more anti-American sentiment in Latin America. There are daily condemnations of the war by many Latin American governments who see no need to criticize Iraq's UN violations. President George W. Bush particularly is the target of blame and the most affected in terms of image, as shown in *Latinobarómetro* polls.

There is another factor adding fuel to the fire of anti-Americanism. As a result of global economic meltdown, poverty and hunger were reaching overwhelming new levels throughout the region. After a decade of experimenting with American free market reforms, countries became very disillusioned with the process. Nations that once were racing to accept American-style democracy and economic values are waking up to the reality that it has not worked for many of them. A poll conducted in 20 different countries around the world has shown that Latin America has become the most critical region in the world regarding free trade policies (*La Nacion* 2006).

Borón (2004) characterized the reasons for the irruption of these new civil society players in the following way. First, the economic failure intensified the contradictions of social and economic policies. Second, the emergence of new-left political expressions is directly related to the failure of the neo-liberal policies and the frustration of the democratic regimes in the region. While the implementation of neo-liberal policies under the new democratic regimes was supposed to produce sustainable economic growth, poverty reduction and less inequality, the results were exactly the opposite. Third, Latin American countries also experienced a political representation crisis; the new social protest showed the decline of populist and leftist parties and of the traditional models of trade unions. Fourth, the anti-globalization movement with its high levels of anti-American sentiment consolidated these new forms of participation and protest in which the leaders were neither political parties nor trade unions.

Social resistance was focused on the implementation of the Washington consensus policies at the domestic level and, as well, heterogeneous civil society players gathered transnational networks and coalitions to resist US free trade initiatives in Latin America. These networks and coalitions started to demand participation and they began to exercise their voice in regional integration processes, particularly in the FTAA (Smith and Korzeniewicz 2002).

In summary, the social legitimacy of the FTAA together with the influence of the US on economic policy have been called into question. Such misgivings concur with a context in which many countries within the region have elected left-leaning governments, with the potential for a greater receptivity to the concerns and claims being articulated by civil society groups and social movements (Tussie 2005). However, at the same time many countries in the region, except for the most opposed ones, have negotiated or are negotiating bilateral trade agreements with the US. Despite the fact that Latin American countries are increasingly disillusioned with American leadership, Latin America in general is not distancing itself from values and norms that are characteristic for the US. Democracy, respect for human rights and market-oriented policies are still key for the majority of the governments in the region.

Opposition to US foreign economic policy and the conclusion of free trade agreements with the US are not homogeneous along the region. In the Southern Cone, there are three blocs of countries. The first bloc's members are Argentina, Brazil and Paraguay, who have changed their political inclinations to the left-wing side of the spectrum. In Argentina, the change in the administration was preceded by a long period of social unrest. In Brazil, the arrival of Lula da Silva to the government was part of the building of a more stable and sustainable social movement. Paraguay also experienced an important farmer mobilization before the change in administration. These governments came to power with the popular mandate of finishing or at least softening the implementation of neo-liberal policies. They held anti-liberal speeches yet, at the same time, they came to power through heterogeneous electoral coalitions which play an important part in certain traditional political sectors and economic players who support neo-liberal policies (Algranati *et al.* 2004).

Chile and Uruguay are part of the second bloc of Southern countries. On the one hand, the neo-liberal Uruguayan administration of President Battle tried to accelerate privatizations and intensify its alignment with US policies before the presidential elections that put a left-wing candidate for the first time in the presidency of the country. However, all the signals sent by Tabaré Vázquez, the new Uruguayan president, have shown that he will be inclined to a free market economy and will even be open to signing a bilateral trade agreement with the US. On the other hand, Chile possesses strong ties to the US and is the Southern Cone country with the lowest level of social protest and the highest rate of economic growth. Chile gained notoriety in the region for having chosen not to fully join Mercosur and opted for the US as a trading partner, signing a bilateral agreement.

Concentrated in the Andean area are significant conflicts being waged mainly by indigenous people and farmer movements, principally in Ecuador and Bolivia but also in Peru and Colombia. Key examples of the instability in the Andean region are the social protests being led by white-collar workers from the public sector against the neo-liberal adjustment policies; the polarization that the Venezuelan process is causing; and the popular unrest that forced the Bolivian government to resign and the discussion of the energy policy to be decided through a referendum. The election of the left-wing Indian leader Evo Morales as the Bolivian president has opened many questions about the characteristics of this administration, given the close ties between Morales and Chávez. In general, the public policies in the Andean countries have adopted an anti-neo-liberal, anti-American character, except for Peru and Colombia, which have also signed PTAs with the US.

Conclusion

The legacy of the failure of the Washington consensus policies has left two clear trends in the region that appear to be more intense in South American countries. First, there is the common rejection of IMF policies that is particularly clear in the Argentinean and Brazilian decisions at the end of 2005 to repay their entire debt to the institution in order to gain economic emancipation to move away from neo-liberal policies. Second, there is the loss of confidence in the partnership between Latin American countries and the US, mainly demonstrated in the increasing resistance from civil society actors to the conclusion of an FTAA agreement or bilateral PTAs with the US.

Historically, governments ultimately determined the rules and regulations that would govern international economic transactions. However, their role in that regard is decreasing. The resurgence of resistance against US policies is being guided by civil society groups seeking alternatives to these policies. Non-state domestic and international players are taking an active role in the hemispheric political scene. Even though the historical view on trade relations shows that the development of the current structure of the world trading system is profoundly influenced by interactions between states, other powerful influences have appeared from civil society and applied pressure not only at the domestic level but also at the regional, hemispheric and multilateral levels. In this sense, even though states continue to lead trade negotiations and there is a weakness and even rejection of the neo-liberal ideology supported by the US in the spheres of public and political awareness, neo-liberal ideology persists in the policy-making sphere, sometimes under cover of populist speech.

The ambitious FTAA plan described by President George W. Bush as a 'vital link for prosperity' is mired in disputes that have led to widespread scepticism and opposition about its chances of materializing, not only from governmental sources but also from civil society movements. With large countries in South America such as Brazil and Argentina being firmly opposed to the initiative, the US has clearly redirected its efforts in the last years from the FTAA to bilateral negotiations with a handful of smaller countries in Central America and the Andean region. However, looking farther south, the Andean nations of Bolivia and Ecuador, hit by violent tumult, have little chance of signing a trade agreement any time soon. Even Peru and Colombia, both of which enjoy good relations with the US, have experienced civil society opposition in bilateral negotiations with the US.

The free trade agenda is becoming a serious problem in Latin America and one of the main sources of friction between US and the region. Increasingly, Latin American governments and particularly civil societies are viewing with suspicion any mooted free trade with the US. At the same time, since the failure of the Washington consensus policies the region has shifted to left-wing governments and become increasingly wary of the US's economic prescriptions as growth has flagged and promises of prosperity fail to materialize. The reasons for caution are numerous, from the potent anti-globalization movement that has swept South America, to practical concerns in many Latin American countries about what it would mean for their industries should they open their markets to the world's largest economy, the United States.

The interconnection between governments and civil society in the Americas is nowadays more sophisticated, showing that the trade regime has become a complex, multi-layered arena where social forces and contending political projects compete – a far cry from the simple manifestation of an uncontested hegemonic project for market-driven integration, as initially mapped out by the US. In this scenario, the prospect of finishing a comprehensive, far-reaching agreement at the FTAA is very unlikely. Nowadays, US bilateral trade liberalization strategy is in practice guiding the hemispheric trade agenda with can-do countries.

Anti-Americanism in Latin America was first related to security issues but, after the failure of the Washington consensus policies, this sentiment has become linked mainly with economic issues. Nonetheless, if we take into account that economic policy became much more explicitly linked with security policy (Higgott 2004b), it is not that anti-Americanism has changed its target, but simply that security issues are now intertwined with economic issues and the US is exerting soft power through economic relations with security aims. Since 11 September 2001, security has become a top priority and the US has been criticized for growing distant and detached from the Latin American region, yet anti-Americanism has resurfaced in the spheres of trade and economics, confirming the strength of the link between security and economic issues.

Hemispheric and bilateral US Free Trade Agreement proposals are closely connected to the US's global hegemony strategy. These new bilateral trade agreements proposed by the US are intertwined with the inevitably resulting dissemination of the neo-liberal agenda. However, beyond the expansion of the neo-liberal agenda, the US's interests in the region are related to security and democracy agendas. In this sense, the FTAA negotiations and the proliferation of bilateral agreements proposed by the US embed security-related strategies into broader trade and economic issues. Trade liberalization has become mixed with other causes, including the conflation of markets and political freedom under US leadership (Tussie 2005). In essence, this was the universal projection of the American dream – a vision of economic plenty in the context of political freedom as expressed some decades later in the notion of a 'free world'. Often a menace or an enemy was necessary to garner consensus on further liberalization. The spirit was re-embodied in the *Trade Act 2002*:

> The expansion of international trade is vital to the national security of the US. Trade is critical to economic growth and strength of the US and its leadership in the world. Stable trading relationships promote security and prosperity. Trade arrangements today serve the same purposes that security pacts played during the Cold War, binding nations together through a series of rights and obligations. Leadership by the US in international trade fosters open markets, democracy and peace throughout the world. (*US Trade Act of 2002*: Title XXI)

As the US extends its power and influence abroad, the challenges multiply. What should be apparent is that as developmental values regain legitimacy, the trade arena has become a site of resistance where the weak or under-represented seek windows of opportunity to reshape rules and reduce pressure for policies that they wish to evade or for which they want offsetting concessions. These challenges are not necessarily a general rejection of future co-operation at all times. As they grow in strength and stature, emerging players are investing in becoming technically empowered to resist, confront and shape a number of outcomes. Dealing with the US is less an exercise of helplessness than an exercise of accommodation, where state and non-state players interact and feed off each other in a process which, even though not organic, allows for values to become shared, rules gradually codified and all players to reinvent themselves.

Notes

1 This chapter would not have been possible without the comments and insights of Diana Tussie, through numerous discussions based on a common research agenda. I am also grateful to Mercedes Botto for her helpful comments.
2 Based on a poll of 18,600 people in 17 Latin American countries.

13 Anti-Americanism in Greece

Helena Maragou

If there is a single statement that summarizes the quality of ongoing debates over the nature and causes of anti-Americanism as an international or local phenomenon, this would have to be that such debates are more productive of confusion and fallacy, than of clarity and comprehension. One of the primary factors that compromises understanding of the issues involved is the frequent deployment of the language of emotion where one would expect factual and dispassionate analysis: 'Americans ache to be loved in foreign places and now the world denies us', laments Fouad Ajami, professor of Middle Eastern Studies at Johns Hopkins and advocate of the anti-anti-American argument (2003a). Equally unprofitable is the general tendency to personalize and subjectivize the matter, which appears to typify much of the discourse of America's critics: 'I can no longer stomach America's insidious meddlings across the face of the world ... wherever I go I find myself more and more repelled by the apparently insatiable American urge to interfere in other people's business' (Morris quoted in Hollander 1995: 389).

What such emotionality promotes is an oversimplified view of anti-Americanism which, in both the anti-American and the anti-anti-American camps, expresses and reproduces a will to negate and repress aspects of the phenomenon that do not fit into the narrow mould of either blind support or sweeping critique. Thus, for pro-Americans, the anti-American discourse is unrelated to historical actuality, and expressive of individual and/or collective cases of illogic, unaccounted for by observable fact: 'Anti-Americanism, more often than not, is irrational and misdirected; it consists of attitudes and sentiments that reveal more about those displaying them than about the target of the hostile critiques' (Hollander 1995: xiii). On the other hand, much anti-American rhetoric constructs the United States as a monolithic entity which generates crass materialism, blind interventionism, un-democratic policies, and much more:

> The United States has in fact – since the end of the Second World War ...
> exercised a sustained, systematic, remorseless, and quite cynical manipula-
> tion of power worldwide, while masquerading as a force for universal good
> ... Arrogant, indifferent, contemptuous of International Law, both dismissive
> and manipulative of the United Nations, this is now the most dangerous

power the world has ever known – the authentic 'rogue state'. (Pinter quoted in Hollander 2002: 28)

The frequent failure on the part of many critics of America to come up with a more dispassionate approach to their subject, muddles the terms of their argument and plays right into their opponents' hands by providing them with cause to proclaim the discourse of anti-Americanism a display of personal impulse rather than political insight: 'Anti-Americanism has always been more a matter of attitude than argument. It depends on, it draws its strength from, the wells of passion, not reason' (Kimball 2004: 239). Anti-Americanism is 'an emotive and pathological impulse,[1] which masquerades 'as an analysis ... When hatred of foreign policies ignites into hatred of an entire people and their civilization, then thinking is dead and demonology lives ...' (Gitlin 2003: 103–4). To rephrase such views, anti-American attitudes are by definition unfocused and visceral, because they bear no connection to political and social actuality.

Indeed, the general tendency of anti-anti-American rhetoric is toward neutralization of critiques of the US as a political, social and cultural entity through orchestrated efforts to a-politicize and a-historicize them. Thus, in a rhetorical move that personalizes social experience without running the risk of politicitizing private life, Paul Hollander argues that, when it comes to anti-Americanism of both the domestic and foreign varieties, there is 'a vital connection between "personal troubles" and their "social roots"' (1995: xvii); the common denominator among strands of anti-Americanism is that 'it is a response to some kind of collective or group frustration or grievance which finds relief in holding the US (or a particular aspect of it) responsible for the grievances in question' (Hollander 1995: 389). But while some relegate anti-Americanism to the realm of perverse psychology, others attempt to de-contextualize the phenomenon and to devalue its historical currency by tracing its origins to a past so distant as to be practically untraceable: 'Anti-Americanism is a phenomenon as old, actually even older, than the US itself. Although it has gone through various periods and emphases, the main themes have remained remarkably consistent' (Rubin 2004). By positioning the anti-American critique within the realm of illogic and by depriving it of a historical *raison d'être*, such treatments of the anti-American discourse implicitly negate the possibility of defining the terms of the discussion and render dialogue futile.

Another factor that dooms the anti-Americanism debate to semantic impasse is several analysts' fascinating habit of proposing definitions of this particular -ism by deploying the use of other, equally vague and debatable terms to which it is, supposedly, differentially related: thus, anti-Americanism is seen as the negative response to capitalism, and/or Western culture, and/or modernity, and/or globalization. The inadequacy of this scheme is especially evident in discussions of European anti-Americanism: can one logically claim that Europe is anti-capitalist, or that America for some strange reason is fitter than Europe to stand as the embodiment of Western values? And what does 'modernity' mean anyway? Total confusion dominates in anti-anti-American arguments that attempt to construct critique of the US as negation of modernization:

> To come bearing modernism to those who want it but who rail against it at the same time, to represent and embody so much of what the world yearns for and fears, that is the American burden … To the Europeans … the US is unduly religious, almost embarrassingly so, its culture suffused with sacred symbolism. (Ajami 2003b: 58)

Most importantly, however, for the 'anti-' stance to be meaningful, the term it defines itself oppositionally by needs to prove definable, too: anti-Americanism is rejection of 'Americanism'; if 'Americanism' stands for love of 'America', then which 'America' precisely is being signified? Samuel Huntington's white, Protestant America? America as the neutral ground over which meet multiple strands of cultural pluralism? The problem is evident in some analysts' naïve attempt to construct America as the bodying forth of a single idea: 'America is a nation born not of a common bloodline, but of a common idea about the public weal. Hence to be unalterably opposed to that common idea is to be anti-American by philosophy' (Garfinkle 2004: 301). Assuming that the above were true, is 'Americanism' blind support of the vision of 'America' promoted by the rhetoric of the White House and the military initiatives of the Pentagon? Or is it synonymous with the republican ideal forming the subtext of the Bill of Rights?

What frustrates attempts to address the phenomenon of anti-Americanism, then, is a tendency to essentialize 'America', thus imposing a corresponding unitary meaning onto its opposite. Over and over again, anti-American as well as anti-anti-American discourses resort to a fundamental fallacy based on the idea that generational cycles in America organize themselves round the passing-on of a common tradition, a common identity, a common value system. From this false assumption to the one that conflates 'America' with the national state is just an easy step. Quite astutely, in an attempt to warn of the dangers of oversimplification, organizers of a 1986 conference on international perceptions of America used the title 'Anti-Americanisms' to suggest that what we call 'anti-Americanism' is a phenomenon as complex, multifarious and paradoxical as our perceptions of 'America' itself.[2]

The discussion of Greek 'anti-Americanism' that follows will bypass extremist 'anti-American' rhetoric, which has often been attributed to the Greek media but does not represent accurately Greek reaction to 'America'. Likewise, it will ignore pro-American rhetoric, which also appears on the Greek scene, usually in the form of a nearly unexplainable will to self-flagellate by relegating Greek opposition to US foreign policy to collective guilt over national failures; here, as elsewhere in the world, lovers of the US may prove as blind as its most virulent critics. After all, exaggeration has always a way of obscuring crucial parameters of the subject without illuminating the real causes – whether justified or not – behind the phenomenon. I will also refrain from using the generic term 'anti-Americanism', not only because it is semantically defunct and obstructs rather than facilitates understanding, but also because it signifies a form of bigotry and even violence which do not form part of the Greek majority's response. Instead, the paper's area of investigation is what I would prefer to call the Greek people's – admittedly intense – 'discontent' with US foreign policy, the historical causes, permutations and inherent paradoxes of the Greek stance.

Greek perspectives on US foreign policy

An article published in *Foreign Policy* identifies 'hatred of the United States' as 'a defining feature of [Greek] political life' (Ajami 2003b: 54). The article evokes the supposed authority of one of Greece's most acerbic, and misguided, critics of Greek anti-US attitudes, to support the view that Greek perceptions of 'America' are the result of an explosive brand of 'nativist ethnonationalism' combined with 'fanatical religiosity':

> Greece loves the idea of its 'Westernness' – a place and culture where the West ends, and some other alien world (Islam) begins. But the political culture of religious nationalism has isolated Greece from the wider currents of Western liberalism. What little modern veneer is used to dress up Greece's anti-Americanism is a pretense. The malady here is, paradoxically, a Greek variant of what plays out in the world of Islam: a belligerent political culture sharpening faith as a political weapon, an abdication of political responsibility for one's own world, and a search for foreign 'devils'.[3]

In terms of both tone and content, this article is an almost predictable, albeit ultimately groundless, treatment of Greek 'anti-Americanism'. The reality is that Greece has long been viewed as a problematical US and North Atlantic Treaty Organization ally, mainly because, from the end of World War II all the way to the present, the vast majority of Greeks are known to have entertained often extremely negative perceptions of American foreign policy – a fact once again made evident by the 2005 Eurobarometer report, which shows Greek public opinion of the US at an all-time low, even lower than that accorded by their European counterparts. Indeed the poll shows that 88 per cent of Greeks consider the US as playing a negative role in world peace (the EU-25 average was 58 per cent), with only 5 per cent of Greeks expressing trust in US peace efforts (a percentage significantly lower than the corresponding European average of 22 per cent).

Concerning the contribution of the US to the fight against terror, 83 per cent of Greeks express a negative view (the EU-25 percentage was 40). They likewise appear to be considering the US as causing a negative impact on the world economy (76 per cent), the fight against world poverty (83 per cent) and environmental protection initiatives (77 per cent). Once again, the percentage of negative response per category is significantly higher than the corresponding average for respondents from combined EU countries. Even after the events of 11 September 2001, and irrespective of the expressed sympathy of the Greek government and the vast majority of the Greek people, public opinion registered unwillingness to support

US foreign policy. Indeed 84 per cent opposed US action in Afghanistan, while 94 per cent objected to the war in Iraq (Eurobarometer National Report: Greece 2005: 37–9).

The question is, of course: what essential content is suggested by these and similar poll results? In Greece itself, commentary runs a gamut from self-congratulatory celebrations of Greek 'astuteness' – and bravado – in recognizing and openly condemning US militarism, to facilely drawn arguments which attribute the phenomenon to absurd exaggeration bred by conspiracy theory. The middle ground is occupied by those who, while wisely acknowledging elements of exaggeration and bias, simultaneously point out the historical and political character of the Greek response.

Commentary on 'Greek anti-Americanism' issuing out of the US mass media, on the other hand, has ranged from uncomprehending indignation to wilful distortion of facts. Especially in the wake of 11 September 2001, public polls registering high levels of Greek opposition to US foreign policy were misinterpreted as suggesting the Greek majority's sympathy for (and even support of) international terrorism. A series of Columbia Broadcasting System (CBS) reports vilified the Greek people for displaying a lack of compassion for the victims of 11 September 2001 attacks and for being critical of the 'war on terror', thus automatically abdicating their ties to the West. Reflecting the general view of 'Greek anti-Americanism' in the American media, a *New York Times* article published on 7 April 2003 referred to a poll conducted a few days earlier, according to which 'more Greeks had a positive view of Saddam Hussein than of Mr Bush [while] a majority of those polled believed that the United States was as undemocratic as Iraq' (Carassava 2003: B12). What the article does not really make clear is that Greeks responded in favour of Saddam in the context of a question which asked them to identify who 'represent[ed] a greater threat to world peace' – not who they were 'in favour of' – and Saddam could never logically be perceived by Greeks as being more of a threat than President George W. Bush, given the incomparable military superiority of the US nuclear, biological and chemical arsenal, as well as the US record of military interventions since World War II.

Deplorably, negative views of Greece as an ungrateful ally translated into a number of venomous reports in various US news media predicting the certain disaster of the Athens Olympics as well as the failure of the Greek presidency of the European Union in 2003. As a Greek commentator wrote on 13 January 2002, there was:

> an orchestrated misrepresentation of the causes as well as of the essential character of the anti-American sentiments of an – admittedly – significant portion of the Greek public and the promotion of the view that the so-called [Greek] anti-Americanism is not directed against certain political decisions of Washington, but against the American people themselves. (Zoulas 2002)

Like much of the American mass media, Greek-American newspapers also expressed deep disappointment, and often outrage, for what was perceived as Greek callousness. So wide was the gap that opened up between the Greek and the Greek-American perspectives on the situation that, for the first time in its history, the Greek-American lobby in Washington, DC, suspended its activity to protest against what had been regarded as Greek hostility. A Greek-American journalist wrote:

> As Greek Americans, we need to show to our friends, to our representatives in Congress, to the Government of the United States, and to news media, that we do not share the negative feelings of our compatriots in Greece, that we condemn those attacks against this country, and to declare our loyalty and devotion to this hospitable and blessed land. And when our children and friends ask 'what's wrong with the Greeks,' our answer should be that this is not the country we left behind. It is a place we do not recognize. Indeed, it is a strange place. (Makrias 2003)

And yet, the story of Greek–US relations is not as uncomplicated as it is often made to seem. The US and Greece have strong political, historical and cultural ties, as they share the same democratic vision, a common sense of the meaning of Western culture, and joint historical experiences as allies in World War II, the Korean War and the Cold War. Approximately four million residents of the US are Greek or Greek-American and form a cohesive and powerful community that facilitates and promotes US–Greek co-operation. The Greek economy, which outpaces the growth rate of the EU generally, is based on the principles of free market capitalism, while the Greek government's foreign, and sometimes even domestic, policies have traditionally been aligned with US State Department decisions. In response to the 11 September 2001 attacks, Greece offered its airspace and stated its willingness to contribute to the counter-terrorism campaign. Likewise, during the Athens Olympics, US counter-terrorism, diplomatic and intelligence officials worked with their Greek counterparts to ensure high security standards at the Games.

Despite their tradition of protest against US foreign policy, Greeks understand, now more so than ever, their inevitable connection with America. A poll published in one of the most widely circulating newspapers in Greece is quite revealing: three in four respondents (76 per cent) consider that good relations between the US and Greece are very important. It is noteworthy that this view is not affected by party affiliations, whereas in the past it was only right-wing voters who tended to be in favour of a strong alliance with the US.[4] But today, political 'realism' overpowers party ideology, and Greek society is collectively responding to the necessity of good relations with the US government. And yet, according to a Eurobarometer report, only 4 per cent of Greeks trust the US as an agent of world peace and only 7 per cent support the US fight against terror (Eurobarometer 2003).

A traditional and steadfast ally of the United States, Greece has been politically maintaining a precarious balance between co-operation and opposition. There is no doubt about it: paradox and contradiction characterize the Greek mind's response to America – not only as political entity but also as society and culture. America is viewed – often simultaneously – as Promised Land but also as the embodiment of all the negative energies that shape modern life. News coverage of American police brutality, racial violence, and assaults in American schools, of death penalty and prisoner abuse – all these construct a negative view of the quality of American life, at the same time that media reports extol American technology, medical research and higher education. In other words, on the level of culture, Greece's uncertain stance toward America translates into simultaneous attraction and repulsion. That Greeks cannot perceive the US in a consistent manner, or maybe that the US has failed to represent itself consistently to the world, is epitomized by the Greek society's tendency to view America, on the one hand, as being too liberal to maintain social cohesiveness and, on the other, as being too much given to religiosity and nationalism to be considered a truly liberal country.

Still, if there is a common denominator in the oftentimes contradictory and paradoxical Greek responses to the US, this would have to be an open and widespread disapproval of the way in which the US defines its role in the domain of world politics. At the end of the day, however, protest and opposition expressed by one democratic country toward another should be regarded as a potential basis of debate, in order to promote understanding and mutual self-awareness, rather than as a *de facto* sign of bias and bad faith. After all, Greek 'anti-Americanism' has assumed the form of political critique, rather than 'hatred' or intense animosity as much of the literature on the phenomenon appears to indicate. Beyond the shadow of doubt, disapproval of US foreign policy is evident throughout Greek society – a phenomenon which may not always be entirely justifiable, but is certainly explainable. In the words of a Greek columnist:

> anti-Americanism is something that comes naturally to Greeks. It is the result of a concrete historical process, of a sense of patron–client dependence …
> It derives from awareness of the political cynicism that attended American efforts to capitalize on their – admittedly – significant contribution to the development of post-war Greece. (Papayiannidis 2003)

Greek opposition to US foreign policy, like all such phenomena, has complex permutations and inflections. Historical events and developments that contributed to the phenomenon will be outlined in the following section.

Historical roots

As political scientist Y. Voulgaris says, 'the roots of [Greek] anti-Americanism are political and grow out of the Greek Civil War' (2002: B14). Indeed, the Greek response to US foreign policy is a political tradition reflecting public awareness of US interventionism in Greek domestic and foreign affairs following World War II. Immediately after its liberation from Nazi occupation, Greece plunged into the most traumatic phase of its modern history, a Civil War (1946–49) which erupted when one of the most influential resistance groups, the Communist National Liberation Front (EAM) turned against the armed forces, which were backed by the Anglo-Americans. Historical research has shown that the US and the UK orchestrated the eruption of the Greek Civil War by arming both sides and inciting conflict, in an attempt to weaken EAM before the Greek Communist Party got the chance to win the elections – an event which would have caused the annexation of the country to the Soviet bloc.

The Civil War proved the most destructive in Greece's history, as it devastated not only the country's economy but also the texture of social relations by leaving indelible memories of brutality on all facets of Greek society for generations. The outcome of the Civil War inevitably brought persecutions of leftists and attempts to control centre-liberals for more than two decades. In the 1950s, the US activated in Greece the Truman doctrine which aimed at preventing the spread of communism by directly interfering with Greek governance and politics. Greece's political scene was dominated by right-wing regimes supported by the State Department, which exerted continuous pressure on the Greek political elites for the persecution and marginalization of leftists – a fact which exacerbated social tensions in the post-Civil War climate. There is no doubt that US intervention in post-war Greece saved the country from the clutches of the Soviet Union, but Greece had to pay the cost of having the State Department dictate its foreign relations as well as its domestic policies.[5]

As J. Kofas, author of *Under the Eagle's Claw: Exceptionalism in Post-war US–Greek Relations*, states: 'more than any other West European country, Greece suffered US pressures to maintain high defence expenditures, to pursue a right-wing ideological and political orientation, and to follow free trade and orthodox monetary policies' (2003: 4). Characteristically, in the course of the 1950s, Greece had to spend 40–45 per cent of its national budget on defence, with only 7 per cent being allocated to education (Kofas 2003: 5). While defence expenditures may have served to protect Greece from the communist threat, they obstructed economic development and social progress during a time when Greece was grappling with the challenge of reconstruction. In 1953, Greece and the US signed an agreement that allowed the establishment and operation of US military bases on Greek soil. Maurice Goldbloom, labour information officer of the US economic mission to Greece during the Truman presidency, admitted that 'Greece was thought of primarily as a military base, equipped with an army, and only secondarily as a country inhabited by people ...' (quoted in Kofas 2003: 4).

What compounded Greek resentment of US foreign policy in the Cold War era was the Cyprus controversy. An official colony of Britain since 1923, Cyprus became a sore point in US–Greek relations from the late 1950s, when the Greek-Cypriot struggle for independence pitted Greece against Turkey for control of the island. During this critical time, the State Department's unwillingness to take a decisive stance in favour of Greece, combined with increasing mistrust of US foreign policy, created the conditions for the emergence of an anti-NATO rhetoric which demanded that Greece follow a neutralist path by aligning itself with Tito of Yugoslavia, Nasser of Egypt and centre-leftist parties in Italy and France.

The call for self-determination, which would supposedly put an end to Greece's subservience to the US, was voiced by Andreas Papandreou, son of centrist Prime Minister George Papandreou (1963–65), and a rising star in the Greek political scene. Andreas Papandreou's increasing popularity became a source of concern for many in the State Department, as his charismatic – even flamboyant – personality touched sensitive political nerves among the Greek electorate and there was danger of Greece's drifting away from allegiance to US foreign policy. In his study of US implication in the military coup of 1967, Louis Klaveras (2004) cites evidence that shows the extent to which centrist political trends, embodied in Andreas Papandreou, were perceived as a potential threat by US diplomatic and intelligence operatives. In the words of a senior American intelligence officer:

> We were increasingly concerned about the election [of 1967]. We were concerned that if [George] Papandreou won, Andreas would be in the driver's seat for all practical purposes. He would withdraw Greece from NATO, [and] evacuate the United States bases … Andreas was also charging that the Americans corrupted the Greek economy. His answer would be to restrict the American presence and demand a high price for what remained. (quoted in Klaveras 2004: 8)

Even though there has been widespread speculation as to whether the Johnson administration staged the military coup in order to eliminate the likelihood of the Centre Union's electoral victory, there is no definitive evidence to suggest direct US involvement. Still, the connections between the junta and the Central Intelligence Agency have been sufficiently documented. The junta years loom dark in the Greek collective memory as the time when free elections were suspended, demonstrations and political dissent outlawed, police brutality and the violation of human rights legalized. In recognition of the extent to which, in order to promote its geopolitical interests, America did not hesitate to support a brutal regime, President Clinton apologized for US foreign policy toward Greece during those critical years:

> When the junta took over in 1967 here, the United States allowed its interests in prosecuting the Cold War to prevail over its interests – I should say its obligation – to support democracy, which was, after all, the cause for which we fought the Cold War. It is important that we acknowledge that … (quoted in Klaveras 2004)

President Clinton's apology will not easily erase what has been imprinted on the Greek collective consciousness: that the dictatorship was the result of the country's destructive relationship of clientism and dependence with the US national security state. The fact that Greek political parties themselves had, through a series of erroneous strategic moves, prepared the ground for the military coup is, sadly, an issue that both the Greek political establishment and the people themselves are even nowadays unwilling to face up to. All the same, the Nixon administration's support of the military dictatorship reawakened painful memories from the Civil War and created the conditions for a more intense and widespread mistrust of American foreign policy, as Greek leftists claimed to have been justified in their view of the US, while right-wingers felt betrayed and humiliated.

Before collapsing in July 1974, the Greek junta orchestrated the overthrow of Archbishop Makarios, the democratically elected President of Cyprus (Makarios's attempts to forge connections with non-aligned nations in order to follow a neutralist path were also posing a threat to US interests, given the strategic importance of the island against the backdrop of East–West conflict). Makarios's overthrow paved the way for the Turkish invasion of the island – an event which is another major cause of resentment against the US in Greece, as it is widely believed that the State Department, led by Henry Kissinger, was instrumental in planning and supporting the Turkish invasion and subsequent division of Cyprus. That Greek Cypriots bear some of the blame for the island's military occupation is an indisputable fact, as there were instances of discrimination and even persecution of the Turkish Cypriot minority that provided Turkey with an ideological excuse. All the same, there is nothing to legitimize the military intervention in the Greek mind, especially since the occupation of the northern part of Cyprus (80 per cent of whose population was Greek) was accompanied by ethnic cleansing which, in addition to two thousand civilian casualties, caused the expatriation of many more from the Turkish-occupied part of the island. And even though the UN Security Council has repeatedly denounced the invasion, Turkey has refused to withdraw and the military occupation of northern Cyprus still continues.

The junta's fall in 1974 found Greece challenged by the necessity of rebuilding its parliamentary system and redefining its domestic infrastructures as well as its foreign policy. Under the leadership of conservative Konstantin Karamanlis, the country entered the path of democratic modernization and greater independence, as membership in the European Economic Community offered Greece some diplomatic leverage, thus releasing it from the tight grip of clientism that marked its relationship with the US in the previous three decades. But resentment against the American government, instead of decreasing, now ran deeper and more widespread because of Cyprus and of what was perceived as the US support of Turkey's claim over the Aegean. In 1975, the ultra-leftist group November 17 emerged which, wielding terror as a political weapon, targeted American, British, Turkish, as well as Greek diplomats, politicians, police and intelligence officers, and even businessmen, managing to remain undetected until 2002. The first victim of November 17 was CIA station chief Richard Welch, whose death elicited an official condemnation by both the government and the opposition but not much sympathy by the public who had come to regard the CIA as an enemy.

In 1981 Andreas Papandreou was elected into office, combining a populist agenda with a leftist vision of domestic welfare reform, and a foreign policy rhetoric which mixed affirmation of national pride with condemnation of US im-perialism. Papandreou's demagogic show of opposition to the doctrine of American exceptionalism articulated many Greek people's frustration, not only with the country's long subordination to US geopolitical interests, but also with domestic social and economic problems which Greeks were willing to attribute to America rather than to internal conditions that obstructed progress. Even though Papandreou made a point of pursuing a multilateral foreign policy, which included forging close ties with Arab countries, and every now and then antagonized Washington by flamboyant displays of anti-US rhetoric, he proved to be rather mainstream, as he continued Karamanlis's diplomatic legacy which aimed to turn Greece into a valuable partner in the Euro-Atlantic bloc. In fact, throughout the 1980s and the 1990s, irrespective of public scepticism, Greek governments undertook some unpopular foreign policy initiatives (as, for instance, sanctions against Iraq, participation in the NATO-led Implementation Force in Bosnia, support of the US-led war on Serbia) to comply with NATO decisions and align Greece with Western interests in order to derive benefits from the emerging New World Order. In other words, in the course of the 1980s and the 1990s Greek governments were forced to maintain a precarious balance between the necessity for co-operation with Washington and respect for popular feeling, which, at least up until the mid-1990s, registered continuing scepticism but decreasing negativity toward the US.

Revitalization of anti-Americanism: from 1999 to the present

Whereas in Europe the new 'anti-American' culture has been fundamentally inspired by the George W. Bush administration's unilateral foreign policy, in Greece the onset of a new period of intense opposition to America's exceptionalism coincides with the presidency of Bill Clinton. That President Clinton was not a favourite among Greeks was made evident during his visit to Athens in November 1999 – a visit marked by demonstrations that attracted much notice in the American and European media. Characteristically, a poll conducted a few days prior to President Clinton's visit on behalf of the widely circulating newspaper *Ethnos* showed that only 12 per cent of the Greeks polled had a favourable opinion of Clinton, with 80 per cent registering a negative opinion.[6]

The revitalization of anti-US polemic in Greece was undoubtedly triggered by the US-led intervention in Serbia, a traditional ally, but was also the result of the general climate of instability and fear caused by events associated with the disintegration of the Republic of Yugoslavia. Starting in the early 1990s, ethnic conflicts in Yugoslavia threatened to erupt into a generalized Balkan conflict – a prospect which Greeks (with the memory of two Balkan wars in their modern history) felt extremely apprehensive about. When in 1994 the Clinton administration recognized the Republic of 'Macedonia', the Greek public felt shocked and besieged (the northern part of Greece is also called Macedonia and Greece has been opposing the use of 'Republic of Macedonia' for the Former Yugoslav Republic of Macedonia as an official name of the country). In the years that followed, and while conflict in Yugoslavia spread from Slovenia, to Croatia, to Bosnia, to Kosovo, Greeks remained committed to Serbia, despite evidence of Serbian atrocities against the Muslim population of Bosnia and Kosovo. Turmoil in Yugoslavia and the 'Macedonian' problem made Greeks regard with increasing suspicion and apprehension Germany's and the United States' official recognition of former Yugoslav republics as signs of Euro-Atlantic expansionism in the Balkan region.

President Clinton's implication in what was regarded as an American betrayal of Greece over the 'Macedonian' controversy did not increase his popularity, and had a negative effect on public perceptions of Ambassador Nicolas Burns.

Ambassador Burns, who left Athens fully convinced that Greek anti-Americanism was both irrational and a definite impediment in US–Greek relations,[7] elicited angry responses not only from the Greek press but also from politicians, because the extroverted style of his diplomacy was interpreted as high-handedness. Following the Ambassador's visits to Greek military installations and public agencies, his outspokenness on issues ranging from Greek–Turkish relations to Greek labour law, as well as his public reprimand of the government for its being 'soft on terrorism', even Parliament Speaker Apostolos Kaklamanis protested against the Ambassador's acting like a 'deputy governor'.[8]

With the NATO bombings of Serbia in April 1999, anxiety over a possible destabilization of the Balkans and renewed tension with Turkey, along with reawakened memories of US interventionism, came into focus over what even domestic political commentators referred to as the average Greek's 'pro-Serb paranoia'. Poll results appeared to be justifying this assessment: 95 per cent of Greeks opposed the bombing; 63.5 per cent expressed a favourable view of Milošević, while 94.4 per cent had a negative opinion of President Clinton.[9]

The explanation of the phenomenon, however, is more complex than has generally been assumed, especially by the foreign media. On the surface, the Greek public's sympathy for Serbia appeared to have been the result of nationalist reflexes derived from the fact that Serbia had been a traditional ally of Greece (among other things, in the struggle against the Ottomans and the Nazis), as well as a valuable trading partner and, quite importantly, a fellow member of the Orthodox Christian Church. Another related explanation would have to be that the Greek pro-Serb stance was the result of anti-Albanian bias as a result of an almost frightening influx of illegal Albanian immigrants who, because the Greek economy was too fragile to accommodate them, contributed to an increased crime rate and were experienced as a threat to Greek national homogeneity. Xenophobic attitudes toward Albanian immigrants definitely did not help to raise sympathy for the Kosovo Albanians in Greece.

On another level, Greeks' one-sided view of the matter was the result of the Greek media's news coverage which placed less emphasis on Serbian atrocities against the Albanian Muslims first in Bosnia and then in Kosovo, and primarily focused on the devastation of Belgrade by NATO bombs, on the killing of innocent Serb civilians, the extirpation of hundreds of thousands of Serbs from their ancestral lands in Kosovo, the destruction of the Serb economic infrastructure, and the environmental damage caused by depleted uranium bombs. Images of the thousands of Serbs sitting on Belgrade bridges holding candles as they waited for the NATO bombers constructed Serbia as simultaneously an indomitable defender of the right of national sovereignty and the sacrificial victim of an international conspiracy. As Jon Kofas says, 'Greeks of disparate ideological and political orientations were convinced that the US and NATO were deliberately dividing and weakening Serbia so they could exert hegemony over Orthodox territory ...' (249). The words of a young Greek anti-war protester summarize in more ways than one popular feeling at the time: '[I]t is ludicrous to say the bombing is to help humanity. It's about the US pursuing its own expansionist strategic interests.'[10] To claim that Greek condemnation of the military intervention in Kosovo and Serbia springs from a nationalist sense of allegiance to a fellow-Orthodox country is not inaccurate, but it also constitutes a rather simplistic view of the Greek response (Mihas 2002). For instance, if Greek reflexes were merely a matter of nationalism mixed with fanatical religiosity, there would be no rational explanation either for Greece's repeatedly waging war against Bulgaria (another fellow-Orthodox nation), or for Greek support of Arab nations.

On a deeper level, it was what most Greeks perceived as the Anglo-Americans' unwillingness to seek a constructive political means in order to reach a diplomatic, rather than a military, resolution of the problem that aggravated public opposition to the NATO bombings. The ineffectiveness of war violence as a means of restoring geopolitical stability in Kosovo was voiced in the Greek media over and over again:

> What is tragic [about the Kosovo problem] is that on the one hand it is not feasible to allow Milošević's tyrannical authority over a minority to go unchecked, especially since it is a major cause of instability in the entire region, while simultaneously the 'remedy' offered is equally, if not more, detrimental to the patient. (Dimitrakos 1999: B:04)

In other words, the victimization of the Serbs was not regarded as the appropriate solution to the Kosovo Albanians' victimization. Indeed, Greeks remained cynically unconvinced by the rhetoric of morality that came to support the NATO bombings. After all, Greek sympathy for the persecuted Kurdish minority in Turkey did not cultivate much public confidence in the moral intentions of the US, Turkey's greatest Western ally. Only two months before the bombing of Serbia, the Greek government facilitated the scandalous abduction of Kurdish leader Abdhoulah Otsalan by CIA agents in Nairobi, Kenya. The Greek public, embarrassed by what was regarded as their own government's act of betrayal, unavoidably questioned the righteous rhetoric that supported human rights for the Kosovo Albanians while turning a blind eye to the suffering of 14 million Kurds in Turkey.

A similar sense that a moral double standard underlies the US foreign policy agenda informed Greek public response to 11 September 2001 as well as to the 'war on terror' that ensued, and was repeatedly voiced by the Greek mass media:

> America declared war on Iraq because of its supposed possession of weapons of mass destruction – turning a blind eye on the possession of nuclear weapons by Israel. When the existence of such weapons in Iraq proved to be a lie, the United States justified the war on the basis of Iraq's violation of human rights, ignoring the systematic and blatant violation of such rights in Israel. (Liakos 2004: B42)

Emphasis was also placed on Saddam Hussein's support by the US during the Iran–Iraq war, on bin Laden's prior connections with the CIA, and on America's reliance on the Afghan *mujahedin* forces to counter the Soviet invasion of Afghanistan.

Moreover, unlike the rhetoric of American media, such as Cable News Network (CNN), which de-contextualized the terrorist hit by zeroing in on the horror of the event itself, the Greek public view tended to also place the attack in the context of conditions that emerged as a result of US hegemony in the Middle East, as well as worldwide. As Antonis Liakos, professor of History at the University of Athens, put it: 'After September 11, terrorism [in the official American discourse] was cut off from its political context and imposed as a powerful language construct that shapes reality and dictates attitudes' (2002: B43). Interpreting the terror unleashed by Al-Quaida as a direct result of erroneous American policy decisions, the Greek media, as well as the Greek public, attributed part of the blame to the victim; this explains poll results according to which 30 per cent of respondents stated their belief that 11 September 2001 was the outcome of US foreign policy, 85 per cent opposed US actions in Afghanistan, 94 per cent were against the Iraq invasion, while 75 per cent did not desire Greece to be militarily involved in the 'war on terror' (Carassava 2003: B12).

Thus, despite the Greek government's statement of support and authorization of the use of Greece's airspace as well as of an air force base at Souda Bay on Crete for the refuelling of US planes, the Greek public's scepticism, or even cynicism, concerning the causes behind Muslim terror were interpreted by numerous American political analysts as a sign of callousness, incomprehension and even hostility. Indicative of the considerable embarrassment that Greek 'anti-Americanism' caused in the Greek-American community is the following commentary by Gregory C. Pappas, publisher of *Greek America Magazine*:

> Despite ... Greece's promise to offer any assistance the United States needs in the fight, the vast majority of Greek citizens oppose the US actions in Afghanistan ... there exists in Greece – amongst a large cross-section of mainstream society – a sense of simultaneous 'tragic, yes, but they got what they deserved' mentality. (Pappas 2006)

Such criticism, typical of the general view of American media of all opposition to US policy in the wake of 11 September 2001 misses out on the significance of the critique, by Greeks and by other peoples, of conditions that preceded as well as followed the tragedy of the terrorist attack. Above all, it signifies once again America's reluctance (or inability) to face up to its own complex motives.

Political implications

Greek public reaction to the US combines opposition to US unilateral interventionism with awareness of the need for collaboration between the two countries; according to a 2004 poll, six in ten Greeks believe that Greece cannot carve an independent foreign policy but must take into account US interests.[11] On the other hand, the White House appears to be recognizing in Greece a valuable ally with whom there is total agreement over 'the larger issues', as President George W. Bush stated during the Greek Premier's visit to Washington last year. Indeed, Greece's military insignificance is counterbalanced by its membership in the Eurozone, growing economic and diplomatic role in the Balkans, strong ties with Arab nations but also with Israel, and participation in the UN Security Council.

The US counts on Greece's co-operation in the still unstable Balkan region and on Greek support of Turkey's and other Balkan countries' prospective membership in the EU. On the other hand, it is imperative for Greece that the so-called 'Macedonian' issue be resolved in a manner favourable to Greek national as well as economic interests (Greece is a major investor in the ex-Yugoslav Republic of Macedonia), and for that a strong relationship with the US is a precondition. Likewise, Greece needs US support for a solution to the Cyprus problem and is thus not ready to grant Turkey the monopoly of partnership with the US. Indeed, in the past decade or so, Greek governments have been far more pragmatic and far less ideological in their dealings with the State Department.

All the same, negative views of America in the Greek public realm are constricting the diplomatic leverage of the Greek government, which balances uneasily between not offending the superpower, serving Greek national interest, forging credibility within the EU, and maintaining the support of the electorate by catering to their feelings of distrust toward the US. In other words, Greek foreign policy has a multi-polar orientation, as it seeks the golden mean between protection under the umbrella of the US, a European identity, and national autonomy. This balance will become increasingly precarious if the US continues on the path of unilateral militarism and the rift between it and Europe widens. In the fluid international climate of today, marked, among other things, by the emergence of China as a pole of international influence, the US is called upon to convince the world of its valid claim to power. As Adam Garfinkle says:

> Anti-Americanism matters, for a liberal great power such as the US depends to a considerable degree on the good-will and benign expectations of others. We are wise to act and speak in ways that produce common security for the maximum number of countries and persuade them that their own interests are best served when they run parallel to ours. When we fail to do so, the impact can be significant. The Iraq war is a case in point. (Garfinkle 2004: 303)

Notes

1 Dan Flynn in J. Glazov (2002).
2 *'L'Amérique dans nos têtes: un siècle de fascinations et d'aversions'*, organized by EHESS, Paris, Hachette, 1986.
3 T. Mihas, quoted in F. Ajami (2003b): 55.
4 Poll conducted on 22 May 2004 by VPRC (Greek public opinion research organisation) on behalf of the Athens newspaper *Kathimerini.*
5 See, for instance, T. A. Couloumbis (1966); T. A. Couloumbis *et al.* (1976); T. A. Couloumbis and J. O. Iatrides (1980); Y. P. Roubatis (1987) and I. Stefanidis (2001).

6 Poll conducted on 3–5 November 1999 by ALCO on behalf of the Athens newspaper *Ethnos.*

7 See, for instance, Ambassaror N. Burns's interview in A. Papahelas, 2001.

8 See for instance, D. Mitropoulos (1998).

9 Poll conducted on 20 March 1999 by ALCO on behalf of the Athens newspaper *Ta Nea.*

10 Quoted in A. Stanley (1999).

11 Poll conducted on 22 May 2004 by VPRC on behalf of the Athens newspaper *Kathimerini.*

14 Anti-Americanism in France

Ariane Chebel d'Appollonia

France demonstrated beyond doubt its solidarity with the Americans after 11 September 2001. Echoing Benjamin Franklin who once declared that 'we are citizens of two nations: France and our homeland', Jean-Marie Colombani, the editor of *Le Monde*, proclaimed 'we are all Americans'.[1] Former French President Jacques Chirac and other European leaders rallied around this heroic watchword. Memorial services were organized in Paris and spontaneous demonstrations of sympathy took place in many cities. Thousands of French citizens held candle vigils, rallies and prayer services. The Western alliance suddenly became more than a concept, invoking an emotional sense of community, a widespread feeling of common destiny.

But within a year, both solidarity and team spirit had vanished. They were replaced by mutual resentment, disdain and tension. The media, the politicians and the experts focused on the issues that divide France from the US. The US was depicted as a 'hyperpower'[2] – a term coined by the former Foreign Minister Hubert Védrine – trying to impose a set of strategies and policies deeply resented by many US allies. France and other European countries felt that George W. Bush's administration was forcing them into accepting a Manichean ultimatum: they were either with the United States in its 'war on terror' or against it (Lacorne and Judt 2005) and, by extension, with the terrorists. Despite the Bush rhetoric of continuing close trans-Atlantic co-operation, French officials and public opinion clearly perceived that his actual intention was to leave them no other option but to rally to the side of the US. Reluctance to accept what Stanley Hoffman called America's 'itch of unilateralism' resurfaced even before the turbulence generated by the Iraq War (Hoffman 2005). President Chirac publicly wondered if the Afghan campaign was not, in fact, a way to relegate Europe to the infamous role of 'vassal' of the US. This war was indeed run from Tampa, Florida, and Washington, DC, not from Mons in Belgium (where the military planners of the North Atlantic Treaty Organization are located) and certainly not from Paris. Reluctant to play second fiddle, the French government liked neither the tone used by the 'neo-conservatives'[3] nor the tempo imposed by them at the United Nations meetings.

The connection drawn by Bush between the war on terror and the concept of preventive war, as defined by the National Security Strategy of September 2002, worried the US's allies. The 'Bush doctrine', with its credo of military dominance in perpetuity' was critically perceived as an imperialist doctrine and accelerated the divergence. For French Foreign Ministry official Gilles Andreani, the 'war on terror' was a 'good cause' but a 'wrong concept'. His analysis reflected the dominant perceptions on the French side:

> Calling the fight against terrorism a 'war' entails some major drawbacks [...] The United States bent both its internal judicial rules and international law to accommodate the concept of war on terror [...] The connection drawn by the Americans between the war on terrorism and the concept of preventive war has undermined the anti-terrorist coalition [...] The linkage with the war against Iraq has aggravated the problem, while heightening anti-Western and anti-American feeling in the Middle East and the Islamic world. Finally, the 'war on terror' has detracted from the consideration of some urgent political problems that fuel Middle East terrorism. (Andreani 2004)

Dominique Moisi, deputy director of the Paris-based *Institut Français des Relations Internationales* and fervent proponent of the Western alliance, reluctantly came to the conclusion that 'defending western values takes more than military muscle'. Unfortunately, for the Bush administration, 'what is bad for America can only be bad for the world' (Moisi 2002). Such a narrow-minded bias, concluded Moisi, could only lead to dramatic misunderstandings and increase the process of 'continental drift' driving the United States and Europe apart.

On the US side, France was depicted as a Soviet-style economy, a hypocritical and arrogant second-rank country populated by lazy and ageing citizens. 'French voters are trying to preserve a 35-hour work week', wrote Thomas Friedman in *The New York Times*, 'in a world where Indian engineers are ready to work a 35-hour day'. Conservatives disliked France for its centralism and elitism. Liberals suspected its ability to manage minorities and to fight political extremism. The discussions on the UN Security Council in the fall of 2002 and winter of 2003 accelerated the divergence and triggered an unprecedented wave of Francophobia. Newspapers described France as the most anti-Semitic country in Europe, with a penchant for appeasement (from Munich to the opposition to the Iraq War) and anti-Americanism. Representative of the anti-French coalition, Friedman also declared the US 'at war with France' and asked to 'vote France off' the Security Council of the United Nations and to replace it 'with India' (Friedman 2003b). Richard Z. Chesnoff dissected the 'arrogance of the French' (Chesnoff 2005) while Charles Krauthammer, another champion of Francophobia, declared 'Thank God for not being French'. Jacques Chirac's resistance to the US war policy was countered with the Secretary of Defense's willingness to 'punish' France.

However, France is not, and never was, the only country that opposed the US policies. In 2002, according to the Pew Research Centre, the US was globally perceived as being 'too big, too powerful, too willing to go it alone in the world' (Pew 2002a). The sharp drop in America's global popularity that dated from the start of the military intervention in Iraq has not been reversed in most European countries. In 2005, more than two-thirds of the public in Spain (69 per cent) and Poland (67 per cent) still thought that their countries were wrong to engage in military action in Iraq. In Great Britain, the support for military intervention declined from 61 per cent in 2003 to 39 per cent in 2005. Ninety-two per cent of the French public (83 per cent in 2003) and 87 per cent (80 per cent in 2003) of the German public reaffirmed that the right decision was not to intervene. This negative view of the intervention in Iraq was coupled with an increasing discontent regarding 'US unilateralism'. Overwhelming percentages of people in Europe believed that the United States did not take their countries' interests into account when making foreign policy. While 67 per cent of the US respondents said that their country did pay sufficient attention to the interests of other countries, only 38 per cent of the Germans, 32 per cent of the British, 19 per cent of the Spanish, and 18 per cent of the French believed so (Pew 2005a,b).

Attitudes toward the US remained negative in Europe. A favourable opinion towards the US decreased among the populations of the United States' traditional major European allies: in Great Britain (83 per cent in 1999–2000, 55 per cent in 2005), France (62 per cent in 1999–2000, 43 per cent in 2005), Germany (78 per cent in 1999–2000, 41 per cent in 2005) and Spain (50 per cent in 1999–2000, 41 per cent in 2005). When asked whether the problem was more with President George W. Bush or with America in general, Europeans primarily blamed Bush whose policies were seen throughout Europe as a major driver of anti-Americanism. Those Europeans who said the problem was 'mostly' Bush outnumbered those who said it was 'a more general problem with America' by margins of about two-to-one. This ratio was especially lopsided in Spain, where 76 per cent of those with a negative view of the US blamed Bush while just 14 per cent blamed America (Pew 2005a,b).

Many Europeans depicted President Bush as an inarticulate Texas cowboy who was undemocratically elected, unfortunately re-elected and influenced by a religious fundamentalism. He imposed violated democratic rules within his country (with restrictions on civil liberties and warrantless spying on Americans) and undermined the rule-based multilateral order by imposing a strategy that was at best ineffective and at worst aggravated the problems it was meant to solve. Roughly three-quarters of the publics in Germany (77 per cent) and France (74 per cent) said 'Bush's re-election has made them feel less favourable toward the US'. The front page of the *Daily Mirror*, one of the UK's largest mass-circulation tabloids, simply asked: 'How Can 59,054,087 People Be So DUMB?' (*Daily Mirror* 2004).

Notwithstanding the current widespread anti-Americanism in Europe, it is still a commonplace assertion on both sides on the Atlantic – but especially in the United States – that France is the most anti-American country in Europe, if not in the world. How can we explain this 'French exception'? Why is France perceived as a bastion of systematic opposition to the United States? Is anti-Americanism in France in fact deeper than, or different from, such manifestations in the past? Are France and the United States drifting apart on basic values or on some substantial issues of international politics? Undoubtedly the long history of anti-Americanism in France suggests that French antipathy is not a short-term aspect of French politics; rather it is woven into a deep structural reality of French cultural and political life. But when it comes to evaluating the real impact of anti-Americanism on French policies, a more reserved assessment prevails – as France and the United States appear to be both reluctant allies and competitive partners.

Anti-Americanism 'made in France'

What exactly is 'anti-Americanism'? The term is often used with no precision, a catch-all phrase to describe any number of grievances and arguments. It can encompass opposition to the domestic or foreign policies of the past or current administrations; the global influence of the United States, especially after the collapse of the Soviet Union; 'American' values (such as individualism, market democracy, consumerism); and/or antipathy to Americans as people.[4] Anti-Americanism can designate hatred of America, of Americans or of 'US things', described as a sort of 'pathological symptom of hysteria' by Theodore Zeldin (1990). It can also be defined as 'an unfavourable predisposition towards the United States, which leads individuals to interpret Americans' actions through pre-existing views and negative stereotypes, irrespectively of the facts'.[5] According to this definition, anti-Americanism is a negative predisposition, based on prejudices and stereotypical judgements that influence the perception of America and Americans.

Both are then criticizing for what they are – relative to what they ought to be – and not for what they do. In that case, the behaviour of the United States itself has little to do with the resentment that it has generated in Europe. On the other hand, negative stereotypes can be fuelled by criticisms of US policies – domestic and foreign – of the current administration ('anti-Bushism') and/or by the rejection of the so-called 'American lifestyle'. Both America and Americans are criticized for what they do and not for what they are. Anti-Americanism as a critical opinion and anti-Americanism as a 'pathological' disposition obviously overlap each other; stereotype-driven attacks on America influence criticism of American politics. Furthermore, as pointed out by Robert Singh:

> recent worldwide expressions of anti-Americanism assume distinct forms along a continuum, from passive dislike and private disapproval through mild gestures of resistance (boycotting Nike) to mass activism (protest marches such as those of anti-globalization demonstrations in Seattle in 1999) and violence (wrecking McDonalds and KFC stores and, ultimately, targeting Americans for terrorist strikes). (Singh 2006: 29)

Anti-Americanism takes different forms and may evolve over time (Werz 2004). Consequently, it is more appropriate to refer to 'anti-Americanisms' rather than to consider anti-Americanism as a coherent and monolithic ideology.

Once one recognizes that the sources and expressions of anti-Americanism are diverse and multiple, one can begin to wonder why France is perceived as an 'exception' (Meunier 2000). Is it correct to argue that 'French anti-Americanism is of different character from that of other European countries' (Fabbrini 2002: 4)? Such an assertion is commonly justified by three reasons: the long historical pedigree of anti-Americanism in France; the competition between 'two imperialisms'; and French national pride frustrated by the downgrading of French grandeur or nostalgia for past glory. A brief examination of these arguments suggests that they are mainly unconvincing. In fact, the analysis of French anti-Americanism rarely escapes from the stereotypes that fuel anti-Americanism itself. The result of such a 'mirror-effect' leads to a fallacy: to demonstrate the exceptionalism of French anti-Americanism, mainly defined as the antithesis of American exceptionalism,[6] on the ground provided by the conviction shared by many anti-Americans of all stripes and persuasion that France is an exception.

It is undeniable that French anti-Americanism is as old as, if not older than, the United States itself. Jean-Baptiste Duroselle (1978) and, more recently Philippe Roger (2002) both have respectively demonstrated that the history of conflicting relations between France and the United States began two centuries ago during the American colonial period. Yet, the evaluation of the 'sedimented reservoir of anti-American arguments' (Meunier 2005: 127) requires a distinction between two related but nonetheless distinct registers. The first one is cultural and relates to negative images of American values, negative stereotypes about personal characteristics of American, and contempt for American civilization. The second one is political and refers to the recurrent crises between the US and French governments.

Cultural anti-Americanism

In terms of its image, the United States did not always enjoy a good reputation among the French intellectuals. Cultural animosity towards America originated with the philosophers of the Enlightenment, such as Raynal and Voltaire. Buffon argued for the physical inferiority of the New World by employing his theory of 'alteration' – which predated the scornful discourse on 'degeneration' so popular among French intellectuals during the 1920s and 1930s. The United States was despised for its 'industrialism' (Aron and Dandieu 1931), its 'lack of culture', and its 'mass production' and 'mass society' – all symptoms of dysfunctional modern life, alienation and insecurity. Two typical works illustrated cultural anti-Americanism: Georges Duhamel's *America, the Menace* and André Siegfried's *America Comes of Age*.[7] Both denounced the 'materialism' of American society, its 'mechanical civilization', its excessive urbanization and the problem of ethnic conflicts and integration of immigrants. After World War II, both communist and anti-communist French intellectuals echoed comparable arguments in their anti-American crusade. François Mauriac shared with left-wing intellectuals a deep disdain for the 'mercantile' culture of America. The pro-Soviet Roger Vailland suspected the fridge of being part of an American plot to destroy French culture. *Le Monde* asserted, 'Coca Cola is the Dantzig of European culture'.[8]

Cultural anti-Americanism entailed a rejection of every trait associated with America, from urban violence to mass poverty. The rejection of the 'Coca-Colonization' was followed by attacks against the invasion of France by McDonalds and other symbols of US 'cultural imperialism'. Jacques Thibau, in *La France colonisée* (1980) developed a metaphor of American colonialism in France. Euro-Disney was described, in 1992, as 'a cultural Chernobyl' by the theatre director Ariane Mnouchkine (Pells 1997). Meanwhile, the most disenchanted US writers or film-makers have received the greatest praise: Upton Sinclair or John Dos Passos before World War II, Spike Lee and Michael Moore today. The French welcomed a book like *Bowling Alone* because it reinforced their disdain for the mediocrity of the American middle class – especially its propensity, as Robert Altman put it himself, to watch *Friends* instead of having them. The success of *Bowling for Columbine*, *Super Size Me* or *Fahrenheit 9/11* could also be explained by their equation with the most recurrent anti-American clichés related to violence (from gun shots to the death penalty), political demagogy, corruption, racism, poverty, the influence of the oil industry and bad cuisine.

However, a global assessment of French cultural anti-Americanism should also take into account the pro-US French intellectuals or, at least, those who condemned anti-Americanism. Raymond Aron, for instance, did not subscribe to any anti-US clichés and was perceived as an 'Atlantist'. Jean-François Revel recently qualified anti-Americanism an 'obsession' driven by a deep fixation on an image of the United States. Even Sartre and de Beauvoir expressed ambivalent feelings on the subject. On the one hand, they despised US policies and politics, notably during the McCarthy period, when they were more or less affiliated to the Communist Party. De Beauvoir declared that America was 'becoming Fascist' and Sartre wrote that it 'had gone mad'. On the other hand, they expressed their admiration for US writers, jazz, movies and New York.

Furthermore, French intellectuals, such as André Glucksmann and Pascal Bruckner, recently supported the invasion of Iraq. Together with the film-maker Romain Goupil and the founder of *Médecins sans Frontières*, Bernard Kouchner, they both signed a petition published by *Le Monde* on 3 March 2003. They condemned French opposition to the war by arguing that the intervention against Saddam was a necessary continuation of the fight against past totalitarian regimes and current dictatorships that practised ethnic cleansing.[9] Glucksmann stigmatized the 'demagogy' of the French government, its 'powerlessness' and its immoral appeasement. The essential distinction was not, he wrote, between the supporters of the war and supporters of peace but rather 'between the retarded people of September 10 and the enlightened ones of September 11' (Pew 2005a), between 'nihilism and civilization'. Even Régis Debray, characterized as a champion of anti-Americanism, defined his position as purely political. He pointed out that some of the most vehemently anti-American intellectuals in political terms (himself included) were the most enthusiastic supporters of US culture.

Cultural anti-Americanism has been analyzed as an attempt to protect the cultural supremacy of France. Like Etiemble (1964), who tried to limit the damage of Franglais during the 1960s, outraged defenders of French culture continue to fight. The rhetoric of French cultural exception is frequently discernable in ministerial pronouncements. Successive ministers of culture, like Toubon (Gaullist) and Lang (Socialist) during the 1990s, have tried to restrict the number of English words that could appear in official documents, scientific journals and the media. Despite the support of the *Académie Française*, the attempt to protect French culture though the defence of language purity has failed. Furthermore, this defensive cultural nationalism is declining and the influence and prestige of French intellectuals are decreasing. Ironically, French modern or post-modern theories attract their most enthusiastic followers on American campuses (Cusset 2003). Foucault, Kristeva, Baudrillard, Derrida and Deleuze – all members of the so-called 'French Theory' – enjoy a greater audience in the United States than in France. 'Anti-Americanism today is fuelled by a new consideration and it is no longer confined to intellectuals' (Judt in O'Connor and Griffiths 2006). But the anti-American intellectuals are few in number and, while they dislike US policies or some aspects of American lifestyle, they often watch *The Sopranos* or *Law and Order* on French TV.

French cultural anti-Americanism has been analysed as exceptional because of a purported French peculiarity: 'the French people think of themselves as more universalistic than any other people' (Matsumoto 2004). Pierre Bourdieu, for instance, spoke of Franco–American relations as a fight between 'two imperialisms of the universal' (1998). If so, one can anticipate than anti-American stereotypes are vivid in France when manifestations of 'US imperialism' multiply in the international arena. Does the increasing disapproval of the foreign policy of George W. Bush's administration lead to negative views of the American people? No one can deny that favourable opinion of the United States has declined in France, from 62 per cent in 1999 to 43 per cent in 2005 (Pew 2005).

This trend is confirmed by recent surveys such as the so-called 'thermometer question' elaborated by the German Marshall Fund of the United States for measuring the nations' feelings toward the United States. The largest drop in 'warmth' has been recorded among French respondents, from 60 degrees in 2002 to 50 degrees in 2003–05 (GMF 2002, 2003a, 2003b, 2004, 2005). Yet, cool feelings towards America are balanced by positive images of the Americans. They are described as 'hardworking' by 89 per cent of the French – the highest score in Europe – 'inventive' (76 per cent) and 'honest' (57 per cent). Negative stereotypes receive less support, except a reputation for 'violence' (63 per cent). Americans are 'rude' according to 36 per cent of French people, 'greedy' according to 31 per cent (in contrast to 70 per cent of the US respondents about themselves) and 'immoral' according to only 37 per cent (Pew 2005a). Obviously, French people like Americans – to some extent, more than Americans like themselves – and America, while disliking the foreign policy of George W. Bush's administration. In response to the question 'What's the problem with the US?' 74 per cent answer 'mostly Bush' and only 21 per cent 'America in general'.

Political anti-Americanism

French political anti-Americanism is of comparable vintage. Like its cultural counterpart, it dates back to the eighteenth century. Despite the mythical image of Marquis de Lafayette, the Franco–American relationship experienced difficulties in overcoming a series of crises that originated with the issue of war debts after the

1783 Treaty. It continued during the nineteenth century, with the French support for the disastrous attempt of Maximilian to establish a Catholic empire in Mexico, and France's opposition to the Spanish–American War of 1898. The United States was subsequently blamed for the 'bad treaty' imposed by President Wilson in 1918 and resentment increased with the dispute over war debts. The United States was criticized as being isolationist, in contrast to previous periods when it was accused of being imperialist.

The period after 1945 was marked by numerous trans-Atlantic tensions. The US atomic bomb was demonized and the two countries clashed over the issue of the European Defence Community (EDC) project. Eisenhower's refusal to help French troops trapped at Dien Bien Phu in 1954, and then the Suez crisis of 1956 poisoned Franco–American relations. The humiliation over each colonial crisis was accompanied by resentment at the prospect of accepting US charity. According to a Gallup poll conducted after the announcement of the Marshall Plan, 47 per cent of respondents thought motives of the United States were self-interest: it wanted to improve Europe's standard of living so that it could reopen markets for US products (Gallup 1947). Rancour developed against the United States, resulting in what Philippe Roger called a 'double denegation': denial of intention (the US did not do it for us) and denial of fact (the Marshall Plan was not helpful anyway).

When de Gaulle returned to power in 1958, he developed a kind of 'sovereignist' anti-Americanism designed to restore both national sovereignty and grandeur. He thus sabotaged Kennedy's grand design for an Atlantic partnership, twice vetoed the British candidacy to the European Economic Community, withdrew France from the integrated military command of the North Atlantic Treaty Organization, and attempted to undermine the dollar's convertibility. Accusations of American imperialism multiplied, with visions of power and authority being projected onto the United States. De Gaulle seized up every opportunity to challenge US foreign policy, condemning the war in Vietnam, siding with the Arabs during the Six-Day War and shouting *'Vive le Québec libre!'* from a balcony in Québec City. The resignation of de Gaulle in 1969 did not result in a dissipation of Franco–American tensions. Economic crises multiplied, from the issue of the reform of the Common Agricultural Policy to the crisis over US extraterritorial legislation (such as the *Helms-Burton Act* or the *Libya Sanctions Act*). The two countries quarrelled over a succession of issues: bananas, iron, wine, cheese, chicken, beef hormones and genetically modified organisms. Foreign policy tensions included the US bombing of Libya in 1986, US reluctance to support the Land Mine Treaty, the Kyoto Protocol on global warming, the treaty establishing the International Criminal Court and the Comprehensive Test Ban Treaty. Serious French reservations about a discernible unilateralist trend in US foreign policy can thus be traced back to the mid-1980s.

Furthermore, there are a variety of shades of political anti-Americanism, because Communist Party members and Gaullists, members of a Green Party or supporters of the National Front blame 'America' for different reasons. 'Sovereignist anti-Americanism is often associated with Gaullism and focuses on the defence of national independence and international prestige. Communists and Socialists share a social anti-Americanism' (Meunier 2005), portraying the United States as an unequal society in which a growing number of disadvantaged people suffer from social and economic exclusion, a lack of welfare protection and an inferior education. Both leftist and rightist proponents of the French republican model of integration despise the 'ghettoization' of American society.

Some supporters of Jean-Marie Le Pen dislike America's pro-Israeli foreign policy (described as an illustration of the influence of the US Jewish 'lobby') but welcome the war on terror as part of the 'clash of civilizations' between Christianity and Islam. The partisans of French secularism (*laïcité*) oppose what they regard as US religious messianic rhetoric and the 'Godly Republicans'. Globalization is interpreted in varied circles (from the extreme left to the mainstream rightist parties) as a new instrument used by the US to reinforce its domination. The linkage between 'Americanization' and globalization is therefore made by nationalist conservatives, leftist ecologists and anti-capitalist movements (such as the French section of Association for the Taxation of Financial Transactions in Aid of Citizens (ATTAC)). As Sophie Meunier states, the reason why 'France has long appeared as incorrigibly anti-American is because of the costless ways in which anti-Americanism has been used for political benefit' (2005). French political parties can indeed employ anti-Americanism in many ways, in supporting different policy agendas, for minimally four objectives: identity-building, policy legitimation, scapegoating and as a rallying focal point (Meunier 2005). But, if the political use of anti-Americanism in French politics is undeniable, does this mean that French policies are always anti-American?

As Hubert Védrine noted, 'France's relations with the United States always seem to reflect a mixture of fascination, sympathy, admiration and exasperation' (quoted in Serfaty 2005) – a condition that Védrine found to be 'normal'. The question 'Can America trust the French?' was not asked by Condoleezza Rice but by James Baker, Secretary of State during the George H. W. Bush administration, to the then-Foreign Minister Roland Dumas on the eve of the Gulf War (Gonzales 1999). The French were indeed reliable partners during the first Gulf War, as they were reliable during the most demanding crises of the Cold War. De Gaulle was pro-'Atlantist' during the Cuban crisis despite his anti-Kennedy stance. Mitterrand was in favour of deploying NATO missiles in Germany in 1983, and more French (44 per cent) than Germans or British declared themselves pro-American in 1984. France supported the United States after the end of the Cold War, and during the wars in Bosnia (1992–95) and Kosovo (1999). Despite disagreements over NATO, French–American relations remained publicly collaborative and France decided to rejoin NATO's integrated command in 1995. Chirac expressed resentment about US policy in Afghanistan but never questioned the necessity of intervening there. Like 55 per cent of the French public, he believed that this war, under a UN mandate, was 'justified' and 'legitimate' (GMF 2004). As Jean-David Lévitte, former French Ambassador in the United States, pointed out to an American audience, 'we are showing solidarity in Afghanistan. We have 5,000 troops deployed; we have forces in Mazar-e Sharif. We have forces in Kabul and so on.

Only France is training the new national army of Afghanistan with the United States' (Brookings Institution 2002).

By contrast, opposition to the war in Iraq has poisoned Franco–American relations. In the United States, this opposition was described either as an implicit support for Saddam or as another expression of obsessive French anti-Americanism. *The Washington Post*, for instance, stigmatized 'Europe's decline', its 'economic anaemia and further military impotence', pouring scorn on the Europeans, and especially the French, who 'did all in their power to keep Saddam Hussein in power, which makes them accessories to tyranny – and war crimes' (Will 2003). This claim fails to take into account the fact that both Colin Powell and Dominique de Villepin participated in the drafting of the UN Resolution of November 2002, and France was ready to intervene if the UN authorized the use of force against Iraq. 'The French faced the realistic possibility that the inspections would fail … in which case Paris was ready to join Washington in military action. The carrier *Charles de Gaulle* was sent to the Middle East by Chirac for that eventuality' (Wall 2004: 131). But the French Foreign Ministry never fully accepted the US thesis that Iraq and 11 September 2001 were connected. For President Chirac, a link between terrorism and weapons of mass destruction was speculative and the doctrine of pre-emptive war espoused by George W. Bush's administration was unacceptable.

'US unilateralism', then, fuelled French resentment, in addition to the fear that a 'crusade against Islam' would increase anti-Western feelings in Muslim countries. The lack of UN approval exacerbated the opposition to the war in Iraq in French official circles and enabled Chirac to size the illusory mantle of speaking on behalf of French and European people. Indeed, in 2002, only 27 per cent of the French believed that US troops should not have invaded Iraq, while 63 per cent said that the United States should have intervened 'with UN approval and support of its allies'. Once the initial stage of the war was over, the French government assumed a co-operative attitude in the UN, voting for a resolution authorizing the US military occupation. But Chirac insisted that the UN must play a central role while 63 per cent of the French still said that they 'would support French's military forces to Iraq if the UN approved a multinational force to assist with security and reconstruction in Iraq' (GMF 2004).

Effects of anti-Americanism on French policies

Is it thus reasonable to claim that the French–US argument over foreign policy lacks substance and that 'the differences are indeed reconcilable'?[10] Superficially, the French anti-American critique of US foreign policy is based on the defence or promotion of 'multipolarity' and 'multilateralism', allegedly designed to oppose US unilateralism and imperial ambition. However, an ambiguous *détente* has followed the clash over military intervention in Iraq. The French Foreign Ministry insisted that the two countries, despite a difference in style, were working collaboratively on 95 per cent of the questions on the international agenda, notably those important matters that came before the UN Security Council such as the war against terrorism, peacekeeping, nuclear proliferation and the reconstruction of Iraq. Howard Leach, former US Ambassador to France, wrote in *Le Figaro* that trans-Atlantic relations were back to normal and Védrine pointed out that, 'on the whole, divergences and suspicions reappear when we have theoretical discussions, but concrete cooperation is going well' (Védrine 2001: 51).

Yet, no one can deny that serious disagreements still exist, notably over the Middle East crisis in general and the Israel–Palestine question in particular. Divergence in this matter dates back to de Gaulle's attitude during the Six-Day War and fuelled anti-Americanism in France. The effect has been most pronounced among radical Muslims who have been promoting a virulent anti-Americanism since 11 September 2001. Conversely, the support for the Palestinian people is perceived in the United States as a form of French anti-Semitism. Popular sympathy towards Israel and the Palestinians contrasted in France and the US. Warm feelings towards Israel in 2003 stood at 43 degrees in France and 60 degrees in the United States; warm feelings towards the Palestinians stood at 45 degrees in France and 39 degrees in the United States (GMF 2003b).

Paradoxically, beyond the 'multipolar' rhetoric adopted by France in the 1990s, French foreign policy remained extremely unilateral when national interests were at stake. Indeed, France's enthusiasm for multilateralism did not prevent military interventions in traditional spheres of influence such as the Democratic Republic of Congo, Ivory Coast, Chad and Rwanda. French foreign policy opposed US Manifest Destiny but still genuflected towards its own *mission civilisatrice* in African countries. As a result, France and the United States argued not only because of their differences but also on the basis of their similarities. French unilateralism was even supported by the US, for example during the intervention in the Democratic Republic of Congo (with American logistical support) and Chad. France and the US also collaborated in 1983 in Lebanon and in 1997 in the co-ordination of peacekeeping initiatives in Africa. The rhetoric of French multipolarity could be depicted as 'disguised anti-Americanism' and French unipolarity could be perceived as a hypocritical attempt to preserve French interests. It seems, however, that France has remained aware that US support was often a necessity while the United States has recognized that France could be a useful partner. Complementarity rather than competition is currently an ideal shared by large majorities in France, Europe and the United States – where 58 per cent of public opinion welcomed a stronger EU and one able to co-operate with Americans.

Furthermore, France has helped the US more in intelligence matters and the war on terrorism than have most other countries. Soon after 11 September 2001, French anti-terrorist police detained 11 people in connection with the attacks. France and the United States collaborated on the Zacarias Moussaoui case as they did on the Ahmed Ressam case in 1999 – an Algerian man arrested at the US–Canadian border and suspected of plotting to bomb Los Angeles International Airport. The adoption by George W. Bush's administration of a new anti-terrorist package after 11 September 2001, however, raised a series of concerns in France as it did elsewhere in Europe. The most controversial application was, of course, the treatment of prisoners held at Guantanamo Bay, where the refusal to treat Taliban and

Al-Qaeda prisoners as prisoners of war raised fears of the US's disregarding international laws. Apart from humanitarian concerns, European tempers were inflamed by the US decision to classify the 'detainees' as 'unlawful combatants'.

The Europeans insisted that no such category exists in international laws and that the captives were entitled either to the rights of prisoners of war, or be treated as common criminals. Tempers were further inflamed by Defense Secretary Rumsfeld's reaction ('I don't feel the slightest concern at their treatment') and by the statement of an American diplomat who told the British media that European subjects held at Guantanamo would face the prospect of death penalty if found guilty by US military courts.[11] The Guantanamo controversy was closely linked to the issue of US opposition to the International Court of Justice. In 2002, in an unprecedented move, Bush withdrew the US as a signatory to the International Criminal Court's statute, which was ratified by all other Western democracies. He then demanded that American nationals be awarded immunity from International Criminal Court prosecution. For the French, the refusal to adhere to international law seriously undermined both US legitimacy and US democracy.

On the issues of human rights and civil liberties, France emphasized – with a mix of condescendence and sincere concern – that the new regulations (such as the *Homeland Security Act* and the *US Patriot Act*) violated the primary ingredients of the American Creed: faith in liberty, constitutionalism and democracy. Furthermore, even though the torture of the prisoners detained at Abu Ghraib caused a controversial debate in the United States, Europeans were outraged by the attitude of some American politicians and right-wing media figures who claimed that torture was acceptable, if not advisable. 'This is not Sunday school. This is interrogation. This is rough stuff' declared (Rep.) Senator Trent Lott (*Democracy Now* 2004). On this issue, the Bush administration stigmatized the French hypocrisy (after all, France had used torture during the Algerian War) and harmful idealism. Americans also pointed to the fact that France had negotiated an exemption for its own troops from prosecution under the International Criminal Court's rules.

While no one should dismiss these concerns, it is nevertheless worth noting that abrogations of civil liberties, privacy and spying are not new in France. The adaptation of the judicial system and intelligence services to terrorist threats began in the aftermath of a new wave of terrorist attacks ordered by Iran and Syria in the mid-1980s. The 1986 anti-terrorist law was completed by a series of exceptional security amendments adopted after 11 September 2001. France favours a judicial approach over the US-style 'war on terror' but the French legislation allows a permissive wiretapping system, intrusive police powers, and limitations both on civil liberties and privacy (Haubrich 2003). The catch-all character of this legislation is surprisingly similar to its American counterpart.

In the realm of economic policies, anti-Americanism is comparably familiar. Big Mac has replaced Coca Cola as the main focus for demonization but the current equation between Americanization and globalization was preceded by criticism of US 'global capitalism' (Kuisel 1993). American firms were the object of considerable negative perception for at least two decades following World War II. In the aftermath of the Marshall Plan, the increasing number of US corporations that invested in France strengthened the belief that US capitalism was exceptionally aggressive. In his book entitled *The American Challenge*, Jean-Jacques Servan-Schreiber warned France – and the rest of Europe – of a possible American takeover of Europe's industrial apparatus (1968). This situation began to change in the mid-1960s when French multinationals engaged in a corporate policy of globalization, partly as a by-product of European integration. Yet, anti-globalization and its related anti-American stereotypes are still vivid in France, championed by José Bové who became internationally notorious after the destruction of a McDonald's structure in Millau in 1999. Notwithstanding the facts – McDonald's in France relies on local producers, does not use US hormone-treated beef and is directed by a French chief executive officer – Bové (who spent his childhood in Berkeley) and the Farmers' Confederation mounted a campaign designed to use the Big Mac as a symbol of both global production and junk food, in order to protect French agricultural products (notably Roquefort cheese) against World Trade Organization and US trade legislation (Bodnar 2003).

Beyond this controversy, France and the United States are economic partners. Trends in foreign direct investment (FDI) reveal the dynamism of their bilateral relationship; total French FDI stocks in the United States exceeded US$170 billion in 2001, in comparison to US$43.4 billion for US investments in France. French companies employ over 600,000 American workers, while US companies employ a similar number of French workers (Serfaty 2005: 87). The two countries participate in the G8's management of the world economy, and even the perception of globalization – and thus of Americanization – has changed in France. Twenty-four per cent of French people surveyed in 1999 believed that 'economic globalization was bad', the highest score in Europe, but 49 per cent said 'it was a good thing' (PIPA 2000). The French appear to be more open than Americans to foreign investment (53 per cent and 43 per cent respectively) but a majority (72 per cent) characterized the United States as unco-operative. Paradoxically, the United States is criticized by French respondents not for its globalized economic policy but for its protectionism. Another recurrent concern relates to the social aspects of US policies; 76 per cent of French respondents said that the US system 'neglects too many social problems because of a lack of job security and few employment benefits for many workers' – an opinion notably shared by a large majority of Americans.

Conclusion

The French are neither 'all Americans' nor 'all anti-American'. While there are many forms of political anti-Americanism, there are also limits to the political use of anti-Americanism. As Simon Serfaty points out:

> France is no more guided by an obsessive anti-American instinct than the United States by an alleged exasperation with France; French attitudes toward the United States are no more defined by reminiscences of past grandeur than are US attitudes by national ambitions of imperial expansion […] In any case,

the widespread public opposition to the use of force found even among the 'pro-American' governments in Europe suggests that bottom-up aversion to the war exacerbated Europe's anti-American sentiments rather than caused them. (Serfaty 2005: 85)

French political parties and diplomats sometimes attempt to legitimate their own agendas by invoking anti-Americanism, but 'few parties actually embrace openly anti-American stances' (Meunier 2005: 138). Economic spats between the two countries are recurrent and will continue, but there are now more European–US arguments than Franco–US ones. Social and cultural issues remain central – such as the debate on the death penalty, abortion, access to welfare state protection and the role of religion in politics. These issues are grounded in irreconcilable differences, both between and within French and Americans because of their comparable internal 'cultural wars'. Arguably, the divisions are greater within the two countries than between them. Meanwhile, France and the United States face similar policy challenges, such as on the issues of immigration and integration, a substantive debate on national identity and questions related to their respective 'exceptionalism'.

In terms of perceptions, the so-called 'Americanization' creates an illusory feeling of proximity which, in turn, strengthens an ambivalent love–hate relationship with America. But *West Wing* doesn't really help Europeans to understand American politics and *Sex and the City* doesn't provide a relevant picture of America society either. In terms of actions, France and the United States will remain rivals as long as their national interests are at stake. To take trans-Atlantic solidarity for granted would be a mistake. No one should forget, however, that solidarity is more often based on common enemies and threats rather than on common values. France and the United States are thus likely to remain reluctant allies and competitive partners.

Notes

1 J. M. Colombani (2001). One year after this editorial, Colombani questioned this assertion in his book (2002) *Tous Américains? Le monde après le 11 septembre 2001* (Paris: Fayard). He wondered 'what is the true face of America? The one that our parents knew, liberating and generous on the beaches of Normandy, or the one our generation knew, stupid and cruel in Vietnam?' (p. 9).

2 It is worth noting, however, that the prefix 'hyper-' in English has a negative implication that is absent in French.

3 Also lost in translation: The 'neo-cons' in French also means the 'neo-jerks'.

4 See R. Singh (2006: 27–8). See also B. O'Connor (2004: 421–6).

5 S. Meunier (2005: 27). See also P. Katzenstein and R. O. Keohane (eds) (2006).

6 S. M. Lipset (1996). Interestingly, Francophobia is also supposed to be exceptional. According to Simon Serfaty (2005: 74, 78), 'no other country in the world endures a comparable "discourse of disparagement", suffers the same kind of "cultural bashing"

and faces the same system of demeaning and even outright hostile clichés, prejudices, obsessions, sensitivities and allergies [...] Americans tend to like France but not the French [...] The French tend to like Americans but not America'. See also J. Vaïsse (2003: 18–33).

7 G. Duhamel (1930); André Siegfried (1927).

8 *Le Monde* (1950) 29 March. And my own book (1991).

9 They were both in favour of the US–NATO bombings of Kosovo and Serbia in 1999. See R. J. Golsan (2004: 391–404).

10 Irwin M. Wall (2004: 137).

11 See T. Karon (2002); *Le Monde* (2002) 17 February. Capital punishment is forbidden in France.

Bibliography

Abbott, T. (2004) Transcript of Interview with Health Minister, Tony Abbott, on Australian Broadcasting Corporation, *Lateline*, 3 August. Available from www.abc.net.au/lateline/content/2004/s1168231.htm

Abelson, D. E. (2006) *A Capitol Idea: Think Tanks and US Foreign Policy*, Montreal and Kingston: McGill–Queen's University Press.

Adomeit, H. and Aslund, A. (2005) 'Introduction', in Hannes A. and Anders Å. (eds) *Russia versus the United States and Europe – or 'Strategic Triangle'? Developments in Russian Domestic and Foreign Policy, Western Responses, and Prospects for Policy Coordination*, Berlin/Moscow: Carnegie Moscow Center. Available from http://www.carnegie.ru/en/pubs/books/73367.htm

Ahmad, A. (2003) 'Contextualizing Conflict: The US "War on Terrorism"', in Thussu D. K. and Freedman D. (eds) *War and the Media: Reporting Conflict 24/7*, London: Sage Publications, pp. 15–27.

Ajami, F. (2003a) 'The Anti-Americans', *The Wall Street Journal*, 3 July. Available from http://www.travelbrochuregraphics.com/extra/the_anti_americans.htm

—— (2003b) 'The Falseness of Anti-Americanism', *Foreign Policy* 138: 52–61.

Albinski, H. S. (2001) 'Cultural Reflections', *Australian Journal of International Affairs* 55: 275–85.

Albrechtsen, J. (2004) 'On Uncle Sam, Latham's Spots Aren't Changing', *The Australian*, 4 August.

Alchon, G. (1985) *The Invisible Hand of Planning: Capitalism, Social Science, and the State in the 1920s*, Princeton: Princeton University Press.

Algranati, C. J. *et al.* (2004) 'Disputas Sociales y Procesos Políticos en América Latina', *Observatorio Social de América Latina* V (13), January–April.

Allard, T. and Wilkinson, M. (2004) 'US Gets Upper Hand in Trade Deal', *The Age*, 10 February.

—— (2005) 'Our New Nightmare: The United States of America', *The Sydney Morning Herald*, 29 March.

Allard, T. and Williams, L. (2005) 'Our New Nightmare: The United States of America', *The Sydney Morning Herald*, 29 March.

Altvater, E. and Mahnkopf, B. (2002) *Globalisierung der Unsicherheit*, Muenster: Verlag Westfälisches Dampfboot.

Andreani, G. (2004) 'The "War on Terror": Good Cause, Wrong Concept', *Survival* 46 (2): 31–50.

Angrisani, L. (2003) 'More Latin, Less America? Creating a Free Trade Area of the Americas', *The National Interest*, Fall.

Applebaum, A. (2005) 'In Search of Pro-Americanism', *Foreign Policy*, July–August, 32–40.

d'Appollonia, A. C. (1991) *Histoire politique des intellectuels en France (1944–1954)*, Bruxelles: Complexe.

Armus, S. (2007) *French Anti-Americanism: Critical Moments in a Complex History*, Lexington Books.

Arndt, R. T. (2005) *The First Resort of King*, Washington, DC: Potomac Books.

Arnove, R. F. (ed.) (1980) *Philanthropy and Cultural Imperialism*, Boston: GK Hall.

Aron, R. and Dandieu, A. (1931) *Le cancer américain*, Paris: Rieder.

Asmus, R. (2003) 'Rebuilding the Atlantic Alliance', *Foreign Affairs*, September–October, 82 (5): 20–31.

Associated Press (2000) 'Bush Turns to Foreign Policy Experts', 16 December.

Augé, É. (2002) 'Hollywood Movies: Terrorism 101', *Cercles* 5: 147–63.

Austin, A. (2005) 'War Hawks and the Ugly American', in Hamm, B. (ed.) *Devastating Society: The Neo-Conservative Assault on Democracy and Justice*, London: Pluto Press.

Australia, Department of Foreign Affairs and Trade (2005) US Fact Sheet, May.

Australian Broadcasting Corporation (ABC), News Online Report (2004) 'US Takes Hard Line on Australian Sugar', 23 January.

Ball, A. M. (2003) *Imagining America: Influence and Images in Twentieth-Century Russia*, New York, Oxford: Rowman & Littlefield Publishers.

Baucus, M. (2004) 'America Must Not Leave Asia in a Trade Blind Spot', *The Financial Times*, 15 December, p. 15.

BBC (2002) 'Canada PM Criticises "Arrogant" West', 13 September. Available from http://news.bbc.co.uk/2/hi/world/americas/2254761.stm

—— (2003a) 'Poll Suggests World Hostile to US', 16 June.

—— (2003b) 'Two-Thirds Share "Unfavourable Attitude" Towards President Bush', 16 June. Available from http://news.bbc.co.uk/2/hi/world/americas/2254761.stm

—— (2005) 'Global Poll Slams Bush Leadership', 18 January.

Beate, J. (2004) 'The Power of Culture in International Relations', in Gienow-Hecht, J. and Schumacher F. (eds) *Culture and International History*, New York, Oxford: Berghahn Books.

Bell, C. (1988) *The American Alliance and the Revolution in Military Affairs*, Sydney: Australian Centre for American Studies.

—— (1991) 'Australia's Alliance Options: Prospect and Retrospect in a World of Change', *Australian Foreign Policy Papers*, Canberra: Australian National University.

—— (1994) *Dependent Ally: A Study in Australian Foreign Policy*, Sydney: Allen & Unwin, 3rd edn.

Bell, D. (2000) *The End of Ideology: On the Exhaustion of Political Ideas in the Fifties*, Cambridge: Harvard University Press.

Bello, W. and Engelhardt, T. (2005) *Dilemmas of Domination: The Unmaking of the American Empire.* Metropolitan Books.

Bellow, W. (2005) *Anti Globalisation*, London: Zed Books.

Berghahn, V. R. (2001) *America and the Intellectual Cold Wars in Europe: Shepard Stone between Philanthropy, Academy, and Diplomacy*, Princeton: Princeton University Press.

Bergsten, F. Commentary: The Move Toward Free Trade Zones, available at: https://www.kansascityfed.org/publicat/sympos/1991/S91bergs.PDF

Berman, E. H. (1983) *The Influence of the Carnegie, Ford and Rockefeller Foundations on US Foreign Policy*, New York: Monthly Review Press.

Berman, R. A. (2004) *Anti-Americanism in Europe*, Stanford: Hoover Institution Press.

Bhagwati, J. (1998) 'The Capital Myth: The Difference between Trade in Widgets and Dollars', *Foreign Affairs* 77 (3): 7–12.

Biden, J. R. (2000) 'Unholy Symbiosis: Isolationism and Anti-Americanism', *Washington Quarterly* 23 (4): 7–14.

Billington, J. (1998) *The Nature of the Russian Transformation: The Search for Legitimacy in a Time of Trouble*, Henry M. Jackson Memorial Lecture, Henry M. Jackson Foundation. Available from http://www.friends-partners.org/CCSI/resource/blllspee.htm

Bobrow, D. (1996) 'Complex Insecurity: Implications of a Disease Metaphor', *International Studies Quarterly* 40 (4): 435–50.
—— (2001) 'Visions of (In)Security and American Strategic Style', *International Studies Perspectives* (2): 1–12.
—— (2005) Center for Policy Studies, Central European University, Working Paper Series, http://www.ceu.hu/cps
Bobrow, D. and Boyer, M. (2005) *Defensive Internationalism: Providing Public Goods in an Uncertain World,* Ann Arbor: The University of Michigan Press.
Bodnar, J. (2003) 'Roquefort vs Big Mac: Globalization and Its Others, *Archives of European Sociology* XLIV (1): 133–44.
Boltanski, L. and Chiapello, E. (1999) *Le nouvel esprit du capitalisme*, Paris: Gallimard.
Borón, A. (2004) 'La izquierda latinoamericana a comienzos del siglo XXI: nuevas realidades y urgentes desafíos', *Observatorio Social de América Latina* V (13), January–April.
Bourdieu, P. (1998) *Acts of Resistance: Against the Tyranny of the Market*, New York: New York Press.
Boym, S. (1995) 'From the Russian Soul to Post-Communist Nostalgia', *Representation – Special Issue: Identifying Histories: Eastern Europe before and after 1989*, 49 133–66.
—— S. (2001) *The Future of Nostalgia*, New York: Basic Books.
Bromke, A. and Nossal, K. R. (1983–84) 'Tensions in Canada's Foreign Policy', *Foreign Affairs* 62 Winter: 335–53.
Brookings Institution (2002) Debate 'France after the Elections', 24 June.
Brown, G. and Rayner, L. (2001–02) 'Upside, Downside: ANZUS: After Fifty Years', Parliament of Australia, Parliamentary Library, Current Issues Brief 3.
Bryan, D. (1991) 'Australian Economic Nationalism: Old and New', *Australian Economic Papers* 57.
Brzezinski, Z. (2007) *Second Chance: Three Presidents and the Crisis of American Superpower*, New York: Basic Books.
Bu, L. (2003) *Making the World Like US*, Westport: Praeger.
Bulmer-Thomas, V. (1998) 'El Área de Libre Comercio de las Américas', *Revista de la CEPAL*, Número Extraordinario 243–58.
Callinicos, A. T. (2003) *The New Mandarins of American Power*, London: Polity.
Campbell, D. (1992) *Writing Security*, Manchester: Manchester University Press.
Capling, A. (2001) *Australia and the Global Trade System: From Havana to Seattle*, Cambridge: Cambridge University Press.
—— (2005) *All the Way with the USA: Australia, United States and Free Trade*, Sydney: University of New South Wales Press.
Carassava, A. (2003) 'Anti-Americanism in Greece Is Reinvigorated by War', *The New York Times*, 7 April.
Carranza, M. (2004) 'Mercosur and the End Game of the FTAA Negotiations: Challenges and Prospects After the Argentine Crisis', *Third World Quarterly* 25 (2): 319–37.
CBC News (2002) 'Canadian Official Called Bush "a Moron"', 26 November. Available from http://www.cbc.ca/stories/2002/11/21/moron021121
—— (2004) 'Parrish Sticks by "Idiot" Comment', 27 August.
Ceaser, W. J. (1997) *Reconstructing America: The Symbol of America in Modern Thought*, New Haven: Yale University Press.
—— (2003) 'A Genealogy of Anti-Americanism', *The Public Interest*, 23 July.
—— (2004) 'The Philosophical Origins of Anti-Americanism in Europe', in Hollander, P. (ed.) *Understanding Anti-Americanism: Its Origins and Impact at Home and Abroad*, Chicago: Ivan R. Dee, pp. 45–64.
Centre for International Economics (2004) 'Economic Analysis of the AUSFTA: Impact of the Bilateral Free Trade Agreement with the United States', a study commissioned by the Department of Foreign Affairs and Trade, April.
Chadha, K. and Kavoori, A. (2000) 'Media Imperialism Revisited: Some Findings from the Asian Case', *Media, Culture & Society* 22 (4): 415–32.

Chesnoff, R. Z. (2005) *The Arrogance of the French: Why They Can't Stand Us – And Why the Feeling Is Mutual*, New York: Sentinel.

Churchward, L. (1979) *Australia and America, 1977–1972: An Alternative History*, Sydney: Alternative Publishing Cooperative Limited.

Clarke, H. D. *et al.* (1984) *Absent Mandate: The Politics of Discontent in Canada*, Toronto: Gage.

Clarke, R. A. (2004) *Against All Enemies: Inside America's War on Terror*, New York: The Free Press.

Clarkson, S. (1985) *Canada and the Reagan Challenge: Crisis and Adjustment, 1981–85*, Toronto: James Lorimer.

Cohen, B. J. (1998) *The Geography of Money*, Ithaka and London: Cornell University Press.

—— (2004) 'Globalist: The Almighty Dollar Looks Mighty Vulnerable', *International Herald Tribune*, 11 December.

Colebatch, T. and Wilkinson, M. (2004) 'Labor Warns It May Block Trade Deal', *The Age*, 20 May.

Coleman, P. (1989) *The Liberal Conspiracy: The Congress for Cultural Freedom and the Struggle for the Mind of Postwar Europe*, New York: Free Press.

Colombani, J.-M. (2001) 'Nous sommes tous Américains', *Le Monde*, 13 September 2001.

Commonwealth of Australia Parliamentary Debates (2003) House of Representatives, Official Hansard, 5 February.

—— (2004) House of Representatives, Official Hansard, 3 August.

Connor, D. W. (2004) 'Anti-Americanism in Post-Communist Russia', in Hollander, P. (ed.) *Understanding Anti-Americanism: Its Origins and Impact at Home and Abroad*, Chicago: Ivan R. Dee.

Conologue, R. (2005) 'Loose Cannon', *Saturday Night*, March: 48–53.

Conze, E. (2004) 'States, International Systems, and Intercultural Transfer (A Commentary)', in Gienow-Hecht, J. and Schumacher F. (eds) *Culture and International History*, New York, Oxford: Berghahn Books.

Cooper, R. (2002) 'The Post-Modern State', in Leonard, M. (ed.) (2002) *Re-ordering the World*, London: The Foreign Policy Centre.

—— (2003) *The Breaking of Nations: Order and Chaos in the XXI c.* New York: Grove Press.

Coser, L. (1965) *Men of Ideas*, New York: The Free Press.

Couloumbis, T. A. (1966) *Greek Political Reaction to American and NATO Influences*, New Haven: Yale University Press.

Couloumbis, T. A. and Iatrides, J. O. (eds) (1980) *Greek American Relations: A Critical Review*, New York: Pella.

Couloumbis, T. A. *et al.* (1976) *Foreign Interference in Greek Politics: An Historical Perspective*, New York: Pella.

Council on Foreign Relations (2003) 'Finding America's Voice: A Strategy for Reinvigorating US Public Diplomacy', New York.

Cox, M. (2003) 'Kagan's World', *International Affairs* 79 (3): 523–32.

—— (2005) 'Beyond the West: Terrors in Transatlantia', *European Journal of International Relations* 11 (2): 203–3.

—— (2006) Symposium: 'Terrors in Transatlantia: The Future of Transatlantic Relations', *European Political Science* 5 (1): 33–68.

Coyne, A. (2003) 'Parrish Says What Chrétien Thinks', *National Post*, 3 March.

Cozens, C. (2001) 'Viewers Greet September 11 Coverage with Cynicism', *Guardian*, 26 October.

Creighton, D. (1976) *The Forked Road: Canada, 1939–1957*, Toronto: McClelland and Stewart.

Crockatt, R. (2003) *America Embattled: September 11, Anti-Americanism and the Global Order*, Routledge: London and New York.

—— (2006) 'Anti-Americanism and the Clash of Civilization', in O'Connor and Griffiths, M. (eds) *The Rise of Anti-Americanism*, London: Routledge, pp. 48–85.

CTV News (2004) 'Martin and Harper Trade Barbs on Tax Issues', 25 May.

Cunliffe, M. (1986) 'The Anatomy of Anti-Americanism', in Kroes R. and Van Rossem, M. (eds) *Anti-Americanism in Europe*, Amsterdam: Free University Press.

Cusset, F. (2003) *French Theory: Foucault, Derrida, Deleuze & Cie et les mutations de la vie intellectuelle aux Etats-Unis*, Paris: La Découverte.

Daalder, I. H. and Lindsay, J. M. (2003) *America Unbound: The Bush Revolution in Foreign Policy*, Washington, DC: Brookings Institution Press.

Daily Mirror (2004*)*: 'How Can 59,054,087 People Be So DUMB', 8 November.

Daniels, B. C. (1998) 'Younger British Siblings: Canada and Australia Grow Up in the Shadow of the United States', *American Studies International* 36: 3.

Davis, M. (1986) *Phönix im Sturzflug: Zur politischen Ökonomie der Vereinigten Staaten in den achtziger Jahren*, Berlin: Rotbuch.

DeConde, A. (2000) *Presidential Machismo: Executive Authority, Military Intervention and Foreign Relations*, Boston: Northeastern University Press.

Dee, P. (2004) The *Australia–US Free Trade Agreement: An Assessment*, Canberra: Australian National University, June.

DeFleur, M. H. and Melvin, D. (2002) 'Why They Hate Us …', *Global Beat Syndicate*, 17 October.

de Grazia, V. (1989) 'Mass Culture and Sovereignty: The American Challenge to European Cinemas 1920–1960', *Journal of Modern History* 61 (1): 53–87.

DeLillo, D. (2001) 'In the Ruins of the Future', *Harper's Magazine*, December.

Democracy Now (2004) 'Trent Lott Defends US Actions in Abu Ghraib', 3 June. Available from http://www.democracynow.org/article.pl?sid=04/06/03/142239

Dezalay, Y. and Garth, B. G. (2002) *The Internationalization of Palace Wars: Lawyers, Economists, and the Contest to Transform Latin American States*, Chicago: University of Chicago Press.

Dieter, H. (1998) *Die Asienkrise: Ursachen, Konsequenzen und die Rolle des Internationalen Währungsfonds*, Marburg: Metropolis Verlag.

—— (1999) 'Ostasien nach der Krise: Interne Reformen, neue Finanzarchitektur und monetärer Regionalismus', *Aus Politik und Zeitgeschichte* (37–8): 21–8.

—— (2003) 'Abschied vom Multilateralismus? Der neue Regionalismus in der Handels- und Finanzpolitik', *SWP-Studie*, 4 February.

Dieter, H. and Higgott, R. (2003) 'Exploring Alternative Theories of Economic Regionalism: From Trade to Finance in Asian Co-Operation?, *Review of International Political Economy* 10 (3): 430–55.

Dimitrakos, D. (1999) 'How Ethical Can a War Be?' *To Bhma*, 16 May.

Diner, D. (1996) *America in the Eyes of the Germans: An Essay on Anti-Americanism*, Princeton: Markus Wiener Publishers.

Directors Guild of America (2000) 'DGA Commends Action by Governor Gray Davis to Fight Runaway Production', press release, 18 May.

Dobell, P. C. (1985) *Canada in World Affairs, vol. 17: 1971–1973*, Toronto: Canadian Institute of International Affairs.

Downer, A. (2002) 'The Strategic Importance of a Free Trade Agreement to Australia–US Relations', 29 August.

Downey, J. and Murdock, G. (2003) 'The Counter-Revolution in Military Affairs: The Globalization of Guerrilla Warfare', in Thussu, D. K. and Freedman, D. (eds) *War and the Media: Reporting Conflict 24/7*, London: Sage Publications, 70–86.

Duhamel, G. (1930) *Scènes de la vie future*, Paris: Mercure de France.

Dunn, R. (1987) 'Duffy Links US Bases with Trade', *Sydney Morning Herald*, 15 September.

Duroselle, J.-B. (1978) *France and the United States from the Beginnings to the Present*, Chicago: University of Chicago Press.

Eccleston, R. (2001) 'Powell Backs Canberra – Free Trade Deal a Good Idea Says Secretary of State', *The Australian*, 24 March.

ECLAC (2003) 'Latin America and the Caribbean in the World Economy, 2001–2002'. Available from http://www.cepal.org/publicaciones/Comercio/9/LCG2189PI/lcg2189i.pdf

Economist, The (2004a) 'Keep an eye on it; The dollar', 10 July, p. 66.

—— (2004b) 'Yankee stay home; East Asia diplomacy', 11 December, p. 50.

—— (2005a) 'The View from Abroad', Special Report on Anti-Americanism, 17 February.

—— (2005b) 'The Old Slur', Lexington, 17 February.

—— (2005c) 'Still Not Loved. Now Not Envied', 23 June.

—— (2005d) 'Democracy's Ten-Year Rut', 27 October.

—— (2006) 'Puritans or Pornographers?', Lexington, 23 February.

Edwards, J. (1989) 'US and Australia on a Collision Course', *The Sydney Morning Herald*, 5 October.

Edwards, L. (1997) *The Power of Ideas: The Heritage Foundation at 25 Years*, Ottawa, Illinois: Jameson Books.

English, R. (2000) *Russia and the Idea of the West: Gorbachev, Intellectuals, and the End of Cold War*, New York: Columbia University Press.

Environics Research Group/Focus Canada (2003) Poll conducted for the Association for Canadian Studies in February. Available from www.acs-aec.ca/Polls/Poll43.pdf

Etiemble, R. (1964) *Parlez-vous franglais?*, Paris: Gallimard.

Eurobarometer (2005) 'National Report: Greece', *Standard Eurobarometer* 64, Brussels: European Commission.

Eurodata TV (2000) '1999: Une année de cinéma dans le monde'.

European Audiovisual Observatory (2002) 'The Imbalance of Trade in Films and Television Programmes between North America and Europe Continues to Deteriorate'.

Faath, S. (2006) *Anti-Americanism in the Islamic World*, Princeton: Markus Wiener Publishers.

Fabbrini, S. (2002) 'The Domestic Sources of European Anti-Americanism', *Government and Opposition* 37 (1): 3–14.

—— (2004) 'Layers of Anti-Americanism: Americanization, American Unilateralism and Anti-Americanism in a European Perspective', *European Journal of American Culture* 23 (2): 79–95.

—— (ed.) (2006) *The United States Contested: American Unilateralism and European Discontent*, New York: Routledge.

Fagan, D. (2003) 'Beyond NAFTA: Towards Deeper Economic Integration', in Carment, D. *et al.* (eds) *Canada Among Nations, 2003: Coping with the American Colossus*, Toronto: Oxford University Press, pp. 32–53.

Financial Times, The (2003) 22 September, p. 13.

—— (2004) 11 February, p. 7.

Flynn, S. (2005) *America the Vulnerable: How Our Government Is Failing to Protect Us from Terrorism*, New York: Harper Perennial.

Forsberg, T. (2005) 'German Foreign Policy and the War on Iraq: Anti-Americanism, Pacifism or Emancipation', *Security Dialogue*, 36 (2): 213–31.

Fray, P. (1989) 'Hawke May "Eat Crow" over Bush's Farm Policy', *Sydney Morning Herald*, 24 May.

Friedman, T. L. (1999) *The Lexus and the Olive Tree: Understanding Globalization*, London: Harper Collins Publishers.

—— (2003a) *Attitudes and Longitudes*, London: Penguin.

—— (2003b) 'Our War with France', *The New York Times*, 9 February.

Frum, D. (2003) *The Right Man: The Surprise Presidency of George W. Bush*, New York: Random House.

Frum, D. and Perle, R. (2004) *An End to Evil: How to Win the War on Terror*, New York: Random House.

Fukuyama, F. (2004) 'East Asia: 6 – 1 = a New Regional Force', *International Herald Tribune*, 10 December.

Gaddis, J. L. (1997) *We Now Know: Rethinking Cold War History*, Oxford: Oxford University Press.

Gallup Poll (1947) 'Public Opinion Surveys', New York: Gallup Poll Organization.

—— (1998) 27 August as reported by CNN. Available from www.cnn.com/ALLPOLITICS/1998/08/27/poll/

Garfinkle, A. (2004) 'Peace Movements and the Adversary Culture', in P. Hollander (ed.) *Understanding Anti-Americanism: Its Origins and Impact at Home and Abroad*, Chicago: Ivan R. Dee.

Garnaut, R (2002) 'An Australia–United States Free Trade Agreement?', *Australian Journal of International Affairs* 56, April.

Gedmin, J. and Kennedy, C. (2003) 'Selling America, Short', *The National Interest*, Winter.

Gelb, L. H. (2003) 'Finding America's Voice: A Strategy for Reinvigorating US Public Diplomacy', New York: Council on Foreign Relations, v–vi.

German Marshal Fund of the United States (GMF) (2002) 'Worldviews'. Available from http://www.worldviews.org/

—— (2003a) GMF's Annual Report.

—— (2003b) 'Transatlantic Trends'. Available from http://www.transatlantictrends.org/trends/doc/2003_english_key.pdf

—— (2004) 'Transatlantic Trends'. Available from http://www.transatlantictrends.org/trends/doc/2004_english_key.pdf

—— (2005) 'Transatlantic Trends'. Available from http://www.transatlantictrends.org/trends/doc/TTKeyFindings2005.pdf

Gibson, J. (2004) *Hating America: The New World Sport*, New York: Regan Books.

Gienow-Hecht, JCE and Schumacher, F. (eds) (2003) *Culture and International History*, New York: Berghahn Books.

Gilbert, S. P. (1977) *Soviet Images of America*, New York: Crane, Russak & Company, Inc.

Gilpin, R. (2000) *The Challenge of Global Capitalism: The World Economy in the 21st Century*, Princeton: Princeton University Press.

Gingrich, N. and Schweizer, P. (2003) 'We Can Thank Hollywood for Our Ugly-American Image', *Los Angeles Times*, 21 January.

Gitlin, T. (2003) 'Anti-Anti-Americanism', *Dissent* 50: 103–4.

Glazov, J. (2002) 'Anti-Americanism', *FrontPageMagazine.com*, 11 November. Available from http://www.frontpagemag.com/Articles/ReadArticle.asp?ID=4489

Gleason, A. (1995) *Totalitarianism: the Inner History of the Cold War*, New York: Oxford University Press.

Globe and Mail (1997) 10 July.

Glucksmann, A. (2003) *Ouest contre ouest*, Paris: Plon.

Goldberg, J. (2002) 'Frogs in Our Midst', *National Review*, 16 July. Available from http://www.nationalreview.com/goldberg/goldberg071602.asp

Goldgeier, J. M. and McFaul, M. (2003) *Power and Purpose: US Policy toward Russia and the Cold War*, Washington, DC: Brookings Institution Press.

Golsan, R. J. (2004) 'Preliminary Reflections on Anti-antiaméricanisme: André Glucksmann et compagnie', *Contemporary French and Francophone Studies* 8 (4): 391–404.

Gonzales, M. (1999) 'Can America Trust the French', *Wall Street Journal*, 23 November.

Gordon, P. H. and Shapiro, J. (2004) *Allies at War: America, Europe and the Crisis over Iraq*, New York: McGraw-Hill.

Gramsci, A. (1971) *Selections from the Prison Notebooks*, New York: International Publisher.

Granatstein, J. L. (1985) 'Free Trade between Canada and the United States: The Issue that Will Not Go Away', in Stairs, D. and Winham, G. R. (eds) *The Collected Research Studies/The Royal Commission on the Economic Union and Development Prospects for Canada, vol. 29: The Politics of Canada's Economic Relationship with the United States*, Ottawa: Supply and Services Canada: 55–94.

—— (1996) *Yankee Go Home? Canadians and Anti-Americanism*, Toronto: HarperCollins.

Granatstein, J. L. and Bothwell, R. (1991) *Pirouette: Pierre Trudeau and Canadian Foreign Policy*, Toronto: University of Toronto Press.

Grantham, B. (1998) 'America the Menace: France's Feud with Hollywood', *World Policy Journal* 15 (2): 58–66.

Grattan, M. (1988) 'Duffy Thrives on Being the Outside', *The Age*, 25 January.

Grémion, P. (1995) *Intelligence de l'anticommunisme. Le Congrès pour la liberté de la culture à Paris (1950–1975)*, Paris: Fayard.

Griffiths, F. (ed.) (1987) *Politics of the Northwest Passage*, Montreal and Kingston: McGill–Queen's University Press.

Grosser, A. (1980) *Western Alliance: European–American Relations since 1945*, London: Macmillan Press.

Gudkov, L. and Dubin, B. (2005) 'Russia's Distinctive Brand of Nationalism', *Pro et Contra Journal*, Nationalism and Racism in Russia (in Russian), 9 (2): 29 September–October. Available from http://www.carnegie.ru/en/pubs/procontra/73309.htm

Guilhot, N. (2005) *The Democracy Makers: Human Rights and the Politics of Global Order*, New York: Columbia University Press.

—— (2006) 'A Network of Intellectual Friendships. The Fondation pour une Entraide Intellectuelle Européenne and East–West Cultural Dialogue, 1957–1991', *Minerva* 44 (4): 379–409.

—— (2007) 'Reforming the World. George Soros, Global Capitalism and the Philanthropic Management of the Social Sciences', *Critical Sociology* 33 (3): 447–77.

Haass, R. (ed.) (1999) *Transatlantic Tensions: The United States, Europe, and Problem Countries*, Washington DC: Brookings Institution Press.

Hagen, M. von (2004) 'Empires, Borderlands, and Diasporas: Eurasia as Anti-Paradigm for the Post-Soviet Era', *American Historical Review* 109: 445–68.

Hakim, P. (2006) 'Is Washington Losing Latin America?', *Foreign Affairs*, January–February.

Halper, S. A. and Clarke, J. (2004) *America Alone: The Neo-Conservatives and the Global Order*, Cambridge: Cambridge University Press.

Handelsblatt (2003) '*Weltweit sinken die Direktinvestitionen*', 171, 5 September, p. 10.

Harris, S. (1998) *Will China Divide Australia and the US?*, Sydney: Australian Centre for American Studies.

Haseler, S. (1985) *The Varieties of Anti-Americanism*, Washington DC: The Ethics and Public Policy Center.

Haubrich, D. (2003) 'September 11, Anti-Terror Laws and Civil Liberties: Britain, France and Germany Compared', *Government and Opposition*. Available from http://www. blackwell-synergy.com/doi/pdf/10.1111/1477-7053.00002?cookieSet=1

Hawke, R. J. L. (1994) *The Hawke Memoirs*, London: Heinemann.

Hayek, F. A. (1994) *The Road to Serfdom*, Chicago: University of Chicago Press.

Hays, W. (1927) 'Supervision from Within', in Kennedy J. P. (ed.) *The Story of the Films as told by Leaders of the Industry to the Students of the Graduate School of Business Administration, George F. Baker Foundation Harvard University*, Kennedy. Chicago: A. W. Shaw Company, pp. 29–54.

Hertsgaard, M. (2002) *The Eagle's Shadow: Why America Fascinates and Infuriates the World*, New York: Picador.

Hesse, H. (1990) 'Außenwirtschaftliches Gleichgewicht: Ursachen und Bewertung von Leistungsbilanzsalden', *Aus Politik und Zeitgeschichte* B 18: 39–46.

Higgott, R. (1989) 'The Ascendancy of the Economic Dimension in Australia–American Relations', in Ravenhill, J. (ed.) *No Longer an American Lake*, Sydney: Allen & Unwin, pp. 132–68.

—— (2004a) 'After Neo-Liberal Globalisation: The Securitisation of US Foreign Economic Policy in East Asia', *Critical Asian Studies* 36 (3): 425–44.

—— (2004b) 'Multilateralism and the Limits of Global Governance', paper prepared for the conference 'Learning from the Crisis: Where Do We Go for Global Governance?', Buenos Aires, May.

Higley, J. (2006) 'The Bush Elite: Aberration or Harbinger?', in O'Connor B. and Griffiths, M. (eds) *The Rise of Anti-Americanism*, London: Routledge, pp. 155–68.

Hitchens, C. (2000) *Unacknowledged Legislation: Writers in the Public Sphere*, London: Verso.

Hoare, Q. and Nowell-Smith, G. (1971) *Selections from the Prison Notebooks of Antonio Gramsci*, London: Lawrence and Wishart.

Hoffman, S. (2005), 'American Exceptionalism: The New Version', in: Michael Ignatieff (ed.), *American Exceptionalism and Human Rights*, Princeton University Press, pp. 225–240.

Hollander, P. (1992) *Anti-Americanism: Critiques at Home and Abroad 1965–1990*, New York: Oxford University Press.

—— (1995) *Anti-Americanism: Irrational and Rational*, New Brunswick: Transaction Publishers.

—— (2002) 'The Politics of Envy', *The New Criterion*, November. Available from http://www.travelbrochuregraphics.com/extra/politics_of_envy.htm

—— (2004) 'Introduction: The New Virulence and Popularity', in P. Hollander (ed.) *Understanding Anti-Americanism: Its Origins and Impact at Home and Abroad*, Chicago: Ivan R. Dee.

—— (2005) *Understanding Anti-Americanism: Its Origins and Impact at Home and Abroad*, Chicago: Ivan R. Dee.

Holmes, J. W. (1981) *Life with Uncle: The Canadian–American Relationship*, Toronto: University of Toronto Press.

Hozic, A. (2001) *Hollyworld: Space, Power, and Fantasy in the American Economy*, Ithaca: Cornell University Press.

Huntington, S. (1996) 'The Goals of Development', in Inkels A. and Sasaki M. (eds) *Comparing Nations and Cultures: Readings in a Cross-Disciplinary Perspective*, New Jersey: Prentice Hall.

Hywood, G. (2004) 'Has Latham Already Lost the Election?', *The Age*, 15 July.

Ikenberry, J. (2001) *After Victory: Institutions, Strategic Restraint and the Rebuilding of Order after Major Wars*, Princeton: Princeton University Press.

International Federation of Journalists (2001) 'Les journalistes du monde entier produisent un rapport sur les médias, la guerre et le terrorisme', 23 October.

International Herald Tribune (2002) 23 July, p. 1.

—— (2004) 10 December, p. 8.

Isaacson, W. (1992) *Kissinger*, London: Simon and Schuster.

Ishihara, S. (1989) *The Japan That Can Say No*, New York: Simon and Schuster.

Israelyan, V. L. (1993) 'New Russia and the United States', in Ginsburgs, G. *et al.* (eds) *Russia and America (From Rivalry to Reconciliation)*, New York: M. E. Sharpe Inc.

Ivie, R. L. (2000) 'A New Democratic World Order?', in Medhurst, M. J. and Brands, H. W. (eds) *Critical Reflections on the Cold War: Linking Rhetoric and History*, College Station, TX: Texas A&M University Press.

Jack, A. (2004) *Inside Putin's Russia*, Oxford: Oxford University Press.

James, H. (2001) *The End of Globalization*, Cambridge, Massachusetts: Harvard University Press.

Joffe, J. (2004) 'The Demons of Europe', *Commentary Magazine*, 117, January.

—— (2006) *Überpower: The Imperial Temptation of America*, W. W. Norton & Co.

Johnston, E. (1950) 'Messengers from a Free Country', *Saturday Review of Literature*, 4 March, 9–12.

Jordan, J. M. (1994) *Machine-age Ideology: Social Engineering and American Liberalism, 1911–1939*, Chapel Hill: University of North Carolina Press.

Judt, T. (2005) 'A New Master Narrative? Reflections on Contemporary Anti-Americanism', in Judt, T. and Lacorne, D. (eds) *With US or against US: Studies in Global Anti-Americanism*, Basingstoke: Palgrave.

—— (2006) 'Anti-Americanism Abroad', in O'Connor B. and Griffiths, M. (eds) *The Rise of Anti-Americanism*, London: Routledge, pp. 203–12.

Kagan, R. (2002) 'Power and Weakness', *Policy Review*, June–July.

—— (2003) *Paradise & Power: America and Europe in the New World Order*, London: Atlantic Books.

Kaplan, E. and Rodrik, D. (2000) 'Did the Malaysian Capital Controls Work?', paper prepared for an NBER Conference on Currency Crises, Mimeo: December.

Karon, T. (2002) 'Why Guantanamo Has Europe Hopping Mad', *Time Magazine*, 24 January.

Katzenstein, P. and Keohane, R. O. (eds) (2006) *Anti-Americanism and Its Consequences*, Ithaca: Cornell University Press.

Kaufman, T. M. (2002) *Soros: The Life and Times of a Messianic Billionaire*, New York: Vintage Books.

Kelly, P. (2003) 'Australian for Alliance', *The National Interest*, Spring: 87–94.

Kelton, M. (2004) 'More than an Ally? Australia–US Relations since 1996', PhD thesis, Flinders University.

Kennedy, D. M. (2002) *Cultural Formations of Postcommunism*, Minneapolis: University of Minnesota Press.

Kennedy, L. and Lucas, S. (2005) 'Enduring Freedom: Public Diplomacy and US Foreign Policy', *American Quarterly* 57 (2): 309–33.

Kennedy, P. (1989) *The Rise and Fall of the Great Powers: Economic Change and Military Conflict from 1500 to 2000*, New York: Random House.

Kent, S. R. (1927) 'Distributing the Product', in Kennedy J. P. (ed.) *The Story of the Films as told by Leaders of the Industry to the Students of the Graduate School of Business Administration, George F. Baker Foundation Harvard University*, Kennedy. Chicago: A. W. Shaw Company, pp. 203–32.

Kimball, R. (2004) 'Anti-Americanism Then and Now', in P. Hollander (ed.) *Understanding Anti-Americanism: Its Origins and Impact at Home and Aboard*, Chicago: Ivan R. Dee.

Kishore, M. (2005) *Beyond the Age of Innocence: Rebuilding Trust between America and the World*, New York: Public Affairs Inc.

Kissinger, H. and Summers, L. H. (eds) (2004) *Renewing the Atlantic Partnership*, New York: Council on Foreign Relations.

Klaveras, Louis (2004) 'Were the Eagle and the Phoenix Birds of a Feather? The United States and the Greek Coup of 1967', *Hellenic Observatory Discussion Paper* 15, London: LSE European Institute.

Kofas, J. V. (2003) *Under the Eagle's Claw: Exceptionalism in Post-war US–Greek Relations*, Westport, Connecticut: Praeger.

Kohut, A. (2003) 'Anti-Americanism: Causes and Characteristics', *Pew Research Center for the People and the Press Commentary*, 10 December.

Konrad, G. and Szelenyi, I. (1979) *The Intellectuals on the Road to Class Power*, New York: Harcourt Brace Jovanovich.

Krastev, I. (2004) 'The Anti-American Century?', *Journal of Democracy* 15 (2) April: 5–16.

Kristol, W. and Kagan, R. (1996) 'Toward a Neo-Reaganite Foreign Policy', *Foreign Affairs* 75 (4): 18–32.

Kroes, R. (2006) 'Anti-Americanism in Europe: What's New? An Appraisal and Personal Account', in Fabbrini, S. (ed.) *The United States Contested: American Unilateralism and European Discontent*, New York: Routledge, pp. 95–109.

Kuisel, F. R. (1993) *Seducing the French: The Dilemma of Americanization*, Berkeley: University of California Press.

Kull, S. *et al.* (2003–04) 'Misperceptions, the Media, and the Iraq War', *Political Science Quarterly* 118 (4): 569–98.

Kunkel, J. (2002) 'Australian Trade Policy in an Age of Globalisation', *Australian Journal of International Affairs* 56.

Kupchan, C. (2002) 'The End of the West', *The Atlantic Online*, November. Available from http://www.theatlantic.com/doc/prem/200211/kupchan

Lacorne, D. and Judt, T. (eds) (2005) *With US or against US: Studies in Global Anti-Americanism*, New York: Palgrave Macmillan.

Lacorne, D. *et al.* (eds) (1990) *The Rise and Fall of Anti-Americanism*, London: Palgrave Macmillan.

La Nacion (2006) 'La Asombrosa Paradoja de China y America Latina', 10 February.

Langbein, L. I. and Lichtman, A. J. (1978) 'Ecological Inference', Sage University papers series. Quantitative Applications in the Social Sciences, No. 10. Beverley Hills, CA: Sage.

Latinobarómetro (2004) 'Encuesta Latinobarómetro 2004 Una Década de Mediciones –Una Década de Evolución.' Available from www.latinobarometro.org

Leffler, M. P. (1992) *A Preponderance of Power*, Stanford: Stanford University Press.

Leger Marketing (2003) 'Canadian Attitudes after the Conflict in Iraq' (May). Available from www.legermarketing.com

Legislative Research Service, Library of Congress (1964) 'The US Ideological Effort: Government Agencies and Programs: Study Prepared for the Subcommittee on International Organizations and Movements of the Committee on Foreign Affairs', Washington, DC.

Legvold, R. (1991) 'Learning in the 1980s', in Breslauer, G. W. and Tetlock, P. E. (eds) *Learning in US and Soviet Foreign Policy*, Oxford: Westview Press.

Le Monde (1950) 'Mourir pour le Coca-Cola', 29 March.

—— (2002) 'Les prisonniers du 11 septembre', 17 February.

Leonard, M. (ed.) (2002) *Re-ordering the World*, London: Foreign Policy Centre.

—— (2004) 'The US Heads Home: Will Europe Regret It?', *The Financial Times*, 26 June.

Lev, G. and Dubin, B. (2005) 'Russia's Distinctive Brand of Nationalism', *Pro et Contra Journal* 9 (2) (in Russian). Available from http://www.carnegie.ru/en/pubs/procontra/73309.htm

Liakos, A. (2004) 'How Did Americans Waste Their Dowry?', *To Bhma*, 6 June, B42.

—— (2002) 'Why 9/11 Changed the World', *To Bhma*, 8 September.

Liam, K. and Scott L. (2005) 'Enduring Freedom: Public Diplomacy and US Foreign Policy', *American Quarterly* 57 (2): 309–33.

Lieven, A. (2004a) 'In the Mirror of Europe: The Perils of American Nationalism', *Current History*, March. Available from http://www.ceip.org/files/Publications/2004-03-01-lieven-curhist.asp?from=pubauthor

—— (2004b) *America Right or Wrong: An Anatomy of American Nationalism*, Oxford: Oxford University Press.

Lipset, S. M. (1960) *Political Man: The Social Bases of Politics*, London, Heinemann.

—— (1963) *Political Man: The Social Bases of Politics*, New York: Anchor Books.

—— (1996) *American Exceptionalism*, New York: Norton.

Lowy Institute for International Policy (2005) *Australians Speak 2005: Public Opinion and Foreign Policy*. Available from www.lowyinstitute.org

Lucas, W. S. (2003) 'A Document from the Harvard International Summer School', in Gienow-Hecht, J. C. E. and Schumacher, F. (eds) *Culture and International History*, New York: Berghahn Books.

Lundestad, G. (1986) 'Empire by Invitation', *Journal of Peace Research*, 23 September 263–77.

—— (2003) *The United States and Western Europe since 1945: From 'Empire' by Invitation to Transatlantic Drift*, Oxford: Oxford University Press.

Lyon, P. V. (1968) *Canada in World Affairs, vol. 12: 1961–1963*, Toronto: Oxford University Press.

McCall, C. and Clarkson, S. (1994) *Trudeau and Our Times, vol. 2: The Heroic Delusion*, Toronto: McClelland and Stewart.

McCarthy, K. D. (1987) 'From Cold War to Cultural Development', *Daedalus*, Winter 93–117.

McFaul, M. (2005) 'Finding Russia's True Friends and Foes', *The Moscow Times*, 18 February. Available from http://www.carnegie.ru/en/pubs/media/72162.htm

McPherson, A. (2006) *Yankee No!: Anti-Americanism in US–Latin American Relations*, Cambridge: Harvard University Press.

Maclean's (1997) 21 July.

Mahbubani, K. (2005) *Beyond the Age of Innocence: Rebuilding Trust between America and the World*, New York: Public Affairs.

Makrias, P. (2003) 'This Is Not the Country We Left Behind', *libertynet.gr*, 20 May. Available from http://www.libertynet.gr/searcharticle.aspx?id=159)

Markovits, A. S. (2003) *European Anti-Americanism (and Anti-Semitism): Ever Present Though Always Denied*, Centre for European Studies, Working Paper Series 108 (3).

—— (2006) 'Twin Brothers: European Anti-Semitism and Anti-Americanism', Jerusalem Center for Public Affairs, 8 January. Available from http://www.jcpa.org/phas/phas-markovits-06.htm

Martin, L. (1993) *Pledge of Allegiance: The Americanization of Canada in the Mulroney Years*, Toronto: McClelland and Stewart.

Matsumoto, R. (2004) 'From Model to Menace: French Intellectuals and American Civilization', *The Japanese Journal of American Studies*, 15: 167.

Mattelart, A. *et al.* (1988) 'International Image Markets', in Schneider, C. and Wallis, B. (eds) *Global Television*, New York: Wedge Press; Cambridge, Mass.: MIT Press, pp. 13–33.

Meacher, M. (2003) 'This War on Terrorism Is Bogus', *The Guardian*, 6 September.

Mead, W. R. (2002) 'The Case against the Europeans', *The Atlantic Monthly*, April.

—— (2003) 'Why Do They Hate Us?: Two Books Take Aim at French Anti-Americanism', *Foreign Affairs*, 82 (2): 139–42.

—— (2006) 'Through Our Friends' Eyes: Defending and Advising the Hyperpower' *Foreign Affairs* 85 (3): 138–43.

Medhurst, M. (2000) 'Introduction', in Medhurst, M. J. and Brands, H. W. (eds) *Critical Reflections on the Cold War: Linking Rhetoric and History*, College Station, TX: Texas A&M University Press.

Melissen, J. (ed.) (2005) *The New Public Diplomacy*, Basingstoke: Palgrave.

Mertler, A. C. and Racel, A. V. (2002) *Advanced and Multivariate Statistical Methods: Practical Application and Interpretation*, Los Angeles: Pyrczak.

Meunier, S. (2000) 'The French Exception', *Foreign Affairs*, 79: 4.

—— (2005) 'Anti-Americanisms in France', *French Politics, Culture & Society* 23 (2).

Meyssan, T. (2002) *Le 11 septembre 2001: l'effroyable imposture*, Chatou: Editions Carnot.

Micklethwait, J. and Wooldridge, A. (2004) *The Right Nation: Why America Is Different*, London: Allen Lane.

Mihas, T. (2002) *Unholy Alliance: Greece and Milošević's Serbia*, Austin: Texas A&M University Press.

Miller, T. *et al.* (2001) *Globalization and Sport: Playing the World*, London: Sage Publications.

Miller, T. *et al.* (2005) *Global Hollywood*, London: British Film Institute.

Milward, A. S. (1984) *The Reconstruction of Western Europe 1945–1951*, London: Methuen.

Mitropoulos, D. (1998) 'He Will Continue to Talk', *To Bhma*, 12 April, A20.

Moisi, D. (2002) 'Why the US Can Not Defeat Terrorism on Its Own', *The Financial Times*, 3 June.

Mowlana, H. (1993) 'Toward a NWICO for the Twenty-first Century?', *Journal of International Affairs* 47 (1): 59–72.

—— (2000) 'The Renewal of the Global Media Debate: Implications for the Relationship between the West and the Islamic World', in Hafez, K. (ed.) *Islam and the West in the Mass Media: Fragmented Images in a Globalizing World*, Cresskill: Hampton Press, pp. 105–18.

Munton, D. and Castle, G. (1992) 'Reducing Acid Rain, 1980s', in Munton, D. and Kirton, J. (eds) *Canadian Foreign Policy: Selected Cases*, Scarborough, ON: Prentice-Hall Canada, pp. 367–81.

Murphy, J. (1993) *Harvest of Fear: A History of Australia's Vietnam War*, Sydney: Allen & Unwin.

Nadeau, R. and Blais, A. (1995) 'Economic Conditions, Leader Evaluations and Election Outcomes in Canada', *Canadian Public Policy* 21 (2): 212–18.

Naím, M. (2003) 'The Perils of Lite Anti-Americanism', *Foreign Policy* 136: 95–6.

Navasky, V. (2002) 'Foreword', in Zelizer, B. and Allan, S. *Journalism after September 11*, London: Routledge, pp. xiii–xviii.

Neumann, I. B. (1997) 'Russia as Europe's Other', in Burgess, P. J. (ed.) *Cultural Politics and Political Culture in Postmodern Europe*, Amsterdam/Atlanta, GA: Editions Rodopi.

Newcomb, H. (1996) 'Other People's Fictions: Cultural Appropriation, Cultural Integrity, and International Media Strategies', in McAnany, E.G. and Wilkinson, K.T. (eds) *Mass Media and Free Trade: NAFTA and the Cultural Industries*, Austin: University of Texas Press, pp. 92–109.

Ninkovich, F. (1994) 'Culture, Power, and Civilization: The Place of Culture in the Study of International Relations', in Johnson, D. R. (ed.) *On Cultural Ground: Essays in International History*, Chicago: Imprint.

Nossal, K. R. (1985) 'Economic Nationalism and Continental Integration: Assumptions, Arguments and Advocacies', in Stairs, D. and Winham, G. R. (eds) *The Collected Research Studies/The Royal Commission on the Economic Union and Development Prospects for Canada, vol. 29: The Politics of Canada's Economic Relationship with the United States*, Ottawa: Supply and Services Canada, pp. 55–94.

—— (1994) 'Quantum Leaping: The Gulf Debate in Australia and Canada', in McKinley, M. (ed.) *The Gulf War: Critical Perspectives*, Sydney: Allen & Unwin, pp. 48–71.

Nye, J. S. (2002) *The Paradox of American Power: Why the World's Only Superpower Can't Go it Alone*, New York: Oxford University Press.

—— (2003) 'US Power and Strategy after Iraq'. Available from www.ksg.harvard.edu/news/opeds/2003/nye_usiraq_foraffairs_070103.htm

—— (2004) *Soft Power: The Means to Success in World Politics*, New York: Public Affairs.

Nye, J. S. and Keohane, R. O. (1993) 'The United States and International Institutions', in Keohane, R. O. *et al.* (eds) *After the Cold War: International Institutions and State Strategies in Europe 1989–1991*, Boston: Harvard University Press.

O'Connor, B. (2003) 'The Last Respectable Prejudice?, *Australian Book Review*, October: 21–2.

—— (2004) 'Are We All Americans Now? The Superpower and Its Critics', *Australian Journal of Political Science* 39 (2): 421–6.

—— (2006) 'The Anti-American Tradition: A History in Four Phases', in O'Connor B. and Martin (eds) *The Rise of Anti-Americanism*, New York: Routledge, pp. 11–24.

O'Connor, B. (ed.) (2007) *Anti-Americanism: History, Causes, Themes*, Greenwood World Publishing.

O'Connor, B. and Griffith, M. (eds) (2006) *The Rise of Anti-Americanism*, New York: Routledge.

O'Neil, A. (2006) 'American Grand Strategy: The Quest for Permanent Primacy', in O'Connor B. and Griffith M. (eds) *The Rise of Anti-Americanism*, New York: Routledge, pp. 140–54.

Oakes, L. (2004) 'The Bomber's American Mission: Kim Beazley's Return to the Labor Frontbenches as Defence Spokesman Allows Mark Latham to Reinvent His Relationship with the US', *The Bulletin*, 20 July.

OECD (2004) 'Economic Outlook', 75.

Office of the United States Trade Representative (USTR) (2004a) *2004 National Trade Estimates Report*.

—— (2004b) 'Free Trade "Down Under": Summary of the US–Australia Free Trade Agreement', *Trade Facts*, 8 February.

Paggi, L. (ed.) (1989) *Americanismo e riformismo. La socialdemocrazia europea nell'economia mondiale aperta*, Torino: Einaudi.

Papahelas A. (2001) 'Nicholas Burns: The Greeks and I', *To Bhma*, 29 July, A14.

Papayiannidis, A. D. (2003) 'The Temptation of a New Anti-Americanism, *To Bhma*, 2 February.

Pappas, G. C. (2006) 'Greece's Attitude: Commendable and Deplorable, All in the Same Breath', *GreekAmerica.net*. Available from http://www.greekamerica.net/pastissues/7-2/terror_hits_home.wu

Parmar, I. (2000) 'Engineering Consent: The Carnegie Endowment for International Peace and the Mobilization of American Public Opinion 1939–45', *Review of International Studies* 26 (1): 35–48.

—— (2002) 'American Foundations and the Development of International Knowledge Networks', *Global Networks* 2 (1): 13–30.

—— (2004a) *Think Tanks and Power in Foreign Policy*, Basingstoke: Palgrave.

—— (2004b) 'Institutes of International Affairs', in Stone D. and Denham, A. (eds) *Think Tank Traditions*, Manchester: Manchester University Press, pp. 19–34.

—— (2005a) 'American Foundations and Anti-Americanism Today', *Working Paper Series*, Centre for Policy Studies, Central European University, Budapest.

—— (2005b) 'Catalysing Events, Think Tanks and American Foreign Policy Shifts: A Comparative Analysis of the Impacts of Pearl Harbor 1941 and 11 September 2001', *Government and Opposition* Winter: 1–25.

—— (2005c) 'I'm Proud of the British Empire: Why Tony Blair Backs George W. Bush', *The Political Quarterly*, April: 218–31.

—— (2006a) 'Conceptualising the State–Private Network in American Foreign Policy', in Laville, H. and Wilford, H. (eds) *The US Government, Citizen Groups, and the Cold War*, London: Frank Cass.

—— (2006b) 'Challenging Elite Anti-Americanism and Sponsoring Americanism in the Cold War: US Foundations, Henry Kissinger's Harvard International Seminar, and the Salzburg Seminar in American Studies', *Traverse*.

Pells, R. (1997) *Not Like US: How Europeans have Loved, Hated, and Transformed American Culture since World War II*, New York: Basic Books.

Pew Research Center for the People and Press (2002a) 'What the World Thinks in 2002', The Pew Research Center for the People and the Press, 2 December. Available from http://people-press.org/reports/display.php3?ReportID=165

—— (2002b) 'Among Wealthy Nations … US Stands Alone in Its Embrace of Religion'.

—— (2003a) 'America's Image Further Erodes, Europeans Want Weaker Ties', 18 March. Available from http://pewglobal.org/reports/pdf/175.pdf

—— (2003b) 'Different Faiths, Different Messages'.

—— (2003c) 'Views of a Changing World', June.

—— (2004a) 'Trouble Behind, Trouble Ahead? A Year of Contention at Home and Abroad', Year-End Report.

—— (2004b) 'A Year after Iraq War Mistrust of America in Europe Ever Higher, Muslim Anger Persists', 16 March. Available from http://pewglobal.org/reports/pdf/206.pdf

—— (2005a) 'US Image Up Slightly, But Still Negative', 23 June. Available from http://pewglobal.org/reports/pdf/247.pdf

—— (2005b) 'American Character Gets Mixed Review. US Image Up Slightly, But Still Negative', *Nation Pew Global Attitudes Survey*, 16 June, p. 3.

—— (2006) 'America's Image Slips, But Allies Share US Concerns over Iran, Hamas', 13 June. Available from http://pewglobal.org/reports/pdf/252.pdf

Phillips, N. (2003) 'The Rise and Fall of Open Regionalism? Comparative Reflections on Regional Governance in the Southern Cone of Latin America', *Third World Quarterly* 24 (2): 217–34.

Pilger, J. (2003) 'We See Too Much, We Know Too Much, That's Our Best Defense', *Independent*, 6 April.

Pillar, P. R. (2001) *Terrorism and US Foreign Policy*, Washington, DC: Brookings Institution Press.

PIPA (Program on International Policy Attitudes) (2000) 'Americans on Globalization: A Study of US Public Attitudes', 28 March. Appendix C: Comparison with European Attitudes.

—— (2003) 'Misperceptions, the Media and the Iraq War'.

—— (2004) 'US Public Beliefs on Iraq and the Presidential Elections'.

Pipes, R. (2004) 'Flight from Freedom: What Russians Think and Want', *Foreign Affairs* May–June. Available from http://www.foreignaffairs.org/20040501facomment83302/richard-pipes/flight-from-freedom-what-russians-think-and-want.html

—— (2005) *Russian Conservatism and Its Critics: A Study in Political Culture*, New Haven: Yale University Press.

Pius XI (1936) 'Encyclical Letter of Pope Pius XI on the Motion Picture Vigilanti Cura'. Available from www.vatican.va/holy_father/pius_xi/encyclicals/documents/hf_p-xi_enc_29061936_vigilanti-cura_en.html

Pollack, K. M. (2002) *The Threatening Storm: The Case for Invading Iraq*, New York: Random House.

Posner, R. A. (2001) *Public Intellectuals: A Study of Decline*, Cambridge: Harvard University Press.

Powdermaker, H. (1950) *Hollywood: The Dream Factory: An Anthropologist Looks at the Movie-makers*, Boston: Little, Brown and Company.

Preble, C. (2004) *Exiting Iraq: Report of a Special Task Force on Exiting Iraq, Sponsored by the Cato Institute*, Washington, DC: The Cato Institute.

Project for the New American Century (PNAC) (2000) 'Rebuilding America's Defenses', Washington, DC: Project for the New American Century.

Pushkov, A. (1993) 'Letter from Eurasia: Russia and America: The Honeymoon's Over', *Foreign Policy* 93: 76–90.

Putnam, R. D. (1988) 'Diplomacy and Domestic Politics', *International Organization* 42: 427–60.

Rae, J. (2006) 'Ambivalent Anti-Americanism', in O'Connor B. and Griffith M. (eds) *The Rise of Anti-Americanism*, New York: Routledge, pp. 48–85.

Ravenhill, J. (2001) 'Allies But Not Friends: The Economic Relationship', *Australian Journal of International Affairs* 55 (2): 249–59.

Rehman, S. S. (2004) 'American Hegemony: If Not US, then Who?', *Connecticut Journal of International Law* 19: 407–22.

Renouf, A. (1979) *The Frightened Country*, Melbourne: Macmillan.

Renshon, S. A. (2004) *In His Father's Shadow: The Transformations of George W. Bush*, New York: Palgrave Macmillan.

Revel, J.-F. (2003a) *Anti-Americanism*, San Francisco: Encounter Books.

—— (2003b) 'Europe's Anti-American Obsession', *American Enterprise* 14 (8): 18–25.

Richmond, Y. (2003) *Cultural Exchange and the Cold War: Raising the Iron Curtain*, University Park: The Pennsylvania State University Press.

Ripp, V. (1990) *Pizza in Pushkin Square: What Russians Think about Americans and the American Way of Life*, New York: Simon & Schuster.

Risse, T. (2004) 'Beyond Iraq: The Crisis of the Transatlantic Security Community', in Held D. and Kosnig-Archibugi M. (eds) *American Power in the 21st Century*, Cambridge: Polity Press.

Robinson, H. B. (1989) *Diefenbaker's World: A Populist in Foreign Affairs*, Toronto: University of Toronto Press.

Roger, P. (2002) *L'ennemi américain: généalogie de l'antiaméricanisme français*, Paris: Seuil.

—— (2005) *The American Enemy: The History of French Anti-Americanism*, Chicago: University of Chicago Press.

Ross, A. (2004) 'The Domestic Front', in Ross, A. and Ross, K. (eds) *Anti-Americanism*, New York: New York University Press.

Ross, A. and Ross, K. (ed.) (2004) *Anti-Americanism*, New York: New York University Press.

Rosten, L. C. (1947) 'Movies and Propaganda', *Annals of the American Academy of Political and Social Science* 254: 116–24.

Roubatis, Y. P. (1987) *Tangled Webs: The US in Greece, 1947–67*, New York: Pella.

Rowley, G. D. (1997) 'Aleksandr Solzhenitsyn and Russian Nationalism', *Journal of Contemporary History* 32 (3): 321–37.

Roy, A. (2001) 'The Algebra of Infinite Justice', *Guardian*, 29 September.

Rubin, B. (2004) 'Understanding Anti-Americanism', Foreign Policy Research Institute, 20 August. Available from http://www.fpri.org/enotes/20040820.west.rubinb.antiamericanism.html

Rubin, B. and Rubin, J. C. (2004) *Hating America*, New York: Oxford University Press.

Rubin, J. C. (2004) 'The Five Stages of Anti-Americanism', *Foreign Policy Research Institute e-Notes*, 4 September.

Rüland, J. (2000) 'ASEAN and the Asian Crisis: Theoretical Implications and Practical Consequences for Southeast Asian Regionalism', *The Pacific Review* 13 (3): 421–51.

Sachs, J.D. (1997) 'Power Unto Itself', *Financial Times*, 11 December.

Sakr, N. (2001) *Satellite Realms: Transnational Television, Globalization and the Middle East*, London: IB Tauris.

Sapolsky, H. M. (2005) 'A Nuisance Neighbour', *National Post*, 27 July, A15.

Sardar, Z. and Davies, M. W. (2002) *Why Do People Hate America?*, Cambridge: Icon Books.

Satloff, R. (2004) *The Battle of Ideas in the War on Terror*, Washington, DC: Washington Institute for Near East Policy.

Saunders, F. S. (1999) *Who Paid the Piper?: The CIA and the Cultural Cold War*, London: Granta Books.

Schulze, J. and Elliott, G. (2004) 'Big Three Will Run World's Media, Says Murdoch', *The Australian*, 12 February.

Scott-Smith, G. (2002) *The Politics of Apolitical Culture: The Congress for Cultural Freedom, the CIA and Post-War American Hegemony*, London: Routledge.

Serfaty, S. (2005) 'Terms of Estrangement: French–American Relations in Perspective', *Survival* 47 (3): 74–8.

Servan-Schreiber, J.-J. (1968) *The American Challenge (Le défi américain)*, London: Hamish Hamilton.

Shanahan, D. (1999) 'US Fury at Our Failings', *The Australian*, 17 September.

Sheridan, G. (2004) 'Labor's Anti-Americanism Won't Wash', *The Australian*, 17 June.

Shiraev, E. (2005) '"Sorry, but ...": Russia's Responses in the Wake of 9/11', in Shlapentokh, V. *et al.* (eds) *America: Sovereign Defender or Cowboy Nation?*, Aldershot, UK: Ashgate Publishers.

Shiraev, E. and Zubok, V. (2000) *Anti-Americanism in Russia: From Stalin to Putin*, New York: Palgrave Macmillan.

Shires, D. and Sargent, S. (1986) 'The Gloves Come Off in the Fight for Wheat Sales', *Australian Financial Review*, 25 July.

Shlapentokh, V. (1988) 'The Changeable Soviet Image of America', in Thornton, P. T. *The Annals: The American Academy of Political and Social Science, Special Issue: Anti-Americanism: Origins and Context*, Sage Publications.

—— (1998) '"Old", "New", and "Post" Liberal Attitudes Toward the West: From Love to Hate', *Communist and Post-Communist Studies* 31 (3): 119–216.

Shleifer, A. and Treisman, D. (2004) 'A Normal Country', *Foreign Affairs* March–April. Available from http://www.foreignaffairs.org/20040301faessay83204/andrei-shleifer-daniel-treisman/a-normal-country.html?mode=print

Shoup, L. H. and Minter, W. (1977) *Imperial Brain Trust: The Council on Foreign Relations and US Foreign Policy*, New York and London: Monthly Review Press.

Siegfried, A. (1927) *Les Etats-Unis d'aujourd'hui*, Paris: Armand Colin.

Singh, R. (2006) 'Are We All Americans Now? Explaining Anti-Americanisms', in O'Connor B. and Griffith M. (eds) *The Rise of Anti-Americanism*, New York: Routledge, pp. 23–47.

Smith, C. W. and Korzeniewicz, P. R. (2002) 'Transnational Social Movements, Elite Projects, and Collective Action from Below in the Americas', in Fawcet, L. and Serrano, M. (eds) *Regionalism's 'Third Wave' in the Americas*, New York: Routledge Press.

Smith, S. (1844) *The Works of the Rev. Sydney Smith*, Philadelphia: Carey and Hart.

Solzhenitsyn, I. A. (1985) 'The Moral Poverty of the West', in Haseler, S. (ed.) *The Varieties of Anti-Americanism: Reflex and Response*, Washington: The Ethics and Public Policy Center.

Soros, G. (1997) 'The Capitalist Threat', *The Atlantic Monthly* 279 (2): 45–58.

—— (2002) *On Globalization*, New York: Public Affairs.

Spanger, H.-J. (2005) 'Western Theories: What Is Their Explanatory Value?', in Hannes A. and Anders Å. (eds) *Russia versus the United States and Europe – or 'Strategic Triangle'? Developments in Russian Domestic and Foreign Policy, Western Responses, and Prospects for Policy Coordination*, Berlin/Moscow: Carnegie Moscow Center. Available from http://www.carnegie.ru/en/pubs/books/73367.htm

Speaker's Advisory Group on Russia, United States House of Representatives 106th Congress (September 2000) 'Russia's Road to Corruption: How the Clinton Administration Exported Government Instead of Free Enterprise and Failed the Russian People'. Available from http://www.fas.org/news/russia/2000/russia/part04.htm

Standard and Poors (2002) *Industry Surveys: Movies and Home Entertainment*, 14 November.

Stanley, A. (1999) 'NATO Bombing Tears at Greek Loyalties, Reawakening Anti-Americanism', *The New York Times*, 25 April.

Stark, J. (ed.) (2001) *The Challenge of Change in Latin America and the Caribbean*, Coral Gables: University of Miami North–South Center Press.

Stefanidis, I. (2001) 'Pressure Groups and Greek Foreign Policy, 1945–67', *Hellenic Observatory* Discussion Paper no. 6, London: LSE European Institute.

Steinmetz, G. (1999) 'Introduction: Culture and the State', in Steinmetz G. (ed.) *State/Culture (State-Formation after the Cultural Turn)*, Ithaca: Cornell University Press.

Stephen, A. (ed.) (2006) *The Americanization of Europe: Culture, Diplomacy, and Anti-Americanism after 1945*, New York: Berghahn Books.

Stiglitz, J. (2000) 'What I Learned at the World Economic Crisis', *The Insider: The New Republic*, 17 April. Available from http://www.mindfully.org/WTO/Joseph-Stiglitz-IMF17apr00.htm

—— (2001) 'Failure of the Fund: Rethinking the IMF Response', *Harvard International Review*, Summer: 14–18.

—— (2002a) *Die Schatten der Globalisierung*, Berlin: Siedler Verlag.

—— (2002b) 'Whither Reform? Towards a New Agenda for Latin America'. Available from http://www2.gsb.columbia.edu/faculty/jstiglitz/download/santiago.pdf

Strange, S. (1987) 'The Persistent Myth of Lost Hegemony', *International Organization* 41 (4).

Strode, L. (2000) 'France and EU Policy-making on Visual Culture: New Opportunities for National Identity?', in Ezra, E. and Harris, S. (eds) *France in Focus: Film and National Identity*, Oxford: Berg Publishers, 61–75.

Summers, A. (1986) 'Aggro Will Stalk the San Francisco Conference on the ANZUS Alliance', *Australian Financial Review*, 8 August.

Summers, L. (2004) 'America Overdrawn', *Foreign Policy*, July–August: 46–9.

Sweig, J. E. (2006) *Friendly Fire: Losing Friends and Making Enemies in the Anti-American Century*, New York: Public Affairs.

Teinowitz, I. (2004) 'Keith Reinhard Critiques US Diplomatic PR Efforts', *AdAge*, 24 August.

Thibau, J. (1980) *La France colonisée*, Paris: Flammarion.

Thomas B. Fordham Foundation (ed.) (2003) 'Terrorists, Despots and Democracy', Washington, DC: Thomas B. Fordham Foundation.

Todd, E. (2003) *After Empire: The Breakdown of the American Order*, New York: Columbia University Press.

Tomlin, B. W. (2001) 'Leaving the Past Behind: The Free Trade Initiative Assessed', in Michaud, N. and Nossal, K. R. (eds) *Diplomatic Departures: The Conservative Era in Canadian Foreign Policy, 1984–1993*, Vancouver: University of British Columbia Press: 45–58.

Tow, W. (2001) 'Australia and the United States', in J. Cotton and J. Ravenhill (eds) *The National Interest in a Global Era: Australia in World Affairs, 1996–2000*, Oxford: Oxford University Press.

Tow, W. and Albinski, H. (2002) 'ANZUS – Alive and Well after Fifty Years', *Australian Journal of Politics and History*, 48 (2): 153–73.

Trenin, D. (2004a) *Through Russian Eyes and Minds: Post 9/11 Perceptions of America and its Policies*, Berlin/Moscow: Carnegie Moscow Center. Available from http://www.carnegie.ru/en/pubs/media/70180.htm

—— (2004b) *Moscow's Realpolitic*, Berlin/Moscow: Carnegie Moscow Center. Available from http://www.carnegie.ru/en/pubs/media/69778.htm

Tulchin, J. (1997) 'El Narcotráfico y la Seguridad Hemisférica', *Paz y Seguridad en las Américas*, Newsletter No. 15, December.

Tussie, D. (2005) *Developmental Opposition in International Trade Regimes: Regional Groupings, State and Civil Society Coalitions*, Ridgway Center for International Security Studies: University of Pittsburgh.

Tussie, D. and Quiliconi, C. (2005) 'The Current Trade Context', Background Paper for the *Human Development Report*.

Ulich, P. C. and Simmers, L. (2001) 'Motion Picture Production: To Run or Stay Made in the USA', *Loyola of Los Angeles Entertainment Law Review* 21: 357–70.

UNCTAD (1995) 'Trade and Development Report'.

UNDP (2004) 'La Democracia en América Latina, Hacia una democracia de ciudadanas y ciudadanos', Buenos Aires: Aguilar, Altea, Taurus, Alfaguara.

Vaïsse, J. (2003) 'American Francophobia Takes a New Turn', *French Politics, Culture & Society* 21 (2): 18–33.

Valenti, J. (2003) 'Intellectual Copyright Piracy: Links to Organized Crime and Terrorism', Testimony before Sub-Committee on Courts, the Internet, and Intellectual Property Committee on the Judiciary US House of Representatives, 13 March.

van der Pijl, K. (1984) *The Making of an Atlantic Ruling Class*, London: Verso.

Védrine, H. with Moisi, D. (2001), *France in an Age of Globalization*, Washington, DC: Brookings Institution Press, 2001.

Vickers, R. (2000) *Manipulating Hegemony: State Power, Labour, and the Marshall Plan in Britain*, London: Macmillan.

Vogel, H. (2005) *How Should We Deal with Russia? Prospects for Coordination of Western Politics*, Global Business Network. Available from http://www.gbn.com/ ArticleDisplayServlet.srv?aid=27731

Volker, R. and Berghahn, V. R. (2001) *America and the Intellectual Cold Wars in Europe*, Princeton, NJ: Princeton University Press.

Vonnegut, K. (2004) 'I Love You, Madame Librarian', *In These Times*, 6 August.

Voulgaris, Y. (2002) 'Anti-Americanism in Greece', *Apogevmatini*, 10 March.

Wall, I. M. (2004) 'The French–American War Over Iraq', *Brown Journal of World Affairs*, X (2).

Wallerstein, I. (2003) *Decline of American Power: The US in a Chaotic World*, New York: New Press.

Wanger, W. (1950) 'Donald Duck and Diplomacy', *Public Opinion Quarterly* 14 (3): 443–52.

Waxman, C. I. (ed.) (1968) *The End of Ideology Debate*, New York: Funk & Wagnalls.

Wenders, W. (1991) *The Logic of Images: Essays and Conversations*, London: Faber and Faber.

Werz, M (2004) 'Anti-Americanism and Ambivalence: Remarks on an Ideology in Historical Transformation', *Telos*, 129 Fall–Winter: 75–95.

Whitaker, B. (1974) *The Foundations*, London: Eyre Methuen.

Will, G. F. (2003) 'Europe's Decline', *The Washington Post*, 11 April.

Williamson, J. *et al.* (2003) 'Should Capital Controls Have a Place in the Future International Monetary System?', paper prepared for the International Monetary Convention organized by the Reinventing Bretton Woods Committee, 13–14 May, Madrid.

Wolf, M. (2002) 'Self-Satisfied, Simplistic, Cogent', *Financial Times*, 10 July, p. 19.

Wood, G. (2002) 'An Australia–US Free Trade Agreement: Balancing of Regional and Multilateral Interests', Australia APEC Study Centre, Monash University. Available from http://www.apec.org.au/docs/fta2woo.pdf

Wright Mills, C. (1959) *The Sociological Imagination*, New York: Oxford University Press.

Yurchak, A. (2006) *Everything Was Forever, Until It Was No More: The Last Soviet Generation*, Princeton: Princeton University Press.

Zea, L. (2001) 'De la Guerra Fría a la Sucia', in Modak, F. (ed.) *11 de septiembre de 2001*, Buenos Aires: Grupo Editorial Lumen, pp. 5–10.

Zeldin, T. (1990) 'The Pathology of Anti-Americanism', in Lacorne, D. *et al.* (eds) *The Rise and Fall of Anti-Americanism*, London: Palgrave.

Zlobin, N. (2005) 'The Special Russian Way: The Origin and Evolution of Russian Perceptions about the United States', in Judt, T. and Lacorne, D. (eds) *With US or against US: Studies in Global Anti-Americanism*, Basingstoke: Palgrave Macmillan.

Zoellick, R. (2002) Letter to Dennis J. Hastert, Speaker of US House of Representatives, 13 November.

—— (2003) quoted in *Inside US Trade*, 16 May.

Zogby International (2004) 'Impressions of America 2004: How Arabs View America, How Arabs Learn About America: A Six-Nation Survey Commissioned by the Arab American Institute'.

Zoulas, S. (2002) 'The Danger of Anti-Hellenism', *Kathimerini*, 13 January. Available from http://www.kathimerini.gr

Index

T - #0111 - 270225 - C0 - 234/156/14 - PB - 9780415746700 - Gloss Lamination